SISTERS AND SOLIDARITY

SISTERS AND SOLIDARITY

Women and Unions in Canada

JULIE WHITE

THOMPSON EDUCATIONAL PUBLISHING, INC.
Toronto, Ontario

Orders may be sent to:

Canada   or   *United States*
11 Briarcroft Road   240 Portage Road
Toronto, Ontario   Lewiston, New York
M6S 1H3   14092

For faster delivery, please send your order by telephone or fax to:
Tel (416) 766–2763 / Fax (416) 766–0398

Cataloguing in Publication Data

White, Julie
    Sisters and solidarity : women in unions in Canada

Includes bibliographical references and index.
ISBN 1-55077-045-4

1. Women in trade-unions - Canada. 2. Trade-unions - Canada - Minority membership. I. Title.

HD6079.2.C2W55 1993   331.4'78'0971   C93-093547-0

Printed in Canada.
1 2 3 4   95 94 93

Table of Contents

For Allan, Hannah and Noah

Preface

In the late 1970s I wrote a book that attempted to summarize the situation of women within the union movement in Canada, *Women and Unions* (1980). Ten years later, the book was not only out of print, but also out of date, and despite many useful publications no other attempt has been made to assess the overall position of women in the labour movement. My tentative inquiries as to the usefulness of a new version of the book met with enthusiasm.

Sisters and Solidarity is, then, a second effort to examine the role of unions for women in the labour force and the position of women inside the labour movement. New issues have developed, different legislation has been enacted, and women have increased their voice substantially within their unions. Moreover, there has been increasing recognition of the important influence that unions may exert on the status of women who work for pay. Changes occurring since the first book have been so extensive that a mere revision of *Women in Unions* could no longer encompass all the issues. *Sisters and Solidarity* is, of necessity, an entirely new book.

The first chapter remains an historical analysis of the early development of the union movement around the turn of the century. New historical research has permitted a more detailed look at the situation of employed women between 1881 and 1921, and why unions did not readily include them. I now consider the debate around union support of the family wage, and include more analysis of the social and economic diversity that the general term "women" tends to obscure.

The second chapter briefly traces both the changes in women's employment from the turn of the century to the present, and the changes in the union movement. There continues to be a dearth of research on women and unions for this time period, and I focus upon the impact of the organization of public sector workers in the 1960s and 1970s, the dramatic shift that brought large numbers of women into the union movement for the first time.

It no longer seemed appropriate to ask the question "Does Unionization Benefit Women?" the heading of a chapter in the 1980 book. There is now a much broader acceptance that unions have an important role to play in improving pay and conditions for employed women, and so the chapter that examines these issues is called simply, "The Advantages of Unionization." It considers what unions have or have not acomplished in negotiations with employers with regard to equal pay for women, employment equity, general benefits and conditions, and specific concerns such as parental leave and harassment.

In the earlier book, one chapter posed the question "Why are Women Unionized Less than Men?" and this issue is still relevant, although the gap in the rates of unionization between men and women has narrowed. The same question is now considered within the context of a chapter that examines more generally the situation of "Unorganized Women." Using Statistics Canada data, it is now possible to analyze union membership by sex in much more detail, including industry and occupation, hours of work and size of workplace, and also racial minority status. This chapter also examines employer opposition and labour relations legislation as barriers to organizing the unorganized. To bring to life the statistical analysis, attempts to organize among homeworkers and cleaners are described, as well as the campaign to introduce new labour relations legislation in Ontario.

Two new chapters consider the changes that have occurred for women inside the union movement itself. Chapter 4 looks at the movement of women into union leadership, not just at the top executive level, but also in local unions, on committees and in staff positions. Chapter 5 considers the expanded role of women's committees and some of the problems they face, and then goes on to assess how the union movement has responded to three issues of particular importance to women members — child care and family responsibilities, sexual and personal harassment, and union education. Much of the material for these chapters is based upon interviews that were conducted with the Canadian Labour Congress, the Confédération des syndicats nationaux, the ten provincial Federations of Labour, and thirteen selected unions.

Finally, it was not possible in the 1990s to write a study of women and unions that did not take into account the differences among women and the demands for equality from other disadvantaged groups. Chapter 7 considers the organization among racial minority groups, people with disabilities and gays and lesbians within the union movement, and the responses of unions to their needs. I have also attempted to integrate these concerns throughout the book wherever information was available.

I would like to thank the many union members, officers and staff who gave their time to provide interviews and materials to make this book possible, and in some cases commented on sections of the work as it progressed. I hope that they will find the end product useful. I am again indebted to the Strategic Grants Division of the Social Sciences and Humanities Research Council, for financial support of the research. Judy Fudge, Penni Richmond, Jane Stinson and Rosemary Warskett read the manuscript from start to finish and made innumerable suggestions for improvements. Finally, my family has survived again through the writing of another book, and the support of Allan, Hannah and Noah in my work, as in my life, is always of primary importance. Although the book could not have been written without these many contributions, the final decisions were mine, and therefore I carry responsibility for the weaknesses as well as the strengths.

War work for women. The Assembly
Department, British Munitions Supply
Co. Ltd., Verdun, Quebec, 1916-1918.

*Courtesy of the National Archives of Canada,
PA 24435.*

1

Women and the Early Development of Unions 1881–1921

Women played a lesser role than men in the early development of the union movement. To what extent this resulted from the material conditions of the time, as opposed to the policies of unions, has been the cause of some dispute. This chapter analyzes the ideological, social and economic conditions that prevailed between 1881–1921 that limited the participation of women in unions. It then examines the nature of unions during the period and their response to working women.

The period from 1881 to 1921 was chosen because during these years trade unions were gaining in membership and importance and becoming a significant factor in Canadian life. Although the first unions were organized in Canada in the 1820s, they were few in number before the 1870s, operating in isolation and with little public attention. In 1886 the Trades and Labour Congress of Canada was formed, the first central labour body. International unions, based in America, were well established by this time and continued to play a crucial role in the development of the union movement in Canada. The earlier influence of British unions was already in decline and had disappeared completely by the 1920s.

Although the union movement was developing, still most people remained untouched by unionization. Unions expanded in urban industrial centres, but between 1881 and 1921 Canada remained a predominantly agricultural society. In 1881 three-quarters of the population was rural, declining to just over half by 1921.[1] In 1911 only 5 percent of the total labour force were union members, rising to just 10 percent by 1921.[2] It is important to bear in mind that the union movement affected only a small minority of workers, whether male or female, throughout the years under discussion.

Canada's population was just 4,324,000 in 1881, doubling by 1921 to 8,787,000. This population was highly concentrated in Ontario and Quebec in 1881, with 78 percent of Canada's population in these two provinces alone. By 1921 this concentration had fallen to 60 percent.[3] Industrialization was equally concentrated, with Ontario the most industrialized province throughout the period and Montreal a major industrial centre. Union activity was consequently focused in these areas.

Despite its name, the Trades and Labour Congress of Canada comprised only Ontario unions in 1886, with Quebec unions joining later. By 1902 there were 1,078 local unions in Canada. More than half (547) were located in Ontario, with British Columbia and Quebec each having just over 150, and the other provinces having considerably less than 100 each. Although by 1922 the balance had shifted somewhat to the western provinces, Ontario still had by far the largest number of locals, followed at some distance by Quebec.[4] This regional disparity is reflected in the discussion that follows. Much of the information was drawn from Ontario, some was drawn from Quebec and British Columbia and little was available from the other provinces.

As industry developed the population was increasingly concentrated in urban centres. By 1921 Montreal and Toronto were the major industrial and commercial centres, followed by Winnipeg and Vancouver.[5] Both Montreal and Toronto exceeded 500,000 in population, Montreal having doubled its population in twenty years and Toronto having increased by one and a half times in the same period. Again, because union activity was focused in these large city centres, information from Toronto and Montreal predominates in the following analysis.

Immigration to Canada had been primarily from Western and Eastern Europe and Scandinavia, a situation that was not to change until after World War II. Consequently, the discussion that follows necessarily concentrates on the union response to the white cultural majority. However, historical research on the relationship between unions and non-white cultural groups is just developing. In the west coast fishing industry the indigenous native population was in contact with the developing union movement. Also on the west coast many Chinese workers had arrived to work on the railways, and by 1931 Chinese men comprised 9 percent of the male labour force in British Columbia, working in agriculture, service jobs and as unskilled labour. There was also a small black population, the result of 200 years of slavery in Canada and the movement north of slaves from America. Many black men in the cities worked as porters for the railway companies, where the work force was unionized. The limited information available on these topics will be explored in the discussion that follows. However, thus far, historical research on women from minority racial groups in relation to the union movement is very sparse.

Before examining the response of unions to women workers during this early period, the context of women's employment is briefly outlined, including the prevalent ideology concerning employed women, the actual work that women did, the composition of the female work force and the role of employers. All these factors influenced the part played by women in the early development of the union movement.

Traditional Ideology Concerning Women and Women Workers

Victorian and Christian ideology defined women as inferior to men, fragile, emotional and in need of protection. This ideology was as prevalent in English Canada as an import as it was in Britain. The ideal of womanhood combined religious piety, moral purity, and — first and foremost — a complete commitment to domesticity. A woman's primary role, her natural contribution, was as a wife and mother. These beliefs were held even more strongly in Catholic Quebec, where the strength of the family was regarded as the root of national survival. Of this Mona-Josée Gagnon has written:

> Quebecers refused to accept the idea that women could have any vocation other than serving the family, the bulwark against the invasion of an Anglo-Saxon and materialistic culture.[6]

Consequently, in Quebec women gained their rights more slowly than elsewhere, and traditional ideology retained much of its force even into the 1960s.

Clearly, women who worked outside the home stood in direct contradiction to the prevailing ideology, and as a result provoked much concern and discussion. Employed women were perceived by middle-class women's organizations, reformers and factory inspectors as a "social crisis," creating problems of cleanliness, morality and health for future mothers.[7] Various organizations were established by well-meaning middle-class women to help the "working girl." They included the National Council of Women, the Saint Jean Baptiste Society and several Christian groups. Factory inspectors concerned themselves with cleanliness, separation of male and female workers including separate lavatories, and seats for shop clerks so that they need not stand all day (to prevent damage to reproductive organs). The requirement for morality was uppermost. Madame Provencher, a factor inspector in Quebec, recommended: "Every working girl caught using certain words or raising improper questions should be immediately discharged."[8]

Although by 1921, 20 percent of women over 14 years of age worked outside the home,[9] the following comments appeared in the 1922 Annual Report of the Quebec Department of Labour:

> Woman's work, outside of her home, is one of the sad novelties of the modern world; it is a true social heresy ... Such singularities are due to a fleeting crisis, the social crisis of the present day ... With regard to the work of single women, it would be wonderful if society could, some day or another, find an economic formula capable of doing away with it.[10]

Public discussion of the position of employed women ignored the rights of women as workers, their economic role and their class position in relation to male workers, concentrating only on the effects of work on the maternal role.

During the period 1881–1921, women in English Canada were gaining economic, legal and political rights. Although many activities were undertaken by feminists during this period, the struggle for the right to vote was the most sustained and widely publicized. Before appraising the ideology concerning women prevalent in the union movement, it is instructive to consider the ideology of feminists at this time. While a small group of women "sought to compete with men on men's terms hoping in the process to etch a new role for women,"[11] most feminists accepted the idea that women had a special maternal role and sought only to extend its influence beyond the narrow confines of the family.[12] They argued that women's mothering instincts should be applied in the political sphere and would benefit society by ensuring the protection of family stability. Only by participation in public life, they argued, could women properly fulfill their special duty to ensure the welfare of their children and their homes.

The best known suffragette, Nellie McClung, wrote indignantly of the opponents of women's votes that they would prevent from voting "the wife and mother, with her God-given sacred trust of molding the young life of our land."[13] While the importance

Nellie McClung on "tender-hearted gentlemen" in 1915

These tender-hearted and chivalrous gentlemen who tell you of their adoration for women, cannot bear to think of women occupying public positions. Their tender hearts shrink from the idea of women lawyers or women policemen, or even women preachers; these positions would "rub the bloom off the peach" to use their own eloquent words. They cannot bear, they say, to see women leaving the sacred precincts of home—and yet their offices are scrubbed by women who do their work while other people sleep—poor women who leave the sacred precincts of home to earn enough to keep the breath of life in them, who carry their scrub-pails home, through the deserted streets, long after the cars have stopped running. They are exposed to cold, to hunger, to insult — poor souls — is there any pity felt for them? Not that we have heard of. The tender hearted ones can bear this with equanimity. It is the thought of women getting into comfortable and well-paid positions which wrings their manly hearts.

Nellie McClung, *In Times Like These*, (Toronto: University of Toronto Press, 1972), first published in 1915, p.52.

attached to motherhood may seem outdated today, the struggle for the vote was undoubtedly progressive at the time and met with massive opposition. It was not until 1916 that women in Manitoba obtained the right to vote. Most provinces followed Manitoba's lead within a few years, although in Quebec women could not vote until 1940.

Given the ideology of the women's rights movement of the period, it is perhaps not surprising to find contradictory positions within the union movement. There is no question that unions operated within the prevailing ideology concerning women, but to be aware that this was also true in certain respects of the suffrage movement helps to place the discussion within an historical context.

The Work Done by Women

The first census to provide information on the occupations of women was 1887. Table 1-1 shows the ten leading occupations for women in 1891 and 1921.

During the 30 years between 1891 and 1921, clerical work expanded rapidly and developed into the leading occupation for women, pushing domestic service from first to second place. Another important development was the growth of factory workers in the textile and clothing industries, together the largest industrial employer of women. Teaching and the needle trades continued among the top ten occupations for women, while nursing developed into a major occupation over these 30 years. Throughout the period, most of the work women did had two characteristics that presented great obstacles to unionization: it was highly fragmented and it was generally unskilled.

Between 1881 and 1921 the large majority of employed women worked either in total isolation or in workplaces with few other workers. This lack of collectivized work inhibited collective action, making it extremely difficult, if not impossible, to unionize. In 1891 fully 41 percent of employed women were domestic servants.[14] Although some of these women had the company of perhaps one or two other servants, most worked as "general helps," alone and in isolation. This isolation militated against unionizing attempts:

> In contrast to the factory or office, which brought workers together, revealed their common interests, and provided a base of action, the private home separated the domestic employee from her sister workers and overemphasized the personal aspect of her relationship with her employers.[15]

Despite such adverse circumstances, organizing attempts were made by female domestic servants, although none could be sustained for very long.[16] As servants they lacked free time for meetings and could communicate only with great difficulty between individual houses. They were vulnerable to retaliation by their employers, having no effective means to protect themselves. As well, the turnover of workers in domestic service was rapid. For most women, the long hours, arduous work, close supervision, lack of personal freedom and low status meant that women left domestic service as soon as they could obtain any other work. Finnish women were an exception since they did not regard domestic work as low status and, by establishing their capability for the work, were able to obtain some leverage with which to

TABLE 1-1: Leading Occupations for Women, 1891 and 1921			
	1891		**1921**
Servant	77,644	Clerical	78,342
Dressmaker	22,686	Servant	78,118
Teacher	14,803	Teacher	49,795
Farmer	11,590	Saleswoman	35,474
Seamstress	10,239	Housekeeper	23,167
Tailoress	7,834	Nurse	21,162
Saleswoman	4,409	Dressmaker/Seamstress	16,612
Housekeeper	4,035	Farmer	16,315
Laundress	3,679	Textile Factory Operative	15,193
Milliner	3,277	Clothing Factory Operative	14,470

Source: 1891 Census of Canada; Janice Acton et al, *Women at Work 1850–1930*, Toronto, Women's Educational Press, 1974, p.267, Table B.

improve their working conditions.[17] But even for Finnish domestics it was common to move from one job to another, obtaining increased wages with each move. While employers were frustrated by the "procession of maids through the kitchen,"[18] the constant turnover frustrated even more surely the stability of any embryo union organization.

Domestic service was not the only occupation fragmented in this way. The second largest employer of women was the clothing and textile industry, and here contract labour and the sweated workshop were the norm. Large and "respectable" firms such as Eaton's contracted out their work to the owners of small shops or to individuals in their homes. The Report Upon the Sweating System in Canada, 1896, stated that in Toronto the proportion of work done in private homes was greater than that done in small shops and far surpassed what was done in factories. The report went on to say that the workers "almost invariably prefer the factory system," well aware that in their individual homes they were subject to extreme exploitation.[19] This system even prevented wage comparison, not to mention unionization. Where women workers were brought together, the numbers were still small. In his excellent study of working women in Toronto from 1896 to 1914, Wayne Roberts states:

Immigrants for domestic service, Quebec City, Quebec, 1911.

In response to the scarcity of servants, private organizations, aided by grants from the Department of Immigration, recruited women in Great Britain and escorted them to Canada.

Courtesy of the National Archives of Canada, PA-126101. Photograph by W.J. Topley.

nineteen establishments shared more than 500 women in shirt, collar and tie making; dressmaking and tailoring each employed more than 1,000 women, who were spread over 402 and 216 establishments respectively.[20]

This is an average of four women in each workplace.

The advantages for employers were many. Small shops were not even covered by the few regulations of the Factory Acts and consequently were not subject to inspection and public scrutiny. More important, unionization was prevented, wages were held down and the potential for strike action was eliminated. Thus profits were secured and increased.

The work done by women was largely unskilled compared to the skilled crafts work of the time, so that any particular worker was entirely dispensable. With high immigration, and with a population moving from the country to the town, a large supply of surplus labour was created. This presented great risks in union organization, since it was a simple matter for an employer to fire any worker who hinted at dissatisfaction and to replace her instantly at no loss to the business. One study reported that such a worker "may at any time be replaced by a younger girl, who may be trained satisfactorily in a few months at the utmost."[21] Roberts reports a case in a laundry in Toronto where women reporting violations of factory legislation to an inspector were fired, "while the employer was let off with a two dollar fine."[22]

Unskilled workers had scant bargaining power with which to face their employers. An analysis of 287 strikes in Montreal between 1901 and 1921 demonstrates the unrelenting power of the employer: 115 of these strikes resulted in the total rejection of employee demands "frequently accompanied by dismissal of the strikers and the employment of scab labour."[23] Unskilled women workers had little leverage to prevent such actions.

Deprived of any interest in or control over their work, closely regimented and without the collective solidarity of unions, many women in factory work, as in domestic service, moved from job to job.

> In the case of women, one observer found floating (i.e. changing jobs) to be the standard technique for staving off the monotony of putting dabs of jelly on cookies or other assorted tasks.[24]

Women worked extremely long hours not only as domestic servants and in the sweatshops, but also as "shopgirls." In 1895 an employer of sweated needleworkers told the hearings of the Royal Commission on the Sweating System:

> I had a grocery store in this city not long ago and a girl came to me and offered her services for two and a half dollars per week, although her hours were longer in that store than those of any girl tailoring for me.[25]

Shopgirls commonly worked 12 hours a day and 16 hours on Saturday. After such exhausting hours, little energy or time could have remained with which to organize.

Three of the leading ten occupations for women in 1921 presented rather different problems as far as unionization was concerned. These were the clerical, teaching and nursing positions that women held in increasing numbers throughout the period. Unions were non-existent in these occupations and where the workers formed organizations to represent their interests, concern with the professional status of the work overshadowed the possibility of collective bargaining for improved wages and conditions.

The burgeoning number of women clerical workers, replacing the male clerks of the nineteenth century, were considerably better paid than most other occupations available to women. Between 1901 and 1921 women clerical workers earned between 37 percent and 45 percent more than the average for all employed women.[26]

Office work also carried some prestige compared to the relative drudgery of domestic service, factory or shop work. These factors, combined with a disciplinarian and individualistic office atmosphere, inhibited the development of unionism among women clerical workers.

> The individualistic strivings of nineteenth-century male clerks, reinforced by small and informal work settings and loyalty to their employer, moulded a pervasive ideology of the office. Trade unionism rarely developed. When women began flooding into offices they inherited this legacy of individualism which had come to define employer-employee relations.[27]

The two professional occupations available to women during this period, nursing and teaching, were of rather dubious stature. While nursing was more respectable in Quebec, being based upon the work of religious orders, in Ontario, student nurses worked long hours for little more than room and board, while trained nurses struggled to distinguish themselves from the untrained "practical" nurses who were often little different from domestic servants. The Canadian National Association of Trained Nurses, formed in 1912, lobbied to obtain government registration of trained nurses. Although the Association did involve itself with the campaign for an 8 hour day, its main objective during this period was to obtain control over training. By 1922 all provinces had some kind of legislation, but it was not until 1951 in Ontario that the Ontario Nurses Association obtained full control over admission and certification.[28]

By the 1880s the feminization of teaching had progressed to the point where in Toronto nine out of ten elementary school teachers were women.[29] Women's salaries were half that paid to men and classes regularly included more than fifty students. In rural communities teachers were isolated and boarded with a local family. Local teachers' associations were formed from the 1880s on and in 1918 the Federation of Women Teachers' Associations of Ontario was constituted. Despite the concern of these organizations with low salaries, and even a strike in one instance, they avoided contact with the union movement. As the Federation phrased it in 1924:

> Our primary concern ... is not with the pros and cons of trades-unionism, but with the problem of creating for teaching a social prestige that will justify its general recognition, by statute if necessary, as one of the major professions.[30]

One exception to the generally professional nature of teachers' organizations was an association of 380 lay teachers in Montreal.

In 1919 they went on strike for improved wages and a collective agreement. However, the school commission refused even to discuss their problems and instead established a professional organization as an alternative. Forty eight teachers lost their jobs because they refused to quit their own association.[31]

The Composition of the Female Work Force

Only a minority of women participated in the labour force during the period from 1881 to 1921. In 1921 just under 20 percent of all women over the age of 14 years were employed in the work force.[32] Women also comprised a relatively small proportion of the total labour force throughout the period. In 1901, women constituted just 13 percent of the total labour force, increasing to only 15 percent by 1921.[33] It was not until the 1940s and 1950s that women became a much more significant part of the work force, and by 1991, 58 percent of women participated in the labour force, while women comprised 45 percent of the total labour force.[34]

Besides being few in number, women workers were predominantly young and single. As Table 1-2 shows, in 1921 the highest participation rates were among women under 24 years old. A comparison with participation rates today clearly shows the different nature of the female work force in the early years of the century. In 1921, while 40 percent of women aged 20–24 years were in the labour force, the figure falls to 20 percent of women aged 25–34 years, and only 12 percent of those aged 35–64 years. By comparison in 1986 there is no dramatic decrease in the participation of women in the labour force after 25 years of age. The participation rate continues to be relatively high at 74 percent for the 25 to 34 year old age group, and 59 percent for the 35–64 year old age group.

The predominance of young women in the labour force in 1921 reflects the fact that women generally left paid employment outside the home when they married and had children, never to return. Although married women contributed to the family income by taking in lodgers and laundry, by growing vegetables and keeping animals, few returned to paid employment outside their homes.[35] Even by 1931, the earliest year for which figures are available, only 10 percent of women in the work force were married.[36] In the same year, of all married women just 3 percent were in the labour force, and by 1941 the figure was still less than 5 percent.[37] One writer in Montreal, Louis Guyon, wrote in 1922:

Table 1-2: Labour Force Participation Rates of Women by Age, for Selected Years, 1921-1986 (%)

	*14\15-19	20-24	25-34	35-64	65+
1921	30	40	20	12	7
1941	27	47	28	15	6
1961	32	51	29	30	6
1981	51	78	66	53	5
1986	50	81	74	59	4

*1921-1961 14-19 years; 1981-1986 15-19 years
Source: Sylvia Ostry and F. Denton, "Historical Estimates of the Canadian Labour Force," 1961 Census Monograph, Queen's Printer, 1967; Statistics Canada, Census Canada 1986, Labour Force Activity, Cat. 93-111, Ottawa, March 1989, Table 1-1.

Happily we have not, in our country, the problem of the married woman in workshops and factories, with a few rare exceptions.[38]

These exceptions were considered to be the "unfortunates," women with dependents who were forced to work because of the death, unemployment or desertion of their men.

Why did women leave the work force upon marriage? In 1895 the Toronto School Board refused to hire either married women or women over 30 years old.[39] However, such compulsion was unnecessary in most cases since women rarely worked outside the home after marriage. The conditions of married life were a serious deterrent. Primitive birth control methods, combined with a lack of domestic technology (or its expense) and subsistence-level family incomes, meant that upon marriage women shouldered an enormous responsibility for the physical survival of an ever-growing family. The strenuous workload of working-class wives and mothers has been documented elsewhere.[40] Indeed few married women chose to work outside the home unless it was absolutely necessary.

The female work force changed every few years as a new generation of women assumed family responsibilities. This constant turnover of women workers was a crucial deterrent to unionization. Given the context of powerful employer opposition, maintaining a union in the face of constantly changing members was extremely difficult.[41] As Joan Sangster has noted with regard to one situation:

It is noteworthy that after the massive 1907 Bell Telephone strike, the operators' attempt to set up an IBEW local floundered not only on employer opposition and the union's ambivalence towards women members, but also because of the rapid turnover of telephone operators at the workplace.[42]

In a report on women and the Catholic unions in Quebec the turnover of members is apparent. In Montreal associations of workers in manufacturing, shops and offices had been formed in 1906 and 1907. In 1922 the manufacturing association had 1,200 members, but 5,000 women workers had passed through the organization since its formation. The shops' association had 107 members in 1922, but 973 members had belonged since its foundation. Likewise among office workers the association of 125 members had seen a total of 1,675 women pass through the organization.[43] The effects were far-reaching. Spending only a few years in the labour force, women were deprived of the opportunity to build experience in collective action, to discuss and pass on knowledge of work relationships, to develop a history of action and to provide leaders with years of work and union experience.

During this period working women constituted only a small and transient section of the labour force, in a society that ideologically opposed their very existence — they were in fact a deviation from woman's dominant role. Roberts describes the impact of this situation:

> Unlike working women of today who can evaluate their experiences in terms of widespread public discussion on the status of women and who can draw inspiration, clarity and legitimacy from a generalized movement, working women before 1914 operated in an ideological vacuum ... They were a small detachment who could not share in the process of re-evaluating sexual standards with any substantial core of the population.[44]

Another factor in the composition of the female work force inhibited unionization. Because unskilled work attracted new immigrants and women who had recently moved to the town from rural areas, in many cases there were cultural and linguistic barriers between working women that hindered moves toward collective action. Of all women employed in gainful occupations in 1911, 24 percent were immigrants.[45] That year 58 percent of domestics in Toronto were immigrants.[46] In the same city Chinese laundries competed with one employing an exclusively Swedish work force and another where only English and Italian women worked.[47] The garment industry, which employed so many women, was fragmented by local divisions between different ethnic groups.[48]

These cultural differences did not improve the chances of organizing. Moreover, as workers threatened by competition from yet more surplus labour when already insecure in their jobs, women shared with men the early anti-immigrant perspectives. In 1901 in Toronto thirty women and five men struck against their employer for hiring immigrants, "revealing that no disdain for nativism differentiated them [women workers] from the rest of the workers."[49]

The Role of Employers

Throughout the period 1881–1921 employers were extremely hostile to any attempts at unionization. Anti-union techniques included firing pro-union workers, blacklisting workers so that they could not obtain employment anywhere, lockouts and hiring workers only on condition that they sign a "yellow-dog contract" agreeing to remain non-union. These were powerful weapons against workers who had no means to survive without a job, and strikers were often starved into submission. Such methods were supported by the courts. Union leaders were imprisoned for "seditious conspiracy," that is for forming a union, until the late 1800s. The courts served injunctions to prohibit striking, picketing and boycotting, thereby rendering unions powerless. Police and militia enforced the injunctions and protected the employer's property more or less violently. As one historian of the trade union movement has said: "Hunger and state coercion — a formidable combination. Employers used it constantly against the unions."[50]

Unionists in Toronto during this period have been called "militants without power" and their situation described as follows:

> When confronting social and economic problems, workers were not passive; they were powerless ... The basic problem confronting labour was the employers' habitual opposition to collective bargaining.[51]

Between 1901 and 1921 the basic issues of union recognition, wages and hours of work dominated union struggles, but most strikes over the period ended in failure.[52]

It is within this context of employer opposition, union weakness and worker insecurity that the early unionization attempts by women must be located. There is some evidence that employers, fearful of losing their source of cheap labour, opposed organizing attempts by women with particular ferocity.

The Fortier Scandal

Evidence under oath of Miss Georgiana Loiselle, cigar maker of Montreal, before the Royal Commission on Relations of Labor and Capital, 1889.

Q: In what factory do you work, Miss?

A: At Mr. Fortier's.

Q: Were you beaten then at Mr. Fortier's?

A: Yes, sir.

Q: Will you tell us in what way you were beaten?

A: It was Mr. Fortier who beat me with a mould cover.

Q: Why did he beat you?

A: I would not make one hundred cigars which he gave me to make. I refused to make them and he beat me with the mould cover.

Q: Did he seize you before beating you?

A: I was sitting, and he took hold of me by the arm, and tried to throw me to the ground. He did throw me to the ground and beat me with the mould cover.

Q: Did he beat you when you were down?

A: Yes, I tried to rise and he kept me down on the floor.

This incident was confirmed by Mr. Fortier himself, as well as the practice of confining young factory apprentices to a dark and damp coal cellar, "the black hole," for hours at a time. The Commissioners commented:

And for all this the law provides no remedy — nay, incredible as it may appear, law, in the person of the Recorder of Montreal, expressly authorized the punishment inflicted. This gentleman on being examined, stated that he had authorized employers to chastise their operatives at their discretion, so long as no permanent injury was inflicted.

Gregory Kealey, *Canada Investigates Industrialism, The Royal Commission on the Relations of Labor and Capital 1889 (Abridged)*, (Toronto: University of Toronto Press, 1973) pp. 42, 222–223.

Women were often more closely regimented at work than men, subject to constant supervision and penalized heavily for small infractions. Such measures served to remind women workers of their vulnerability and powerlessness, further inhibiting thoughts of unionization. Roberts states:

Although employers found this punishment impossible to impose on men, the practice of fining women workers for laughing, talking, using toilet-paper hair-curlers, or damaging work was common, especially in the early years of industrialism.[53]

As an example, Roberts records an incident in 1905 of an employer intending to install a clock timed to the half-second, by which the women workers would lose a half-hour's pay for being one minute late.[54]

Such harassment by the employer was not confined to factory workers. Female teachers were subject to surveillance of their morals, religion, dress and personal habits. One contract specified that the teacher not get married, not ride in a carriage with any man not her relative, not leave town without permission, not smoke or drink, not dye her hair, not dress in bright colours, never wear fewer than two petticoats, not wear make up, wear her dresses no more than two inches above the ankle and not loiter downtown in icecream parlours.[55] In 1895 the Toronto School Board felt compelled to meet to discuss a woman teacher observed wearing bloomers while riding a bicycle;[56] this same board refused to hire women who chewed gum.[57]

In 1886 the government established the Royal Commission on the Relations of Labor and Capital (referred to hereafter as the Labor Commission) to travel across the country and report on factory conditions. Two reports were produced in 1889, and among its many findings the Commission reported that employers subjected women to particular forms of regimentation:

Females and children may be counted upon to work for small wages, to submit to petty exasperating exactions and to work uncomplainingly for long hours.[58]

With regard to the practice of fines for workers in factories and stores the Commission said:

It is worthy of note that the fines are only imposed upon females and children, the most helpless class of operatives. Men will not put up with deductions from wages which they have toiled hard to obtain, and therefore the system is not applied to them.[59]

The methods by which employers suppressed any suggestion of "insubordination" must have taken their toll in undermining the possibility of union organization among women.

Whatever patriarchal attitudes employers harboured, they served to reinforce the basic economic self-interest that lay behind their opposition to unionization. This becomes clear when the work done by women is examined. Apart from domestic service,

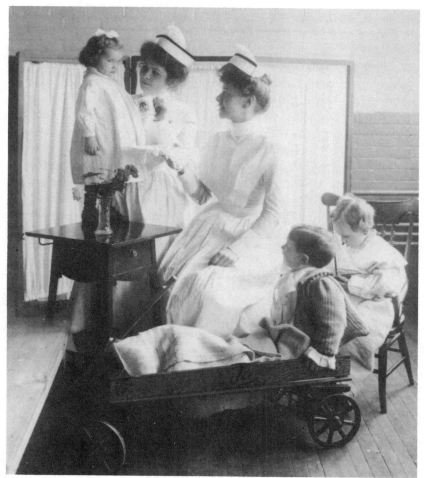

Nurses and patients
on the baby ward
verandah, Hospital
for Sick Children,
Toronto, Ontario,
1905.

*Courtesy of the National
Archives of Canada,
C91070.*

the leading occupations for women in 1891 were in the garment
industry, as dressmakers, seamstresses, tailoresses and milliners
(see Table 1-1). The garment industry as well as the laundries were
engaged in cut-throat competition to supply cheap goods and
services. Not only were the employers' profits increased by cheap
female labour, they often depended upon it.

The use of women as a source of cheap labour was not confined
to factories and workshops. Between 1880 and 1914, 96 new
hospitals were built in Ontario and student nurses were blatantly
exploited as cheap labour. They worked long hours in return for
very low pay and wretched room and board, with minimal actual
education. After two or three years of training the hospitals

replaced them with more student nurses and they were forced into nursing in private homes. It was common practice for hospitals to employ no trained nursing staff at all, a situation that remained a problem until into the 1930s.[60]

In clerical work, teaching and selling, the other leading jobs for women in 1921, rapid expansion had been attended by feminization in each case. During the second half of the nineteenth century, hiring more female teachers at lower wages than men provided the means by which school boards could expand education while keeping costs as low as possible. At the same time, grading systems were introduced within the schools. Teaching of the lower grades was perceived as less skilled work, thereby justifying the low wages paid to the women who taught those grades.[61] In 1889 the average yearly salary for a male teacher was $421 in Ontario and for a woman $296.[62]

A similar process occurred for saleswomen. As department stores expanded, the work became more finely divided, with women allocated to the work considered the least skilled.

> Feminization of the occupation attended the triumph of the large department stores, which restructured the division of labour and patterns of authority of retail staffing.[63]

As stores became larger, each job required less knowledge and held less responsibility. Thus the way was paved for cheap, unskilled labour — in other words, women.

Somewhat later, after 1900, clerical work experienced the same shift from male to female employment and for similar reasons. Economic expansion in the first two decades of the century lead to a rapid increase in clerical work, and tasks were divided and specialized so that less-skilled workers could be hired at lower wages. The result was the massive entry of women into clerical work, replacing the male bookkeepers of the 1800s.[64] In 1901 female clerical workers earned an average annual income of $264, while men earned $496.[65] In all these occupations the lower wages paid to women was the primary motivation for employers to expand the female labour force.

The Union Movement

Before examining what unions actually said and did about working women, it is important to understand the nature of unions in Canada during the period 1881 to 1921. Two characteristics are important: the craft nature of unions and the fact that they were international.

Initiated before the advent of mechanization and the consequent employment of unskilled labour in factories, the early unions were organizations of workers skilled in particular crafts. These craft unions based their bargaining power upon the fact that such workers could not easily be replaced. Restricting access to such crafts was therefore an integral part of maintaining this bargaining power and was a central tenet of craft unionism. Admitting unskilled workers into these unions was not only foreign to their method of operation, it represented a threat to the bargaining power of the skilled members. Organizing on industrial lines (including all workers, skilled and unskilled, within a plant or factory) did not become an integral part of the union movement until the 1930s and 1940s. Table 1-3 shows the predominance of members in craft unions from 1914 to 1921, although there is a significant increase over the period in the "other trades and general labour" group. 1914 is the first year for which such figures are available.

The exclusion of unskilled workers from craft unions affected both women, most of whom were unskilled, and large numbers of unskilled male workers. Craft unions had some reason to be especially threatened by women workers because employers used women as cheap unskilled labour. Consequently, women's entry into an occupation "was the death knell of an artisanal trade. More, they were levers that destroyed its norms, habits and strengths."[66] Such was the case, for example, with women shoemakers:

> They were a direct result of the factory system with its logic of breaking down attained skills into simple, repetitive and mechanical tasks. Where once the shoe trade required long apprenticeships and highly skilled men, now the factory-made shoes simply required highly attentive women to watch the machines.[67]

The fears of craft unions about women are demonstrated by the 1907 Toronto Bell Telephone strike of 400 non-unionized women operators, protesting poor conditions, low wages and an increase in working hours. In her excellent article on the strike, Joan Sangster explains that the International Brotherhood of Electrical Workers (IBEW) had claimed jurisdiction over the telephone operators, but had done little to organize them.[68] The strikers twice passed resolutions to affiliate to the IBEW, but nothing materialized. Convinced that women made poor union members, the IBEW "had developed a strong tradition of inequality." The few American

Table 1-3: Union Membership by Type of Employment (%) 1914 & 1921		
	1914	1921
Railroad Employees	24.9	26.2
Building Trades	18.9	9.8
Metal Trades	8.6	7.4
Mining & Quarrying	8.7	6.8
Printing Trades	4.7	2.6
Clothing, Boots & Shoes	7.0	6.0
Transportation (other than Railways)	8.0	8.8
Public Employees, Personal Service & Amusement	8.2	7.9
All Other Trades & General Labour*	10.7	24.5
	99.7%	100.0%

*Includes unions not specified elsewhere: rubber, unions of general workers like Industrial Workers of the World and One Big Union, some of Quebec National Catholic following and independent locals.
Source: H.A. Logan, *The History of Trade Union Organization in Canada*, University of Chicago Press, 1928, p.127, Table 6.

locals of telephone operators (all women) were denied full autonomy and given only half their voting rights. Sangster describes other fears held by the skilled electricians:

> The electricians claimed that unskilled operators might make foolish decisions on craft matters that they did not understand. There was also a strong apprehension about "petticoat rule:" the large number of operators, it was feared, would come to control the union.[69]

Consequently the union did not help to organize telephone operators, and this was a factor in the failure of the Toronto telephone operators' strike.

The early craft unions have been criticized because of their protectionist policies, because they bargained for workers who were already among the best paid, and because they ignored the growing army of unskilled workers. These criticisms are not unjustified, but it is also necessary to understand the power of employers to influence which workers could organize and bargain.

Unskilled workers were all too easily fired and replaced, and their attempts to organize in the early decades of this century are a story of struggle against overwhelming odds. In his analysis of 287 strikes in Montreal between 1901 and 1921, Copp found:

> Success in the sense of employer acceptance of the demands of the strikers was obtained in only 49 strikes, most of them involving less than 100 workers in highly skilled craft unions.[70]

It is clear from Copp's description of these strikes that in this period even craft workers usually lost their demands, and success depended very much upon the economic climate. For example, a longshoremen's strike for wage increases "was instantly successful, probably because it was timed as the last ships were desperately attempting to clear the Montreal harbour before the freezing."[71] Without such economic leverage, unskilled workers were generally powerless in the face of employer opposition.

If we use the example of the Toronto Bell Telephone strike referred to earlier, it is apparent that employer opposition to unions and to collective action was adamant, in this case despite tremendous public support for the women workers. Bell refused throughout to consult with the workers. Strike-breakers were hired to carry on the work from the first day of the strike, undermining the women's bargaining power. When the strike ended, Bell initially refused to re-employ any of the strike leaders or picketers. This policy was later amended and women connected with the IBEW could resume their positions on condition that they left the union. "Such anti-union victimization was obviously a major factor in discouraging unionization."[72] Fierce employer opposition, and the vulnerability of unskilled workers so easily replaced, gave the craft unions some realistic basis for their reluctance to organize women workers.

Another tradition directly or indirectly worked against the unionization of women. Between 1881 and 1921 unions were almost all international, based in America and affiliated to the American Federation of Labor (AFL). At the Trades and Labor Congress of Canada in 1902, an amendment to the constitution was adopted that stated that no national union would be recognized where an international existed, thus effectively undermining the formation of a national labour movement. In 1912, 85 percent of union members in Canada belonged to international unions; this had dropped to 71 percent by 1921.[73]

It is difficult to assess the influence that the international nature of unionism in Canada had upon the organization of women workers. Certainly Samuel Gompers, president of the AFL, forcefully supported craft unions against industrial unionism, and this hindered the organization of women. Alice Kessler-Harris has examined the ambivalence of the AFL towards women workers and documented many examples of the failure of international unions to support and organize women in America.[74] There is no reason to suppose that the same unions treated Canadian women workers differently. While it is impossible to prove that, left alone, Canada would have developed a more progressive union movement, there is no question that the American influence was a conservative one which did not promote the unionization of women during this period.

To summarize the discussion to this point, from 1881 to 1921, women were never more than 15 percent of the total labour force. Women workers were young, single, and transient, remaining in the labour force only until marriage. Women's role in society was still overwhelmingly domestic, a role reinforced and institutionalized by the prevailing ideology. Unions organized primarily craft workers who, with some justification, regarded the relatively powerless unskilled workers as a threat to their status and wages. Women were particularly threatening because their wages were lower and because employers used female labour to reduce wages. Given this framework, what was the response of the union movement to working women? In fact there was no single response; different and contradictory positions were taken by the union movement, including the exclusion of women from the labour force and the family wage policy, protective legislation, and unionization.

The Exclusion of Women and the Family Wage

The union movement was generally in step with the times in viewing the primary role of women as a domestic one. Women's pages in labour publications were oriented towards the wives and mothers of unionists, providing recipes and fashion discussions. In 1907, an article entitled "The Influence of Women in the Labour Movement" appeared in the *Toronto Labour Day Souvenir Book*. As Klein and Roberts describe it:

> this article deals exclusively with the role that women as consumers, wives and mothers can play in the union movement. There is not

a hint to be gleaned from this article that there is such a thing as the employed female.[75]

Women were encouraged to contribute to the union movement either through the label campaign or women's auxiliaries. The label campaign promoted the purchase of goods with a union label (indicating that the goods were made by unionized workers) and was intended to pressure employers to permit unionization, while penalizing non-union workplaces. Auxiliaries supported the men's unions and commonly organized social activities. While these two activities provided some role for women within the union, they were very limited, and usually relegated to a marginal position.[76]

The union movement did not confine itself to ignoring women in the labour force; the exclusion of women was openly advocated. The Trades and Labor Congress of Canada, as part of its 16-point program in 1898, called for the

abolition of child labour by children under 14 years of age and of female labour in all branches of industrial life, such as mines, work-shops, factories, etc.[77]

The American Federation of Labor (AFL), with which most unions in Canada were affiliated, took the same stand. Kessler-Harris has documented the prevailing policy positions. In 1905 the AFL's treasurer said:

The great principle for which we fight is opposed to taking … the women from their homes to put them in the factory and the sweatshop.[78]

Individual unions followed suit. In 1893 the International Brotherhood of Electrical Workers that represented telecommunications workers formally excluded women workers. This decision was rescinded following some protest, but "although not formally excluded from the union, women were not actively sought as members."[79] In 1904 bookbinders went on strike in Montreal to force the employer to fire the women workers.[80] In the 1920s the Journeymen Barbers International Union still rejected female applicants.[81]

A related response from unions to the issue of women and employment was to advocate the family wage. Men should receive sufficient pay to support a wife and children, so that women did not need to seek employment outside the home. The Western Clarion, a socialist paper, printed these comments in 1908:

Socialists don't believe in mothers working at all. They hold that under a sage industrial system wherein the worker would obtain the full value of his products, the man would earn sufficient to raise and maintain his family under proper conditions.[82]

A labour journal in Toronto, The Tribune, stated in 1913, concerning a proposal for a minimum wage for women: "Give the male workers a decent living wage and a minimum wage for women will be unnecessary."[83]

AFL president Samuel Gompers outlined the economic reasons for exclusion of women from the labour force:

> It is the so-called competition of the unorganized defenseless woman worker, the girl and the wife, that often tends to reduce the wages of the father and husband.[84]

The fear of women competing at lower wages for men's jobs was echoed by various unions that belonged to the Canadian and American central labour bodies, and they had good reason to be fearful. As occupations expanded and employers sought cheap labour to offset the costs of expansion, women were hired, wages fell and men were forced out. As outlined earlier in this chapter, this sequence of events occurred in teaching, clerical work and the retail trade, as well as certain branches of manufacturing.

This labour market competition fostered hostility between male and female workers. A member of the United Garment Workers wrote in the Weekly Bulletin of the Clothing Trades in June 1905:

> It is the men who suffer through the women who are employed in the manufacture of clothing. While the men through long years of struggle have succeeded in eliminating the contracting evil and the rotten system of piece work, the girls ... are now trying to deprive the older members of the Garment Workers of the benefits because [they] ... can afford to work for small wages and care nothing about the condition of the trade.[85]

The threat to wages and jobs from women workers became acute during World War I, when women were drawn into the labour force in unprecedented numbers. In Montreal, by the end of the war women had replaced men in munitions plants, railways, shops, and banks, generally earning from 50 to 80 percent of the wages paid to men.[86] The following sentiments were published in the B.C. Federationist, the journal of the British Columbia Federation of Labour:

> Women have worked for less than men ... and women will continue to work for less than men. Employers have had a taste of cheap labour and will be loath to part with their feminine employees at the close of the war ... The "heroes" will have to accept employment at such work and wages as the employers see fit to give. The work of the trade unions will have to [be] done all over again.[87]

By advocating the exclusion of women from the labour force, unions sought to resolve the problem of labour market competition, while at the same time conforming to the prevailing ideology that women were domestic creatures, to be protected within the confines of the home and economically supported by men.

Exclusion by Race

As society's perspective on women was reflected in unions, so was its perspective on racial minority groups. During the decades around the turn of the century Canada was an overtly racist society. The destruction of native culture was already well advanced, and the small population of blacks were subject to many restrictions, including segregated schools.[88] Immigration policy for Asians was geared to the need for labour, so that for example, while Chinese men obtained entry to work on the Canada Pacific Railway, Chinese women were excluded. The limited evidence available makes it clear that the union movement promoted the exclusion of non-whites from the country, from employment and from the unions.

Alicja Muszynski has described the exploitation of native and Asian workers in the fishing and canning industry on the west coast. By 1882 1,700 native workers, men, women and children, were employed in the industry at the height of the season. "While native labourers, male and female, were paid lower wages than European labourers, women (and children) were paid the lowest wages."[89] After the Canadian Pacific Railway was completed in 1885, Chinese men began to work in the canneries. Most were bound by debt to contractors, who had arranged the journey to Canada, who organized their employment in groups and who then took most of their wages in repayment for as long as ten years. In this situation, combined with language and cultural barriers, Chinese workers were in a particularly vulnerable position and as such they tended to replace the lowest paid workers, namely women and children.

> The Indians ... complain very much this spring and summer of how they are undermined in the labour market by Chinamen, especially in all kinds of light work, where the Indian women and their boys and girls used to be employed.[90]

Chinese, Japanese and East Indian immigrants were used generally as a source of cheap labour, earning one-half to three quarters of the wages paid to white workers.

Native women preparing fish at a salmon cannery, Skeena River, British Columbia, 1890.

Courtesy of the National Archives of Canada, PA 118162.

The response of the union movement was to call for the exclusion of all "orientals" from the country. The Workingman's Protective Association was formed in 1878 in Victoria for "the mutual protection of the working class of B.C. against the great influx of Chinese; to use all legitimate means for the suppression of their immigration."[91] Moreover, this position was not confined to specific unions or regions. The central body of the emerging labour movement, the Trades and Labour Congress, appointed a delegation at the 1890 convention in Ottawa to lobby the government for oriental exclusion.[92] From 1885 head taxes were levied specifically upon Asian immigrants as a deterrent, and in 1923 the Chinese Immigration Act stopped the entry of Chinese workers entirely. This legislation was not repealed until 1947.

In mining, the "willingness" of Asian workers to accept lower wages, work longer hours and in less safe conditions, led the Miners' Union to call for their exclusion from underground work in the mines. In 1898 labour candidates to the government of British Columbia, with additional leverage because the government was in a minority position, obtained the Coal Mines Regulation Act, which prohibited the employment of Chinese workers underground.[93] The Chinese population had no influence over such legal restrictions since they were denied the right to vote in 1875. As immigration from Japan increased, the same restriction was applied to the Japanese population in 1895.

Union negotiated agreements, for example in the lumber mills, entrenched lower minimum wages for oriental workers. This is not to imply that trade unions accepted non-whites as members, because the majority specifically excluded them. In the fishing industry, white, native and Japanese fishers organized separately. When fishers went on strike in 1893 the whites asked the Japanese fishers to join the strike, but would not let them join the association, and actually offered them $500 to set up their own separate union, an offer that was rejected. Native Indian fishermen were also excluded and in one joint strike the whites returned to work without even consulting them.[94]

> European, native and Japanese fishers can all point to instances when one group was striking while another group broke their strike, as well as instances when all three groups acted co-operatively.[95]

Divisions based on racial conflict continued in the fishing industry until after the second World War.

For the same reasons Chinese workers formed their own organizations, the Chinese Canadian Labour Union in 1916, the Chinese Shingle Workers' Union in 1919, and in the 1920s the Chinese Cooks Union and the Chinese Restaurant Workers' Union.[96]

At times the anti-Asian feeling erupted into violence and in 1907 racist rioting in Vancouver caused widespread damage to Chinese and Japanese homes and businesses.[97]

After World War I the more radical One Big Union and Workers' Unity League admitted Asian workers, but this was not the position of the mainstream union movement. In 1921 the Asiatic Exclusion League was formed, which included six unions and the Vancouver Trades and Labour Council as well as soldier and merchant groups.[98] It was not until after the second World War that labour support for such groups declined and oriental wage differentials were eliminated. Until that time, as one researcher has concluded:

> For the most part, the white labour movement excluded Asians from their trade unions, boycotted businesses employing Asians, pressed for legislation to protect jobs for white men, and were at the forefront of the movement to end further Asian immigration.[99]

The situation was no better in other parts of Canada where blacks working on the railways met the same exclusionary policies. Black workers were confined to the position of porter on the sleeping cars and were generally excluded from the higher paying dining car positions. The Canadian Brotherhood of Railway Employees (CBRE) refused membership in the union for the black

Scene following the 1907 race riots in Vancouver. The home of Otomatatsu Sonada, Contractor, 336 Powell Street, Vancouver.

Courtesy of the National Archives of Canada, PA – 67271.

porters, who organized their own union in 1918, the Order of Sleeping Car Porters. An attempt to allow blacks admission to the CBRE at the 1919 Convention failed, although it did succeed at the next Convention. However, admitting black workers to the union did not mean integration, because the locals of dining car workers and porters retained their separate identities and it was still not possible for blacks to move into the dining car positions. This was not changed until 1964 when a complaint under the Fair Employment Practices Act finally forced a merger between the two groups.[100]

On a different note, apparently the Teachers' Association of Canada West, at their fourth annual convention in Toronto in 1864, condemned separate schools for black children and passed a resolution opposing segregation in education.[101] No information is provided on why this occurred or whether it was repeated elsewhere. In any case it had no effect, since segregated schools remained common, particularly in Ontario and Nova Scotia, and the last segregated school in Canada, located in Colchester, Ontario, closed its doors in 1965.[102]

It is clear that during the decades around the turn of the century the union movement supported the exclusion of minority groups, and that this was true not only among individual unions but also at the central Trades and Labour Congress. The mainstream labour movement did not become a more progressive force until after World War II, when the Jewish Labour Committee of Canada worked to gain support for anti-discrimination legislation. The Canadian Labour Congress then organized a National Committee on Human Rights with regional committees across the country. Their work included attacking racial quotas in immigration and pressing for legislation to enforce fairness in all areas.[103]

Protective Legislation

Around the turn of the century, despite union calls for the exclusion of women from the work force, women continued to be employed, often for long hours and in the most appalling conditions. For example, in 1908 a Quebec, textile worker's day began at 6:15 a.m. and entailed non-stop work for 6 hours, followed by a half-hour lunch, and then a further period of uninterrupted labour until 5:30 in the evening. Factory legislation, purporting to protect women and children, offered one means to mitigate some of the worst conditions and to shorten the hours. In common with middle-class women's groups, reformers and factory inspectors, the union movement supported protective legislation for women.

In advocating protective legislation, unionists often worked with organizations such as the National Council of Women and turned to middle-class reformers to aid women workers, rather than to the union or to working women themselves. D.J. Donohue, a labour representative in Toronto, expressed to the National Council of Women "the need of some women of leisure and education to assist women workers to form benefit societies and other organizations for their help and improvement."[104] In British Columbia the Royal Commission on Labour Conditions invited the Vancouver Trades and Labour Council to provide suggestions on legislation for female shop and office workers. This union organization turned

Long Hours of Work for a Shop Clerk

Evidence under oath of a woman shop clerk from Montreal before the Royal Commission on the Relations of Labor and Capital, 1889.

Q: You are engaged in a millinery shop?

A: Yes, as clerk.

Q: What are the hours of work that you are called upon to do?

A: In the sale room it is from 8 o'clock in the morning until 9 o'clock in the evening, and when there is a rush, we begin at 8 o'clock in the morning to knock off — well, that depends at 10 o'clock to half-past 10, 11 o'clock to half-past 11.

Q: When you are not busy, from one end of the year to the other, you close at 9 o'clock?

A: 9 o'clock generally.

Q: What are the hours of rest which you have during the day?

A: Two hours, one hour for dinner and one hour for tea.

Q: Are you allowed to sit during the day?

A: Sometimes, if business allows.

Q: What are the wages generally paid the lady clerks in shops?

A: $3, $4 to $5 (per week), much depending on the season.

Source: Gregory Kealey, *Canada Investigates Industrialism: The Royal Commission on the Relations of Labor and Capital 1889 (Abridged)*, (Toronto: University of Toronto Press, 1973) p.255.

to the middle-class local Council of Women to form a committee, rather than to working women among its own membership. The Council of Women recommended a minimum wage for women of only $5 per week and this finally appeared in the committee's brief, even though the union representative had suggested $16.50 as reasonable. The committee also recommended a female inspector, seats for female employees so that they need not stand all day, and the separation of Caucasian women from Asiatics for reasons of morality.[105]

Union concern with the physical and moral protection of women workers, rather than their low wages, was typical of the period. In Quebec, Catholic unions ran courses for women that included domestic training as well as interest courses and general education. Michelle Lapointe concludes that work for young women, and union involvement, was accepted if it did not interfere with their later role as wives and mothers, the point of view that informed much protective legislation of the period.[106]

When the problems of working women were defined as health and morality some recourse other than negotiation was required, since unions were unable to bargain on these issues. In the struggle against starvation wages, strikes were almost invariably over wages, hours of work or basic union recognition.[107] Many of these strikes were lost and certainly there was little possibility for bargaining on other issues.[108] Meanwhile legislation purported to offer the means to protect women workers from some of the worst health hazards and longest hours.

Apart from "the overwhelming influence of the prevailing ideas of the time,"[109] two other reasons have been suggested for unions' recourse to legislation rather than negotiation to resolve the problems of women workers. One argument is that it was an extension of the exclusionary policies outlined above, the idea being that if women's hours and conditions of work were restricted, then employers would be less likely or able to hire women.[110] For example, in Ontario the 1892 Mines Act directly prohibited the employment of women and girls in or around mines and the Liquor Licence Act of 1906 prohibited women from obtaining a bartender's license.[111]

However, it has also been suggested that male workers pressed for protective legislation for women and children in some industries, aware that because the men's and women's work was interdependent, the same conditions would necessarily be applied to men.[112] In Quebec the Fédération des ouvriers textiles du Canada held as one of its objectives the adoption of laws to the advantage of textile workers "surtout celles qui s'appliquent aux femmes et aux enfants." However, the union's effective lobbying of the government resulted in 1910 in a reduction of hours from 60 to 58 per week for all workers in the cotton and wool factories.[113]

It is difficult to know how working women regarded such efforts to protect them. In strike activity women showed that their concerns were no different from the men's — wages and job security. In some cases protective legislation may have promoted discrimination against women, although more often it was simply ineffective. Most women were not covered by the Factory Acts since they worked predominantly in private homes, stores and sweatshops. Even where it was applicable, the legislation was poorly enforced. Although suffrage organizations opposed protective legislation because it was discriminatory, in later years working class women in the Federation of Women's Labour Leagues (formed in 1924) rejected this position, viewing as desirable any protection against arduous working conditions.[114]

Unionization and Equality

In the 1880s and lasting effectively about a decade, the Knights of Labor was an important organization of working people. Its direct criticism of capitalism and vision of general social reform elicited considerable support not only in Ontario and Quebec, but also in other provinces. Across Canada, the Knights organized 450 local assemblies and twelve district assemblies, and in 1893 forty of the seventy delegates to the Trades and Labor Congress convention represented members of the Knights of Labor.[115]

Contrary to the craft unions, the Knights of Labor was committed to organizing all workers, regardless of their type of work or their sex, an organization that welcomed women members. One researcher has suggested:

> For a few critical years, the cultural divisiveness of race, sex, creed, ethnicity, and partisan politics, was largely overcome by the sweep of the Knights' ideology of labour reform.[116]

However, while the Knights undoubtedly had a significant impact upon the unionization of women, the evidence suggests that the organization in Canada was no less discriminatory against racial minority groups than any other. On the west coast the Knights strongly supported the exclusion of Asian workers from Canada and in 1887 was deeply involved in a campaign to drive Asians out of Vancouver. This campaign involved painting large black Xs on businesses run by or dealing with Chinese people.[117] Moreover the Trades and Labor Congress was supporting exclusionary immigration policies when the influence of the Knights was at its height.

Before the Knights of Labor, women's involvement in unions in Ontario was virtually non-existent. However, it is estimated that women were involved in at least twenty-five of the Knights' Ontario assemblies, including ten that were entirely composed of women.[118]

In Toronto, where almost 5,000 workers belonged to the Knights at its height, two of the Local Assemblies were composed entirely of women who ran their own affairs, as well as serving on the executive board of the District Assembly. They organized social and educational meetings, and investigated the working conditions of women.[119] In 1888, Mrs. Elizabeth Wright was the first woman delegate to the Trades and Labor Congress, representing the Knights' all-women assembly in St Thomas, and she was joined the following year by a second woman delegate, Miss Emma Witt, from the Knights' Toronto District Assembley.

Although the Knights did not favour strikes except as a last resort, unions associated with the Knights gave support to women strikers. In 1882 the first major strike of women workers in Toronto involved women shoemakers from five major factories demanding union recognition, uniform wages and a wage advance. The Wholesale Boot and Shoemakers' Union provided financial support and the men in that union then struck in sympathy with the women.[120] The first national strike in Canada occurred in 1883 when the United Telegraphers of North America demanded wage increases and equal pay for men and women. It collapsed with no gains after four weeks.[121] These two unions were the first to join the Knights of Labor in 1882.[122]

The Knights also influenced the Trades and Labor Congress. At its first convention in 1883 the Congress passed a resolution recommending "the organization of female labor wherever possible, to the end that better wages and shorter hours of labor may be accorded them." It was John Armstrong, a leader in the Knights of Labor, who moved the resolution and spoke strongly in its support. At that time Armstrong presided over "the only women's union in the city" (Toronto), and stated that women "were just as able to conduct the business of a union as most men."[123] Support for this resolution was repeated each year from 1886 to 1889.

The Knights of Labor declined almost as quickly as they had developed, although they lasted longer in Quebec than elsewhere. By 1895 there were still thirty assemblies in Quebec, but only fourteen in Ontario.[124] By 1906 only three assemblies remained, the influence of the Knights having lasted little more than a decade.

In the Trades and Labor Congress the Knights' influence faded in the 1890s and the Congress moved to the right, embracing the American Federation of Labor and a more business unionism approach. As mentioned earlier, in 1898 the Trades and Labor

Garment workers—
interior of a clothing
factory, London,
Ontario, 1912.

*Courtesy of the National
Archives of Canada,
PA – 74737.*

Congress called for the exclusion of women from the labour force
as part of its platform of principles. This position was not altered
until 1914, when it was replaced with "equal pay for equal work
for men and women."[125] At this time, women were entering
industries to replace men during World War I, and the Congress
stated:

> Equal pay for women employed on work usually done by men, as
> men are or were receiving for the same work, will be insisted
> upon.[126]

It was not only in the Congress that changes in policies took
place. The 1902 constitution of the Toronto and District Labour
Council included in its program "equal pay, civil and political rights
for men and women, and the abolition of all law discrimination
against women."[127] By 1905 the women's column of the Tribune
stated:

> Ideas, like conditions, are changing and the old idea that woman
> must confine her attention entirely to the home and the raising of
> children is fast becoming a thing of the past.[128]

In specific instances the traditional union movement, local
unions or groups of male unionists were able to move beyond the
limits of the prevailing ideology and support women's rights as
workers. In 1904 the Journeymen Tailors of St John's went on strike
to demand equal pay for women doing the same work:

The Union would like most emphatically to state that it does not want the services of female help ... dispensed with. What it does object to is females ... being paid very much less than the journeyman on a similar job.[129]

During the Toronto Bell Telephone strike in 1907, bell-boys at a local hotel refused to work when strike-breakers stayed there, forcing the scabs to move elsewhere.[130] In 1912, another strike by women boot and shoe workers over pay reductions was endorsed and publicized by the union and supported by the men, who walked out in solidarity.[131] Ruth Frager tells the story of 65 male members of the International Ladies Garment Workers Union who in 1912 refused to take over the sewing work of the women, stating "We will not take the morsel of bread from the mouths of our sisters."[132] They were locked out by the employer and 1,000 ILGWU factory workers, one-third of them women, then struck in support and the union sent two women organizers to Toronto to help the strikers. Nonetheless after a four month strike, Eaton's prevailed and the ILGWU was seriously weakened as a result.

However, despite examples of worker solidarity and the policies supporting equal pay, union organizing and bargaining were often marked by traditional attitudes. As an example, in Toronto:

General Organizer Sam Landers was embarrassed when reading his manual for the initiation of a local body of women tailors to discover that the wording was exclusively suited to males.[133]

While policy statements might favour equal pay, unions bargained lower increases for poorly paid women workers. In 1907, male bookbinders were to earn from $13.50 to $14.50 a week, while

for 400 female bookbinders a scale of $5.00 per week, $5.25 for the second, and $5.50 for the third year was adopted, no fixed scale having previously been in force.[134]

While that last phrase gives some cause to wonder whether obtaining a fixed scale was in itself an accomplishment for the women, certainly the gap in pay rates is huge. In Vancouver in 1918, the Hotel Employees and Restaurant Employees Union obtained:

A scale of $15 to $18 per week for the waiters, which is an increase of 50¢ per day, and the scale for the chambermaids is $25 per month, being an amount of 17¢ per day over the old wage.[135]

Women comprised more than half the workers in the garment trade in Toronto in the 1920s, were confined to the least skilled jobs and were paid far less than men, even those doing the same work. The strong and left-leaning Jewish labour movement failed to recognize the secondary status of women. Their exclusive focus on class and ethnicity, as well as their acceptance of the traditional role of women, meant that women were generally excluded from the Jewish labour culture and from its leadership.[136] The inclusion of women in unions did not necessarily mean that they were regarded as equals.

Understanding Union Policies on Women

Why were union policies so contradictory? Why seek legislative protection for women if they were to be excluded from the labour force? Why call for unionization and equal pay for women, while also demanding a higher wage, the family wage, for men? The confusion evident within the union movement was echoed by the male factory workers who appeared as witnesses before the 1889 Labor Commission. Some men believed that women should receive equal pay, while others said that this would not be fair because women's work was inferior, while others again saw that low pay was an encouragement for employers to replace men with women:

> In fact there were almost as many opinions about female labour as there were workingmen witnesses. The very diversity of opinion suggests that the male factory workers were unsure just what female labour meant to them.[137]

Even the Knights of Labour, while welcoming women and supporting equal pay, called for the family wage and argued that women would not have to work outside the home in an ideal society.[138]

This confusion can be understood as a reflection of real contradictions. The prevailing belief was that women's place was in the home, but the reality was that a proportion of women were employed in the labour force. In the labour force a conflict of interest existed between men and women over the question of cheap labour, a conflict mediated and exacerbated by employers. Also, I want to argue, conflicting interests existed not only between men and women, but also between different groups of women.

Looking first at the problem of the use of women as cheap labour, it has been suggested that unions, had they been able to overcome the ideology of women's domesticity and dependence, should have unionized women and bargained for equal pay, thereby eradicating the threat of women's cheap labour. By failing to do so, it is argued, unions contributed to the development of women's unequal pay and ghettoization.[139] It has been proposed that the reason unions did not struggle for equal pay for women was because this would have threatened both men's superiority in the labour force and "male domination within the home."[140]

I would suggest that too much emphasis has been placed upon the role of unions in this conception of the problem. First, unions were very few and very weak, and the large majority of men and women were not unionized. Second, it is clear that employers managed to restrict women to certain jobs and pay them lower wages with no help from unions, in those occupations where unions did not exist. The entrance of women into teaching, the retail trade and clerical work all bear testament to this. Third, where unions did exist and attempted to exert some influence they faced the fact that employers simply refused to hire women if it meant hiring them at equal pay to men. This last point deserves further discussion.

As outlined earlier, some unions argued that women should be paid the same wages as men. But in reality, unionization of women and bargaining equal pay could not at the time provide a solution to the undercutting of men's wages. For all the reasons outlined above (employer opposition, the type of work women did and the composition of the female labour force), it was extremely difficult to organize women, and unions confronted all these problems in their attempts to deal with the issue. Moreover, the craft nature of unions did not admit the possibility of organizing workers in the predominantly unskilled and semiskilled jobs in which women worked.

The limited evidence available also suggests that employers not only opposed the notion of equal pay for women, but refused to hire women if the same rates of pay applied. When unions insisted upon equal pay, women were not hired. For example, Jane Scott, observing the situation in the 1890s, noted that women and children had largely replaced men in the cigarmaking industry in Ontario. However, Toronto was an exception and in that city while the women stripped and prepared the leaves, men continued to actually make the cigars,

> The reason being that all the employees belong to the union which insists on all workers being paid alike, and the employers prefer to employ men because they are likely to remain longer in the business.[141]

Because the union insisted upon equal pay for men and women cigarmakers, the employer refused to hire women into that position. Scott concludes that generally in Ontario: "There is no doubt that if women were paid the same rates as the men they would not be so largely employed."[142]

At the Fifth Trades and Labour Congress in Montreal in 1889 the following complaint was made:

> At the present time female labour is manipulated and used as a means of reducing the price of labour in general; and in trades where the female is so used to the detriment of the male labour, as exemplified particularly in the printing business, she is scarcely ever properly taught said trade, or given an opportunity of earning a fair rate of wages, being merely used for the time being as a lever to reduce the price of labour.[143]

Women were not regarded by employers as an alternative source of labour, but only as a cheap source of labour.

An example from England clearly expresses the dilemma in which women were ensnared and the difficulties of unions that might attempt to deal with the problem of cheap labour by demanding equal pay rates. Fierce competition existed between men and women in the hosiery industry in Leicester, and it was the women who insisted upon their lower pay rates.

> At a meeting of circular rib hands the men determined to fix the price of all hose at the men's rate. The women, however, refused to demand the same price as the men and resolved to accept a lower rate, fearing dismissal if they were to charge the same rate as the men charged. The men would not agree to have women charge a lower rate because the men would be replaced.[144]

In fact the men finally agreed that the women would work for a farthing a dozen below the men's rate, but just as the men had feared several firms responded by dismissing men and hiring the lower paid women. When the men had argued for equal pay rates for the women, the employers objected because "the men turned out more work than the women from the same machine."[145] However, once a lower rate for women was agreed upon this argument counted for nothing and the employers proceeded to replace the men with women.

In Canada employers had no compunction about stating their position. Appearing before the 1889 Labor Commission, employers frankly avowed that in order to obtain employment women were required to be "docile, clean, quick, cheap and sober" or they would be replaced.[146] Employers clearly expressed the fact that they favoured female labour only because it was cheap labour and therefore "more profitable to us or we would not employ them."[147]

Did unions at the turn of the century really have an option to bargain for equal pay for women workers? Perhaps the real choice that unions faced, given the intransigent position of employers, was either to allow women to work for lower wages and therefore replace men, or to maintain the wages of the men and see women excluded from the work force. The third possibility was to accept the division of the work with women employed in different jobs at a lower pay rate. The unions, largely unsuccessful even in preventing wage cuts, were in no position to dictate to the employers that women should be hired at the men's rate of pay.

Union support of the family wage has been criticized because it reinforced pay inequality by promoting the belief that men should receive higher wages than women, since women were dependent upon their husbands.[148] It is true that the family wage approach could not accommodate equal pay for women and perhaps helped to legitimize and institutionalize pay inequality. It is also the case that while all men were to receive the family wage, some were not married, while some women were forced to support their families on lower pay rates. Certainly, the idea of a family wage contributed to the prevailing ideology concerning the dependent position of women.

Nonetheless it is important to recall that at the turn of the century less than 5 percent of married women were employed outside the home, so that over 95 percent of married women actually were largely dependent upon their husbands' wages. At the same time men's wages, even among the better paid unionized workers, were barely sufficient to support a family in the minimum of necessities. Living in conditions of chronic poverty and insecurity, a family wage that would offer adequate support must have seemed attractive not only to men, but also to the majority of women who were dependent upon men's wages.

Studies of more recent labour struggles have recognized the legitimate interest that wives may have in union negotiations over their husbands' wages. Among others, Luxton has argued that union activities affect the wives and families of male workers' and has pointed out that wives have often provided important forms of support and solidarity during strikes.[149] If this is the case today when over 60 percent of married women are in the labour force, how much more concerned were women likely to have been when

"A Complaint from Female Teachers"

Letter to *The Mail*,
February 27, 1882.

Sir,

Some time since the lady teachers of the city Public Schools sent a petition to the board of trustees asking for an increase in salary ... However, when the salary list for this year was published we discovered that the increase amounted to only $25 each per annum ...

Our salaries, since the magnificent increase referred to above, range from $350 to $550, while those of the head masters range from $750 to $1,100. We think, of course, that their salaries should rank somewhat higher than ours on account of the responsibility resting upon them, but surely the above difference is altogether too great. Then again, in four of the schools assistant masters are employed who teach a lower grade than the highest lady teachers, and have no responsibility whatever, and yet because of their sex receive $850 per annum, $300 more than the ladies teaching the highest grade in the same schools. Now, we ask you, is this just?

Of course, we know that the world is yet averse to putting women's salaries on a par with those of men but surely in this nineteenth century, with its boasted culture and many improvements, it is time that the common sense of the people should endorse that those who do equal work should receive equal remuneration, be their sex or age what it may. We have to pass the same examinations and undergo the same training as men and no merchant offers us his goods at half price because we are ladies, yet we are expected to be thankful to receive half or less than half as much salary. Some would persuade us that the difference is made because men have families to support. Then, according to that argument, men with large families should get more than those with smaller ones and bachelors should receive much less than either. Anyone can see how absurd this would be. Our motto is "The labourer is worthy of his hire," but even if the above ridiculous argument had any strength, then what about those ladies (of whom quite a number are on our teaching staff) who have families to support?

Yours & c.,

Lady Teachers' Deputation
Toronto, February 27, 1882.

The Board's response to the complaint was final; the secretary was instructed to "respectfully intimate to all the teachers in the service of the Board that it would accept the resignation of those who are dissatisfied with their present positions."

Pat Staton and Beth Light, *Speak With their Own Voices: A Documentary History of the Federation of Women Teachers' Associations of Ontario and the Women Elementary Public School Teachers of Ontario,* (Toronto: Federation of Women Teachers' Associations of Ontario, 1987) pp. 45–46.

less than 5 percent of wives worked outside of the home. At the turn of the century a conflict of interest existed not only between employed women and men, but also between employed single women and married women dependent upon their husbands' pay. The Western Clarion, expressed this contradiction, addressing itself to employed women as follows:

> You are helping to cheapen him (the male worker). You intensify his struggle to live, and, ironical though it may seem, insofar as you crowd him from the industry you aggravate the poverty of your own sex, the wife and daughters dependent upon him.[150]

The evidence now suggests that only a minority of young working women were self-supporting, since a large proportion continued to live at home with their parents. This was certainly true, for example, of young women who worked in the cotton mills in Quebec, one of the major employers of women in the province and where, in 1891, women constituted 55 percent of the work force.[151] These women workers lived at home with their parents between the time that they started work and when they married and left their jobs. Similarly, in 1892 in Toronto only one quarter of all working women were obliged to find board and lodging for themselves.[152] In St John's, in 1921, 54 percent of single working women lived at home with their parents while a further 5 percent lived with female relatives, and 34 percent were live-in domestic servants. In this city less than 5 percent of single working women boarded out, while just 2 percent were themselves heads of households.[153] One researcher has concluded:

> The majority of young women lived at home, accepting parental authority and making significant contributions to the family economy, sometimes turning over all, or most of their wages to their mothers.[154]

Employers understood these realities and exploited them. Where young single women could be employed at the lowest wages there was no reason to pay more than this minimum rate. In the 1914 Report of Labour Conditions in British Columbia,

> employers stressed that women were not expected to have to live on their salaries and, therefore, women's wages had nothing to do with any notion of a living wage.[155]

In circumstances where the rate of pay was established to partially support a young woman living at home with her family, men with dependent families could hardly compete.

However, it was not only men with dependent families that faced this problem; single women not living with their families found it difficult to live on the wages offered. One advantage of domestic service to new immigrants without families was that it avoided the need to find accommodation on wages that were insufficient to meet the cost of daily life. One woman who left domestic service and obtained work in a factory at $4 a week, found that she had to pay $4 a week for board and lodging, leaving her nothing for other expenses.[156] The cost of full board and lodging in Toronto in the 1890s was $2.25 to $5 per week, while women factory workers earned from $2 to $5 per week, waitresses $2-$3, laundresses up to $4, and teachers from $6 to $12 a week.

> The fact that many girls in employment in Toronto live at home and are able to accept small wages makes it rather difficult for those girls who are obliged to board to command good salaries.[157]

It is interesting to note some limited evidence that women themselves were aware of the different material realities and therefore different interests among women. The Federation of Women Teachers' Association of Ontario was formed in 1918 and strongly supported equal pay for women and men teachers. However, the Federation also supported the practice of discharging married women from employment, and as late as the 1930s urged the school boards "to give preference to the unmarried woman except in cases where the married teacher (was) the sole support of the family."[158] This policy was not abandoned until the members called for change during World War II, when teacher shortages lead to increasing number of married women working as teachers. Even later, in the 1940s, women telephone operators in British Columbia organized their own union, and one clause in their 1943 contract stated "Married women not on the permanent staff shall not hold a supervisory position, if they have outside support, and there are single girls to fill the position."[159]

Given these realities it may not be appropriate to speak of the interests of "women" as if that term comprises a homogeneous group and single interest. The interests of married women dependent upon their husbands, women responsible for dependents themselves, single women living with their parents and single independent women were rather different. As Lavigne and Stoddart suggested some time ago:

> The history of women is like all other history, the history of different classes and diverse social and cultural groups, often with conflicting interests. It is time that we stopped analyzing women like a

homogeneous group and studied the particularities of the numerous groups that compose the feminine sex.[160]

Conclusion

Women in the labour force in the period 1881 to 1921 were caught within a cruel irony. Employers would hire them only as cheap labour at the lowest rates of pay, and consequently they were the most in need of collective action to improve their conditions. But the jobs where women most commonly worked were often the most difficult to organize, being isolated and unskilled. At the same time employed women, spending only a few years in the labour force, had little opportunity to build lasting organizations with which to defend themselves. Meanwhile the union movement was hampered by the prevailing ideology of women as domestic and dependent creatures as well as its own craft organization that did not include unskilled workers, male or female. The main exception was the Knights of Labor that did successfully organize women during the 1880s, although there were also examples of individual unions or groups of male workers who supported the demands of working women.

Unions were faced with the reality that single women were a small and transient contingent of the labour force, while the vast majority of married women were dependent upon their men's wages. Confronted with the employers' use of cheap female labour to undercut men's wages, and unable to move beyond the ideology of women's domestic nature, most often unions failed to organize women workers and turned instead to protective legislation and the idea of the family wage to deal with the "problem" of the working woman.

STEWARDESS

IS YOUR :

SMILE, Friendly & Sincere
POSTURE, Erect & Poised
HAIR, Short & Styled
MAKE-UP, Neat & Natural
BLOUSE, Fresh & Pressed
RIBBON, New & Trimmed
NAILS, Manicured & Polished
GLOVES, White & Tailored
UNIFORM, Clean & Pressed
PURSE, Orderly & Polished
SHOES, Repaired & Shined

?

SMILE!

In the 1940s women working for
Frontier Airlines had to meet a number
of requirements as stewardesses.

2

Women and the Changing Union Movement

Women's participation in the labour force is radically different now than in the early decades of the century. Table 2-1 summarizes the major trends, showing that the period during and immediately following World War II initiated a new era of involvement in the labour force for women. While the number of women in the labour force and the percentage of women compared with men was gradually increasing throughout the century, both took a sharp upswing between 1941 and 1951, and that acceleration was then maintained. In 1941 less than 1 million women were in the labour force, but by 1991 that figure had leapt to 6 million. While women were less than 19 percent of the total labour force in 1941, they were over 45 percent by 1991. We are not far from a situation in which women will comprise half the Canadian labour force.

The majority of women are now employed outside the home. In the early decades of the century less than 20 percent of women participated in the labour force; the figure is now 58 percent. Another important change is that employed women are no longer predominantly single. During World War II married women began to enter the labour force in increasing numbers, a trend that continued after the War. In 1941 less than 5 percent of married women worked outside the home, but by 1951 this figure had risen to almost 15 percent, and to 21 percent by 1961. The new trend that was noted for the 1960s was that women's employment pattern followed a "two-phase" profile. Women continued to work outside the home when they married, but commonly left the labour force upon the birth of the first child, so that the participation rate fell

Table 2-1: Major Trends in the Labour Force Participation of Women, 1901 to 1991

Year	Female labour force (000s)	Participation rate of all women in labour force (%)	Participation rate of married women (%)	Women as % of total labour force
1901	238	12.0	-	13.3
1911	365	14.3	-	13.4
1921	489	17.2	-	15.5
1931	665	19.1	3.4	17.0
1941	834	20.2	4.5	18.5
1951	1,164	23.6	14.9	22.0
1961	1,764	29.5	21.9	27.3
1971	2,961	38.7	36.3	34.3
1981	4,898	51.0	51.7	40.6
1991	6,188	58.2	61.4	45.0

Notes:
1901-1911 includes females 10 years and over 1921-1951 includes females 14 years and over 1961-1991 includes females 15 years and over.
The married category includes separated (but not divorced) women for 1901 to 1981. For 1991 the married category includes both divorced and separated women.

Source: For 1901-1961: Department of Labour Canada, *Women at Work in Canada: A Fact Book on the Female Labour Force, 1964*, Ottawa, 1965, p.10, table 1. Dominion Bureau of Statistics, 1951 Census of Canada, *Occupation and Industry Trends in Canada, 1901-1951,* table 9. Dominion Bureau of Statistics, 1961 Census of Canada, *Population: Marital Status, Cat:92-544; and Labour Force: Occupations, 3.1,* Vol.III-Part I; and *Population: General Characteristics,* 1.2, Vol.I, Part 2, table 29. For 1971-1981: Statistics Canada, 1971 Census of Canada, Vol.3, Part 2, *Labour Force,* table 8; and Vol.1, Part 4, *Population,* table 1. Statistics Canada, 1981 Census of Canada, *Labour Force - Industry by Demographic and Educational Characteristics,* Cat.29-921, Vol.1, table 4; and *Age, Sex and Marital Status,* Cat.92-901, Vol.1, table 5.
For 1991: Statistics Canada, *Labour Force Annual Averages 1991,* Cat.71-002, p.B-8, Table 3.

for women in their twenties. However, unlike in earlier decades, a good number returned to the labour force once the children were older, so that the proportion of women in the labour force rose again for women from their late 30s until the age of 49, creating a second phase of employment.[1]

This pattern has altered dramatically again since the 1960s. The continued climb in the participation of married women in the labour force reached 61 percent in 1991, because an increasing number of women with young children remained in the labour force, or took shorter breaks before returning. Among women with children under 16 years of age, 71 percent were in the labour force and for women with pre-school aged children the figure was 64 percent. Even for women with children under 3 years of age, a remarkable 62 percent were in the labour force.[2]

Women working outside their homes are no longer a small and deviant contingent, but part of a large and growing majority. No longer are employed women almost entirely single, leaving the work force upon marriage, but instead continue to be employed outside the home, whatever their marital status or the ages of their children. Contrary to the situation during the early decades of the century, women are now a significant and stable proportion of the labour force.

What jobs have women taken as they have moved into the labour force? The most dramatic increase has been in clerical work, which was recorded as the leading occupation for women for the first time in 1921. Between 1941 and 1981 the proportion of women clerical workers rose from 18 to 36 percent (see Table 2-2). More than one out of every three employed women continues to work in clerical occupations. A more modest increase has occurred in professional work, which includes teaching and nursing. In 1941 16 percent of employed women worked in professional jobs, little changed since the turn of century. However, by the 1981 census one quarter of women in paid work held professional or administrative positions. Although the 1981 Census is not directly comparable with earlier years, still it is possible to identify the general trends, and Table 2-2 shows these changes over the century.

As clerical and professional jobs have risen in importance, personal service and manufacturing work have declined. As previously noted the position of servant was the single most common job for women at the turn of the century, and in 1901 fully

Table 2-2: Percentage Distribution of Employed Women by Occupation, 1901, 1921, 1941, 1981.

	1901-1941			1981	
Occupation	1901	1921	1941	1981	Occupation
Clerical	5.3	18.7	18.3	36.3	Clerical
Professional	14.7	19.1	15.7	25.2	Admin./Prof.
Personal Services	42.0	25.8	34.2	15.7	Service
Manufacturing	29.6	17.8	15.4	10.3	Manufacturing
Commercial/Financial	2.4	8.5	8.8	9.4	Sales
Other	6.0	10.1	7.7	2.8	Other
Total	100.0	100.0	100.0	99.7	Total

Source: Canada, Department of Labour, *Women at Work in Canada, 1964*, Ottawa, 1965, p.28, Table 12; Statistics Canada, 1981 Census of Canada, *Labour Force - Industry by Occupation*, Cat: 92-923, Vol.1, Table 1.

42 percent of all women were employed in personal service jobs. The decline in the use of house servants and housekeepers over the century meant that by the 1981 census only 16 percent of women were employed in the personal services occupations (which included laundry workers, dry cleaners, hairdressers, chambermaids, and babysitters). In manufacturing, at the turn of the century, 30 percent of all employed women held manufacturing jobs, particularly in textiles and clothing. This figure had already fallen to 15 percent by the 1941 census and dropped to only 10 percent by 1981.

The other general occupational category is sales. There was an upswing in the proportion of women employed in sales in the first two decades of the century, but since 1921 the figure across the census years has remained stable at around 10 percent of all employed women.

To summarize the situation today, over one third of all employed women are in clerical jobs, while another quarter work in administrative and professional positions. Fifteen percent of women who work for pay are employed in personal service jobs, while sales and manufacturing each employ about 10 percent of working women. Women are less likely now to work in isolation as they did at the turn of the century, although relatively small workplaces are still common, especially in the personal service occupations, and in small stores and offices. But women are much more likely now than in past decades to work together in large numbers, more often in offices, schools and hospitals than in factories.

Changes in the Union Movement

Labour historians describe three waves of unionism in Canada: the early craft unions, the industrial unions that developed in the 1930s and 1940s, and the public sector unions of the 1960s. Something of the nature of craft unions was discussed in the last chapter. It was not until the 1930s that a new type of union developed to challenge the dominance of the craft organizations. Industrial unionism organized all workers in a workplace, including both skilled and unskilled, and for the first time large numbers of unskilled workers were unionized. Between 1939 and 1945 the number of organized workers doubled, increasing to 725,000.[3] Rising industrial action, and particularly the high number of strikes in 1943, led to the introduction of P.C.1003 in 1944, legislation that recognized the right to unionize and established procedures for the certification of unions approved by a majority of workers. The number of unionized workers continued to expand to just under 1.5 million by 1960.[4] Industrial unions were organized in the logging, mining, electrical, steel, rubber, auto, shipping and textile industries.

Industrial unionism meant important changes in the Canadian labour movement and women were unionized where they worked in tobacco, food, electrical and textile production. There is very limited research available on women and unions during the 1940s and 1950s, particularly in Canada, and still we lack a clear understanding of the role of women as industrial unions developed. Women remained only a small proportion of the new union members. In 1941 only 15 percent of women workers were employed in manufacturing, where the main organizing drive of the industrial unions occurred (see Table 2-2). An attempt

Industrial Organizing in Quebec

The textile industry in Quebec was one of the largest employers of women. In 1946, the six thousand workers at the Dominion Textile plants in Montreal and Valleyfield went on strike for one hundred days. They were led by Madeleine Parent and her husband Kent Rowley, leaders of the United Textile Workers of America. The Primier of Quebec, Duplessis, sent provincial police to intimidate the strikers, and the union leaders were arrested a number of times: Kent Rowley served six months in prison for "seditious conspiracy." However, the strikers emerged victorious, winning certification of the union, their first collective agreement and an eight hour working day.

In 1947, seven hundred employees of the Ayers textile factories in Lachute stopped work. The strike lasted more than five months and ended in defeat. Madeleine Parent and the president of the union were found guilty of seditious conspiracy by a jury and were sentenced to two years in prison. However, they did not serve their sentences; their conviction was quashed because of problems with the court record. But Parent's persecution did not frighten the factory workers at Ayers. In 1947 they joined with workers from Dominion Textile — six thousand people in all — and launched a strike in factories at Montmorency, Sherbrooke, Drummondville and Magog. This time the strikers carried the day.

The tobacco industry also employed large numbers of women. In 1951, the three thousand women employees of Imperial Tobacco went out on strike and their demands were met. But in 1952, the women employees of a textile factory in Louiseville laid down their tools: Duplessis sent in the police to help break the strike. After eleven months the women went back to work, still without a union or collective agreement.

The Clio Collective, *Quebec Women: A History*, (Toronto: Women's Press, 1987) pp. 294–295.

to organize Eaton's, the largest department store in the country, failed[5] and the majority of women employed in shops, offices, schools, hospitals and restaurants were left untouched by the new unionism.

Radical change in the participation of women in unions did not occur until the 1960s with the third wave of unionism, the unionization of the public sector. At the federal and provincial levels, some civil servants had belonged to workers' associations for decades, although they were commonly conservative organizations, not seeking to represent their members as unions. Nurses and teachers had their professional associations, but they were primarily interested in educational standards and professional recognition for their members. With few exceptions, organizations of public sector workers were not generally included in the legislation that gave recognition to unions in the private sector in the 1940s and they had no legislated right to bargain conditions of employment. It was not until the 1960s and 1970s that public sector workers, in a wave of dissatisfaction and militant action, turned to unionization in unprecedented numbers and forced governments to recognize their right to negotiate collective agreements and, in some jurisdictions, their right to strike.

At the federal level, civil service associations had existed since the early 1900s, but they were unable to bargain for their members. They could not negotiate, there was no written contract or arbitration procedure, and the employee associations were generally conservative. For example, the Civil Service Federation of Canada did not call for collective bargaining rights for federal service workers until 1953, and then favoured compulsory arbitration rather than the right to strike. However, the federal government effectively blocked the formation of trade unions for another 14 years after this. The government argued that the state was sovereign ("The Queen does not negotiate"), that unions were inappropriate since the public service was non-profit, and that negotiation was incompatible with the merit system then in operation.

By the 1960s the demand by federal civil servants for some form of collective bargaining had become irresistible and Arnold Heeney was appointed to examine the issues and make recommendations. Just weeks after the 1965 Heeney Report recommended collective bargaining without the right to strike, the inside postal workers walked off the job, illegality notwithstanding.[6] As a result the Public Service Staff Relations Act of 1967 offered a choice between binding arbitration or a conciliation-strike route for negotiations. Because of this legislation 120,000 federal public service workers obtained the right to bargain collectively for the first time. The Public Service Alliance of Canada was formed in 1966 by a merger of the former civil service associations in response to the forthcoming legislation. Non-existent in 1966, in 1967 the Alliance became the fourth largest union in the country. The union had 98,000 members and over one-quarter of them (28 percent) were women.[7]

At the provincial level, collective bargaining by government employees only became legally permissible between 1965 and 1975, with the exception of Saskatchewan. In that province the Co-operative Commonwealth Federation government (predecessor of the New Democratic Party) included civil servants in its Trade Union Act of 1944, giving them, somewhat to their consternation, the right to bargain collectively and the right to strike.[8] In other provinces the right to bargain was gained only after long campaigns and conflicts. The B.C. Government Employees Association wanted collective bargaining from its inception in 1944 and regarded the Saskatchewan situation with envy. In 1959, still with no right even to bargain, the Association went on strike for one half day, until their picketing was pronounced illegal. With militancy mounting among its members, the name of the organization was changed to the B.C. Government Employees Union in 1969, and two strikes occurred in the first years of the 1970s. Finally, in 1973, new legislation provided for full collective bargaining and the organization was then able to negotiate as a union for the first time.[9]

By 1975 government workers in all the provinces had the right to negotiate a collective agreement. However, in provinces such as Ontario and Alberta, legislation permitted public service workers to bargain, but not to strike. Despite these restrictions, in 1974 the Civil Service Association of Ontario threatened illegal strike action to obtain its wage demands and a year later signified its new, more militant approach by changing its name to the Ontario Public Service Employees Union.[10] In Alberta the Civil Service Association also changed its name to the Alberta Union of Provincial Employees, and there were strikes of liquor board workers, hospital workers, and in 1974 18,000 civil servants walked off the job for two days.[11]

Municipal government workers also organized and developed a new militancy. In 1963 the Canadian Union of Public Employees (CUPE) was created from the merger of two previous unions, and continued its organizing efforts among municipal, education and health workers. Of this merger Grace Hartmann has written:

> Public employee unions were not really of great news interest at that time. Our new union caused little reaction in the labour movement because I don't think the industrial unions took us too seriously at that time.[12]

Perhaps the labour movement was taking the CUPE more seriously by 1975, when it became the largest single union in Canada. It continues to be the largest union in Canada, and is also the union with the largest number of women members.

Over the same period the professional associations of nurses and teachers, increasingly frustrated by poor wages and working conditions, were pressing for the right to negotiate improvements. In British Columbia the Registered Nurses Association approved

The 1963 convention in Winnipeg that created the Canadian Union of Public Employees.

At this time women were 32 percent of the membership, since increased to over 50%.

Courtesy Canadian Labour Congress.

the principle of collective bargaining in 1946, but like nurses in other provinces, waited until the second half of the 1960s for legislation permitting them to negotiate.[13] In most provinces the legislation stopped short of permitting nurses the right to strike. Nonetheless, in 1974 the newly formed Ontario Nurses Association stated its dissatisfaction with the low wages obtained through compulsory arbitration and gave notice that its members would strike illegally if substantial wage increases were not obtained. Strike votes were held and pickets organized, but the hospitals capitulated before the strike deadline. Nurses unions in other provinces threatened militant action if their low wages were not improved. In New Brunswick, since strikes were still illegal, 1,300 hospital nurses out of 1,600 resigned collectively in 1975 to force their demands for higher wages.[14]

Teachers associations were undergoing a similar transformation. In Ontario negotiations for wages were only possible on an individual school basis, until they were consolidated into school boards in the 1960s. When this process was completed in 1968, collective bargaining became a more feasible undertaking, but still the teachers had no right to strike. Increasingly teachers resorted to the use of mass resignations to obtain settlements, and as a result the Ontario government introduced legislation that would invalidate mass resignations, deny collective bargaining and establish compulsory arbitration instead. In solidarity the five teachers' federations closed elementary and secondary schools across the province on the 18th December 1973, and marched in protest in the largest demonstration ever held in Toronto. The offending legislation was withdrawn, but dissatisfaction continued and the following year teachers walked off the job in York County, Windsor and Thunder Bay. In 1975 Ontario teachers obtained the right to negotiate and to strike.[15]

In Saskatchewan the situation for teachers was quite different since school board consolidation had occurred in the 1940s and teachers obtained the right to negotiate in 1944. However, there was an unprecedented wave of strike activity between 1968 and 1973, when the provincial government imposed a new form of area bargaining. The Saskatchewan Teachers' Federation supported a combination of province-wide and local bargaining, and in 1973 legislation allowed the Federation to negotiate with the government for all teachers across the province for the first time.[16] In British Columbia after 1966 the Social Credit government introduced a series of measures that restricted educational resources and limited the teachers' right to negotiate. As a result the B.C. Teachers' Federation took a political stand against the Social Credit government and worked actively, and successfully, to defeat that party in the 1972 election.[17]

Nowhere was the entrance of the public sector into the union movement more indicative of profound change than in Quebec. There the nurses association had lobbied for collective bargaining as early as the 1940s, and in 1946, twenty years before other provinces, legislation in Quebec recognized the right of nurses associations to bargain collective agreements. Several nurses unions developed to bargain for improved wages and hours.[18] Although not legally permitted to strike before 1965, in 1963 nurses at the Sainte-Justine Hospital in Montreal were on strike for a month to support their demands.[19] Among teachers, their professional organizations followed conservative, professional policies, with the exception of the more militant association of Montreal teachers. This group was on strike for a week as early as 1949, dissatisfied with their arbitrated contract. In 1959 the Montreal teachers were re-integrated into the provincial corporation of teachers, although it was not until 1963 that this organization supported the right to strike. But the new militancy mounted quickly and, although illegal, teachers were on strike in 1963 (Sainte-Foy), 1964 (Sherbrooke) and 1965 (Quebec City). At the same time, by 1964 pressure from Quebec government workers had pushed the predecessor of the Confédération des syndicats nationaux to support the right to strike for provincial civil servants.[20]

Between 1964 and 1965 public sector workers in Quebec, including government workers, nurses and teachers obtained the right to strike. However, when the Quebec Teachers Corporation struck in 1967 they were legislated back to work, the existing salaries frozen and further strikes prohibited for 16 months. In 1971 the Confédération des syndicats nationaux, the Quebec Federation of Labour and the Quebec Teachers' Corporation joined to form the Common Front to negotiate for all public sector workers in the province. Dissatisfaction with the negotiations resulted in a strike in 1972 that included Quebec government employees, hospital and school workers, teachers and nurses. According to one source, it was the largest strike in Canada's history.[21]

Between 1965 and 1975 large numbers of public sector workers joined the union movement, including federal and provincial

Table 2-3: Women Union Members, 1962 to 1989

Year	Number of women union members	Women as % of all union members
1962	248,884	16.4
1964	276,246	16.7
1966	322,980	17.0
1968	438,543	20.4
1970	513,203	22.6
1972	575,584	24.2
1974	676,939	25.2
1976	750,637	27.0
1978	835,263	28.7
1980	932,883	30.2
1982	985,376	32.3
1984	1,219,065	35.5
1986	1,310,000	36.4
1988	1,418,900	37.5
1989	1,518,500	39.1

Source: Statistics Canada, *Corporations and Labour Unions Returns Act, Part II*, Cat:71-202, Ottawa, Reports for 1962-1989.

government employees, municipal workers, workers in schools and hospitals, and nurses and teachers. The impact upon the union movement has been profound. All these groups include large numbers of women workers and the composition of the union movement was radically altered as a result. For the first time women became a significant sector of the Canadian labour movement.

Women and Unions Today

The rapid increase in women union members after the early 1960s is shown in Table 2-3. In 1962 under 250,000 women belonged to unions, a figure that had increased to one and a half million by 1989. The number of women union members grew by 510 percent over this period. The participation of men also increased during these years, but not nearly so rapidly. The number of men belonging to unions rose from 1,269,000 to 2,362,500, a growth of 86 percent. In other words, while the number of women in unions multiplied by five times, the number of men did not double. Since women have been joining unions at a faster rate than men, their proportion of the total number of union members has risen. Thus, while women were just over 16 percent of all union members in 1962, they were 39 percent by 1989.

The rapid unionization of the public sector has entailed changes in the industrial composition of the union movement. There has been a dramatic shift away from unions and union members in the manufacturing sector, and towards unions in the service sector. In 1966 (the first year for which such figures are available) 39 percent of union members worked in manufacturing and 9 percent in services. By 1989 union members in manufacturing had dropped to 19 percent, while the proportion in services had increased to almost 34 percent. However, it is women members who are primarily responsible for this shift, since 57 percent of women union members were employed in services in 1989, compared to only 19 percent of men. Manufacturing continued to be the industry with the largest proportion of male unionists (25 percent), but less than 10 percent of women unionists worked in manufacturing.

The unionization of the public sector also entailed a shift away from international unions. The Statistics Canada data used in this chapter provides information on three types of unions: international unions have their headquarters in the United States and members on both sides of the border; government employee organizations represent workers employed at different levels of government, and necessarily include only Canadian workers; and national unions include all other unions representing only Canadian workers. Since the international unions primarily represent workers in manufacturing and construction, and the organization of public sector workers entailed a shift away from those sectors, the internationals have experienced a decline in their relative importance. In 1962 the percentage of union members in interna-

Table 2-4: Distribution of Union Members by Type of Union and Sex, 1962 and 1989 (%)

Type of Union	1962			1989		
	Female	Male	Total	Female	Male	Total
International	47.8	69.2	65.9	20.4	40.0	32.3
National	33.8	20.2	22.3	62.8	48.4	54.0
Government	18.4	10.6	11.8	16.8	11.6	13.7
Total	100.0	100.0	100.0	100.0	100.0	100.0

Source: Statistics Canada, *Corporations and Labour Unions Returns Part II*, Cat: 71-202, Reports for 1962 and 1989.

tional unions stood at 66 percent, but has fallen to 32 percent in 1989. While both men and women are less likely to belong to internationals now than in the early 1960s, women's membership of this type of union is lower than for men. In 1989 only 20 percent of all women members belonged to internationals, compared to 40 percent of men (see Table 2-4).

The predominance of women in Canadian unions is also reflected in the internal composition of the three types of union. In 1989 women were 25 percent of the membership of international unions, 46 percent in the national unions and 48 percent of all members in the government unions.[22]

As well as the shift away from the manufacturing industry and from international unions, a third change resulting from increased public sector unionization has been a decline in the number of union members affiliated to central labour organizations. One important reason is that nurses and teachers unions have not joined the Canadian Labour Congress or, in Quebec, the Confédération des syndicats nationaux. Only 57 percent of all unionized workers were affiliated to the Canadian Labour Congress in 1989, down from a high of 70 percent in earlier years. One out of every five union members (20 percent) belonged to unions that were not affiliated to any labour central. More women than men belong to unions that are unaffiliated. Of all women union members, 31 percent belonged to unions that were not affiliated with any labour central, compared to only 14 percent of men.[23]

The third wave of unionization in Canada has meant more women, more public sector and service workers, more national unions and more independent, unaffiliated unions. The typical union in Canada is no longer the craft or industrial, blue collar, male, international organization of the earlier decades of the century. Times have changed. The following chapters explore what it has meant for women to become an integral part of the Canadian union movement.

Women bring their own style to the picket line. Members of the United Food and Commercial Workers Union on strike at an IGA supermarket in Huntsville, Ontario, December 1985.

Photo by Bill Reno, UFCW.

3

Bread and Roses — The Advantages of Unionization

It has been thoroughly documented that unions have escaped neither the sexism nor the discrimination to be found in other institutions and organizations in this society. Women active within unions have faced barriers to their participation and to the acceptance of issues of concern to women, and the struggle to overcome these barriers is a continuing one. Nonetheless, there has been increasing recognition of the actual and potential contribution of the union movement to the advancement of women's position in the labour force. It is over ten years ago that McFarland suggested that unions were more of a hindrance than a help, and Baker and Robeson concluded "Considering that unions are dominated by blue-collar men, we cannot expect them to be leaders in women's rights."[1]

While some ambivalence is still expressed, women concerned with labour force issues are no longer discussing whether unions have something to contribute, but rather how much and how best to do it. The following discussion considers control and protection at the workplace, pay and equal pay, benefits and some issues of specific concern to women.

Control and Protection at Work

Unions provide the only mechanism whereby working people can place their concerns directly before the employer, and insist upon a response. During this process unions offer some protection from reprisal, which is critical in dealing with any workplace problems. These basic advantages are essential to any discussion of whether women benefit from unionization, since the capacity to obtain improvements is based upon the rights to collective bargaining and to job security. The advantages of unionization can be summarized as follows:

1. *Negotiating Pay and Working Conditions* — Unionization enables workers to participate in decisions affecting their pay, benefits and any other matter they may wish to negotiate. By law, the employer must negotiate with a certified union. Non-unionized workers have no such control over their conditions of work, since the employer is not bound to discuss these issues.

2. *Legally Binding Contract* — Once a union contract between workers and the employer is signed, its contents are legally binding with penalties for flouting the agreements. For non-unionized workers any customary or verbal agreement, or the contents of a personnel manual are generally not enforceable and the employer may change or disregard them at any time.

3. *Third Party Arbitration* — For unionized workers provision is made for external intervention, by a third party, of any irreconcilable disagreement between employees and the employer. If agreement on contract terms cannot be reached, third party arbitration imposes terms and conditions. For grievances that arise during the time of the collective agreement, a grievance procedure must by law be included in the contract. This procedure provides for independent assessment of the disputes if internal agreement cannot be reached. For non-unionized workers, the employer makes all final decisions, with no outside recourse for workers.

4. *Job Protection* — In a unionized workplace it is more difficult for an employer to fire a worker without a good reason because the worker has the right to submit a grievance if fired. Also, collective bargaining legislation provides for the legal withdrawal of labour by workers (over a collective agreement dispute) and some protection in being rehired at the end of a lawful strike. Workers without a union might appeal an unjust dismissal to a human rights commission or under employment standards legislation, but both are relatively remote to the individual worker, while the delays and complexities involved may require resources not easily available to an individual.

Bread and Roses

The song "Bread and Roses" was inspired by a strike of women textile workers eighty years ago in Lawrence, Massachusetts, who carried a banner "We want bread and roses too."

They won important concessions for all textile workers, men and women. Bread and roses have come to symbolise women's demands for equality and dignity in the workplace and in the union movement.

As we come marching, marching
In the beauty of the day,
A million darkened kitchens,
A thousand mill lofts grey,
Are touched with all the radiance
That a sudden sun discloses,
For the people hear us singing:
"Bread and Roses! Bread and roses!"

As we come marching, marching
We battle too for men,
For they are women's children,
And we mother them again.

Our lives shall not be sweated
From birth until life closes;
Hearts starve as well as bodies;
Give us bread, but give us roses!

As we come marching, marching,
Unnumbered women dead
Go crying through our singing
Their ancient cry for bread.
Small art and love and beauty
Their drudging spirits knew.
Yes, it is bread we fight for —
But we fight for roses, too!

As we come marching, marching,
We bring the greater days.
The rising of the women
Means the rising of the race.
No more the drudge and idler —
Ten that toil where one reposes,
But a sharing of life's glories:
Bread and roses! Bread and roses!

Words: James Oppenheim
Music: Caroline Kohlsaat

5. *Collective Strength* — As a group, workers have greater potential for obtaining improved conditions and benefits than non-unionized individuals bargaining with the employer separately and privately, including the collective strength to disrupt production. Non-unionized workers have no formal opportunity to meet to discuss their work situation. Regular union meetings provide the opportunity for workers to meet, share information about the working conditions and discuss issues of concern.

These are the most basic benefits of unionization. Without the right to bargain, and subject to unjust dismissal, non-unionized workers are relatively powerless to control their working conditions. Upon these provisions depend negotiations for equal pay, benefits for women workers and all other issues affecting the workplace.

Pay and Equal Pay

Pay is perhaps the most important consideration for women working in the paid labour force, since women are concentrated in low-paying jobs, and generally receive 60 to 65 percent of the wages paid to men. Many studies have found that unionization produces higher wages for workers in general; the difference being between 10 and 25 percent.[2] This means that unionization, by itself, provides a substantial advantage in increased pay for both men and women.

Studies on the impact of unionization on the wage gap between men and women are fewer, but suggest that the gap is smaller among unionized than among non-unionized workers. In the late 1960s Gunderson found an average wage gap of 22 percent between men and women doing the same or similar work, and that this differential was reduced by almost half where the workers were unionized. He concluded that unions were effective in promoting equal pay and said "the encouragement of unionization into areas of traditional female employment may do much to narrow male-female wage differentials."[3]

Using the same data base as Gunderson, I compared the pay differentials between men and women in 36 narrowly defined office occupations, covering 425,200 workers in 1977, the last year in which Labour Canada collected this data. On average unionized women office workers were earning $26 more per week than non-unionized women doing the same job — a considerable improvement given that most non-unionized workers were earning less than $200 a week. I also examined the pay differential between men and women doing the same or similar work in these office occupations and found it to be 13.3 percent overall. However, the male-female pay differential for non-unionized workers was 16.8 percent, while for workers belonging to a union the differential dropped to 8.6 percent. I concluded, "Unionized women workers receive higher pay and more nearly equal wages with men, than do non-unionized women."[4]

More recent data suggests the same result. In 1989, looking at all workers employed full-time and full-year, unionized women earned on average $13.98 an hour compared to $10.89 for non-union women. Considering the pay gap between men and women, unionized women workers earned 84 percent of men's wages, while among non-union workers women earned only 70 percent of the wages paid to men.[5] This advantage for unionized women has varied little since 1984, when this survey including wage rates was first conducted. However, this very general data has the disadvantage of not taking into account variables other than unionization that might affect the result, particularly the impact of different occupations and industries.

In a review of the impact of unions in Canada, Britain and the United States, Jain and Sloane concluded that unions in Canada had improved the position of women compared with men, although this was not true in the United States, where there has been a positive impact for blacks but not for women.[6]

Several studies have found that unions reduce wage inequality between higher and lower wage workers.[7] It would be reasonable to assume that this would have a positive effect on the wage gap between women and men, since more women are found in lower paid jobs and benefit disproportionately when general inequalities are reduced. However, it is also an important factor for all workers at the lower end of the pay scale, including the disproportionate numbers of racial minority workers found in low paid jobs. Considering the contribution of unions to equality in employment for women and also for minority groups, Gunderson has suggested: "policies that are conducive to unionization are likely to be policies that will facilitate equality of employment."[8]

To summarize, research on union and non-union rates of pay show that unionization increases pay levels for women, decreases the wage gap between men and women and reduces inequality between the highest and lowest paid workers. However, this gives no indication as to how this occurs, or what policy measures are best oriented to reducing discriminatory pay practices against women. There has been increasing debate over the methods most likely to reduce the pay gap, particularly in response to the introduction of pay equity legislation.

Pay Equity Legislation

It is beyond the scope of this study to analyze this legislation in great detail, and there are other studies that have focused on it exclusively.[9] However, it is important to consider the role of unions with regard to pay equity legislation. There are two types of legislation that provide for equal pay for work of equal value, complaint-based and pro-active.

In 1978 the federal government introduced complaint-based legislation on equal pay for work of equal value, giving workers in the federal jurisdiction the right to make a complaint to the Canadian Human Rights Commission. The Public Service Alliance of Canada (PSAC) that represents federal public service workers was successful in obtaining pay adjustments for several groups of women workers. For example, 470 librarians, predominantly women were compared to historical researchers, predominantly men, and obtained a backdated settlement of $2.3 million, with individual increases ranging from $500 to $6,000. Such settlements encouraged further action and by December 1984 65,000 PSAC members were represented in complaints before the Commission.[10]

Prompted by the potentially enormous cost of settling such complaints, Treasury Board established a joint committee to study the implementation of equal pay for the whole federal public service, a study which involved thirteen unions and took five years to complete. Despite many criticisms of the process and the methods used, the study recommended an average 15 percent increase for women workers, with over $1 billion in retroactive payments. After four months of silence following the release of these results, Treasury Board unilaterally announced retroactive payments of one-quarter of this amount and future payments at one-third of what the study had found to be necessary. The union reactivated its complaints before the Commission and mounted a campaign to press for at least the pay adjustments determined to be necessary by the joint study.[11]

It is now 14 years since the legislation came into force, and after the expenditure of much time and resources, the results continue to be frustrating and incomplete. Moreover, the difficulties and technicalities encountered have posed problems for one of the largest unions in the country. It is next to impossible for unorganized workers to contemplate the process, because of the technical expertise required and because of the fear of reprisals without

Demonstration by members of the Public Service Alliance of Canada to support demands for equal pay, Ottawa, Ontario, 1991.

Courtesy of the Canadian Labour Congress.

union protection. The only other jurisdiction with comparable legislation is Quebec, where it was introduced in 1975, and has resulted in the same delays and frustrations.

The situation changed dramatically when Manitoba became the first province to introduce pro-active legislation on equal pay for work of equal value in 1985, followed by Ontario (1987), Nova Scotia (1988), PEI (1988), and New Brunswick (1989). Instead of a complaints procedure, these laws have in common the requirement upon the employer to develop a pay equity plan, one that involves a comparison of female to male wages on the basis of skill, effort, responsibility and working conditions. It fundamentally assumes that women have been excluded from their rightful place in the job hierarchy, and sets about to insert them more fairly on the ladder. In the case of Ontario, the law is unique because it covers not only the public sector, but also parts of the private sector.

Unions have been at the forefront of lobbying efforts around these legislative changes, working with the women's movement to press for progressive provisions, criticizing the limitations of the laws, and lobbying for improvements.[12] Since the laws require that pay equity plans be negotiated with unions where the work force is organized, the labour movement is intimately involved in the functioning of the legislation. Pay equity legislation has both removed the issue of equal pay from unions, placing it in the hands of politicians and lawyers, and at the same time dropped the issue into the lap of the union movement by forcing them to negotiate it. There is serious and continuing controversy around the advantages and disadvantages of this legislation.[13]

As a result of the legislation some women have received wage increases that have narrowed the gap between their wages and those of men working for the same employer. In Manitoba 4,700 women in the public service received an average pay raise of $1.87 per hour, an increase of 15 percent, and some saw their pay rise by as much as $3.67 per hour.[14] In many locals of the Canadian Union of Public Employees, women working as cleaners, kitchen staff, nursing aides and assistants, clerical workers and secretaries have obtained pay increases. For example, in the York Region Board of Education, head secretaries in elementary schools were compared to technicians and received an hourly pay increase of $4.86, an annual increase of $7,650. At the Ottawa General Hospital, Registered Nursing Assistants were compared to carpenters and received a pay increase of $2.75 an hour. Cleaners at the Women's College Hospital were compared to male cleaners and received a 72 cent per hour increase.[15]

The pay equity legislation has also forced unions to deal with the issue, especially in Ontario where the law affects not only the public, but also the private sector. There has been a veritable deluge of research, educationals and publications on pay equity, what it means, how to understand the law, and how to negotiate it. It is extremely unlikely that the union movement would have committed the same level of energy and quantity of resources without legislative requirement.

The legislation has created a new environment in which some unions have negotiated equal pay adjustments despite the absence of legal imperative. In both British Columbia and Newfoundland the provincial governments have negotiated pay equity plans with public service unions without legislation on the subject. Labour Canada data on negotiated contracts that cover more than 500 workers shows a dramatic rise in the number of collective agreements with clauses on equal pay for work of equal value. In just four years between 1988 and 1992 the number of contracts containing such a clause rose from only 6 to 102 (0.5 to 8.3 percent of all contracts), and the number of workers covered rose from just 0.4 percent to 17.2 percent.[16] Pay equity legislation has raised both the consciousness and the level of activity of the union movement.

Unfortunately, the list of negative factors is longer. Of primary concern has been the large number of women excluded from the legislation. First, pro-active pay equity laws exist in just 5 provinces, and in all but Ontario only the public sector, or parts of the public sector, are included. In Ontario not all of the private sector is covered. Workplaces with fewer than 10 workers are excluded and establishments with fewer than 100 workers are not obligated to produce a pay equity plan. In effect non-unionized workers are excluded, because where there is no union the employer designs the plan, and workers are placed in the position of lodging a complaint. Having examined the attempts of one non-unionized group to challenge their employer's pay equity plan, Keck and Green concluded: "The clearest lesson is that a non-unionized worker needs extraordinary resources of all types to gain access to remedies under the Pay Equity Act."[17]

Even among those workers and workplaces supposedly included under the legislation there are problems. The laws require male comparator groups with which to compare the wages of female-dominated groups, but because so many women work in all-female job ghettoes such male groups often do not exist. In Ontario over 50 percent of the women supposedly included in the legislation are unable to meet this requirement.[18] At the time of writing the New Democratic Party government in Ontario has introduced amendments to the legislation to resolve this problem, although it remains an issue elsewhere.

These various exclusions often involve the women already at the bottom of the heap in terms of wages; namely, private sector workers, the unorganized, those employed in the smallest workplaces, and women who work in female job ghettoes. This in turn involves the exclusion of many racial minority women and immigrant women, who are disproportionately ghettoized in these types of workplaces. Pay equity laws are therefore criticized for failing to help those who are most in need and for acting to widen the wage gap between women, that is between those who will get pay adjustments and those who will not.

In fact it may also serve to widen the wage gap among women who do receive some benefit. Reviewing the gains made by some locals of the Canadian Union of Public Employees (CUPE) provides examples of a school secretary getting an additional $4.22 an hour while the school cleaner got 16 cents; a head secretary earning $3,946 more than the clerk typist before pay equity, and $4,783 more afterwards; a cafeteria manageress getting a raise of $1.14 an hour while the cafeteria worker gained an additional 14 cents.[19] This is not necessarily the direction for all settlements, and a few show greater increases to the lowest paid, or mixed results. In general it will be very difficult to asses the impact of the legislation. In Ontario, for example, there is no requirement to submit pay equity plans, so they are not easily available for examination.

While the legislation only raises some women's wages somewhat, it is not clear that even these gains will be maintained following the period of pay equity adjustments. Some legislation makes no reference to maintenance of pay equity after the adjustments are complete. Ontario's law is confused on this point, but implies that following the implementation of pay equity, bargaining strength will again become the main method of determining wages, a method which has been insufficient to close the gap in the past and offers nothing to unorganized women.

For several reasons, it is feared that despite its many limitations, the legislated pay equity process will be regarded as the complete and final strategy. The technicalities of the procedure cast the false impression that the result is scientific and objective, accurately determining fair wages for women, and therefore the final word on the issue. For unions the costly time and resources employed to implement the legislation will dampen enthusiasm for further measures, as well as the energy to undertake them. There is real concern that we will be left with few gains, and an increased reluctance to continue the struggle.

Other Equal Pay Measures

Comparing women's and men's jobs through complex job evaluation schemes of the whole work force is not the only way to reduce the wage gap, although legislation based on job evaluation has tended to obscure other possibilities. There are other options, possibly preferred options, that do more to reduce inequality and improve the situation for the lowest paid workers.

1. *Across the board increases* provide the same dollar raise in pay to all workers, and although they do not reduce the dollar pay gap, they prevent the disparities from growing. Negotiating percentage pay raises has been condemned for many years because it increases the wage gap between the highest and lowest paid. A 5 percent raise on an income of $20,000 amounts to $1,000, while a 5 percent raise on $40,000 means

an increase of $2,000. The gap in pay is thereby widened from $20,000 to $21,000, and this process has a serious impact over several rounds of negotiations. Since women are commonly found in the lower income positions, the wage gap between men and women is widened. Cost of living allowances (COLA) also widen the gap in pay where they are calculated as a percentage of the wage.

2. *Bottom-end loading* is one term used to mean negotiating larger increases for lower paid workers. It may be a higher percentage increase for workers at the bottom of the scale, or an additional dollar amount above the general pay increase. This has a direct impact on improving the relative pay rates of the lowest paid workers.

3. *Raising base rates* involves equalizing or reducing the differences between the entry level pay rates of different jobs within a workplace. It is often the case that jobs with predominantly female workers have much lower initial rates of pay than those where men are primarily employed, and it can be argued that this difference should be reduced or eliminated. It has been used to close the pay gap between office workers and outside maintenance workers.

4. *Pay increases for specific groups* of workers can result in more equal pay rates. For example, part-time and casual workers tend to be lower paid, or excluded from increments, or receive them at a slower rate. This can be addressed by negotiating a wage adjustment and shortening the waiting period for regular increases. Particular occupational groups found at the bottom of the pay ladder, such as cleaners or kitchen staff, may receive special wage increases

5. *Reducing the number of pay increments* shortens the amount of time needed to reach the top pay rate for the job. It is important here that women, especially office workers, often have the longest wait to reach the top, while men in maintenance or trade or technician jobs are paid the rate for the job either immediately or within a much shorter period of time.

6. *Reducing the number of classifications* reduces pay disparities by merging jobs that were previously separated into the same classification and pay rate. For example, instead of having a Clerk 1 and a Clerk 2 position, it is argued that the two jobs are basically the same, so both become Clerk 2 positions with

the Clerk 2 pay rate. A predominantly female job such as a Cleaner and a predominantly male job of Custodian may be merged into one classification with one job description and one pay rate.

These types of pay arrangements may be characterized as a solidarity approach to wage bargaining.[20] This approach focuses on reducing pay inequalities between workers in general, rather than attempting to fit women into the pay ladder on the same basis as men. It does not rely so much on comparisons with male workers, as on comparisons between the highest and lowest paid. There are examples of successful union strategies based on the solidarity approach, and they have had an important impact upon women's wage rates.

Since the 1960s the Canadian Union of Postal Workers (CUPW) has used a variety of tactics to reduce income differentials between inside postal workers who sort the mail. Across the board rather than percentage increases have been negotiated, specific groups such as mail handlers (predominantly male) and part-time workers (predominantly female) have obtained larger pay increases to equalize their rates with other workers, classifications have been merged, increments have been eliminated, and proposals for different regional rates have been resisted. The impact of these strategies has been profound. The wage gap between the lowest and highest paid workers in the bargaining unit was 35 percent in 1965, but this had been reduced to just 2 percent twenty years later in 1985.[21] It was predominantly women who earned the lowest wages in the Post Office, first as part-time workers and then as Coders in a special lower classification. By its policy of equalizing pay rates for all, the CUPW has eliminated these lower rates of pay for women.

In Quebec, when the Common Front bargained for public sector workers in 1972, the wage demand was for $100 per week for all workers, which had the effect of improving women's position on the pay scale, especially clerical and hospital workers. The Confédération des syndicats nationaux (CSN) has long held to a program of reducing pay inequities, and made several attempts to negotiate salary adjustments for specific jobs where the union judged pay rates to be discriminatory. In 1986 the union obtained agreement that six months before the 1989 round of negotiations a separate bargaining process would consider the relative wages for female dominated job categories. However, the union refused to participate with the government in a joint study of public sector employment. Instead the union carried out its own analysis, using the opportunity to educate workers about the value of women's work and the need for change. Although they did evaluate jobs with the help of the workers, they did not use a formal job evaluation plan or a point system, preferring to make their own assessment as a union and stress the importance of struggle for change, rather than scientific method.

The CSN review proposed a variety of methods for improving the relative pay situation of women, including that basic office staff salaries should be adjusted to the same level as those for services and crafts, that the number of different classifications of office worker should be reduced by half through mergers, that nurses and medical technicians should be adjusted upwards to computer technicians, and that four of the lowest level salary scales for women should receive an increase. The government responded with its evaluation of the whole public sector, which provided pay raises for the majority, but also found that 22 percent of its workers were overpaid, including 12 percent of the women.

The CSN rejected the government's evaluation, and pay equity was one the major issues in a five day strike in the fall 1989, a strike that resulted in severe reprisals. Nonetheless the CSN estimates that it obtained about half its demands, including raising the basic rates for women's jobs and adjustments for nurses and aides, although not for clerical workers. The CSN did not accept the government's new evaluation system and feels that the door was left open for future negotiations, while gains were made in educating members on the issue. Pay equity is still a hot issue, and is expected to reappear in the next round of negotiations. Meanwhile, application has been made to the Human Rights Commission in a further attempt to obtain equal pay for clerical workers.

The Canadian Union of Public Employees (CUPE) has been intimately involved with pay equity legislation, since many of its members in municipalities, hospitals and schools in different provinces are covered. The union's policy has been to participate in the job comparison/evaluation process under the legislation, but also to stress the need for a variety of negotiation tactics as part of the total strategy. Some CUPE locals report avoiding full scale and complex job evaluation systems in favour of merging classifications, or increasing base rates, or making a general pay adjustment for all women in the bargaining unit.

It is not easy to negotiate solidarity types of demands. Employers are strongly opposed to any proposal that infringes upon what they regard as the right of management to organize work, such as eliminating increments, or reducing classifications. They are also opposed because they benefit from the cheap labour involved, whether it be women, or part-time workers, or immigrant workers, or office workers. Whatever the category, employers do not want to lose access to hiring sections of workers at lower rates of pay. Consequently, these demands often lead to strike situations, as has occurred in the examples given above with both the CUPW and the CSN. Another interesting example is the 1981 strike by Vancouver municipal workers, members of CUPE, who were demanding an equalization of base rates between women office workers and the predominantly male manual workers, and the elimination of five years of increment steps for the clerical workers. The employer remained adamantly opposed throughout a thirteen week strike, insisting upon percentage increases. It is particularly interesting that the Employer's Council of B.C., which includes the largest 150 corporations in the province, wrote to the municipal employers to say that a job evaluation study must be carried out if equal pay was to be considered.[22]

But it is not only employers who are opposed to reducing pay inequality. Workers may also be opposed if they will not be among those to benefit. It is critical to educate the members around solidarity proposals, and be clear about the advantages of bringing up the low paid workers. The CUPW argued over many years that lower paid workers and classifications would act as a downward drag on wages for everyone, and this proved to be correct on more than one occasion. The union also pressed the point that it was important politically to avoid the divisions among workers created by the employer through many different classifications and pay levels. More equal rates of pay, it was stressed, would lead to more solidarity, and therefore increased ability to obtain improvements for everyone through negotiations with the employer.

Unions have supported different approaches to bargaining for pay, sometimes stressing the importance of a living wage and a decent standard of living for all workers (the solidarity approach), and sometimes arguing that pay should meet the skills required for the job. Unions may also hold these apparently contradictory positions at one and the same time, pragmatically negotiating whatever seems most advantageous and attainable.

As unions bargain under the pay equity legislation for more equal pay for women, many have continued to negotiate percentage increases. Despite CUPE's strong position on pay equity, most bargaining units are continuing to negotiate percentage increases. While the PSAC was in the midst of its battle with Treasury Board over equal pay, it negotiated percentage increase into the new collective agreement. In interviews for this study with thirteen unions (see Chapter 4), percentage increases remained the most common form of pay demand. This must raise questions as to the level of consciousness and commitment created by the pay equity legislation.

As with pay equity agreements, negotiating reductions in pay inequity from a solidarity approach is necessarily limited because unions usually bargain by individual employer, so solidarity bargaining can take place only on that very restricted basis. There are other mechanisms to achieve a broader-based impact on wage equality, such as an adequate and indexed minimum wage to enable families to survive above the poverty line, and improved employment standards legislation so that non-unionized workers would have better benefits and working conditions. Unionization itself is a means to improve women's wages, and reduce wage inequality.

However, at this moment pay equity legislation has grabbed most of the attention and resources of both the women's movement and the union movement as far as the wage issue is concerned. It remains to be seen whether this will prove to be a consciousness raising exercise that will lead to further action, or a liberal reform that will produce insignificant gains, particularly for those women who need them the most.

As far as the role of unions is concerned, it has been expressed by one researcher as follows:

> It is undeniably true that women continue to face obstacles in promoting our interests through the union movement. It is equally true, however, that virtually every gain women have made in terms of the equal pay issue has been accomplished by unionized women, whether through collective bargaining or through utilizing union support to take advantage of the legislative provisions that do exist.[23]

Having shown a real commitment to equal pay for women, the question remains, despite pay equity legislation, as to what methods the union movement should focus upon, and how best to achieve results.

Employment Equity

Employment equity has received less attention than pay equity, and yet it is an equally critical strategy for improving women's position in the labour force. While equal pay for work of equal value aims to provide fair remuneration for "women's work," the purpose of employment equity is to enable women and other disadvantaged workers to take an equal place in the labour force. Either one of these programs can have only a limited impact without the other. Moreover, employment equity is central because it moves beyond concern only with the secondary position of women and raises the situation of minority groups in the labour force, particularly visible minorities, native people and persons with disabilities.

For unions, employment equity undoubtedly presents more of a challenge than pay equity. Unions are well-attuned to bargaining for wages and there is a long and accepted tradition that unions have a role to play in establishing wage rates. This is not the case with employment equity, which treads into areas always considered to be exclusive management rights: recruitment, hiring, training, transfers, and promotions. These are fundamental elements in management control over the work force. In fact where individuals participate in these decisions they are commonly excluded from union membership because of their close relationship with management functions. In some cases legislation specifically prohibits unions from negotiating on these topics, as with federal government workers and some provincial public servants. Employer opposition to union involvement on these issues is intense.

Unions also face the difficulty of opposition to employment equity among their own ranks. Insisting upon hiring, training and increased opportunities for women and minority groups may be unpopular among the established work force. Insecurities are aroused by discussion of quotas and modifications to the collective agreement. Some unions therefore face resistance in convincing their members that employment equity is important, and some do not try.

Unions have attempted to obtain some control over work force decisions through bargaining the application of seniority. Instead of the employer determining who should be promoted, transferred or laid off, it is decided according to the number of years of employment that workers have with that employer. Although unions have long regarded the negotiation of seniority provisions as a central demand, they have had mixed success. As of January 1992, the majority of workers in bargaining units of more than 500 workers were covered by seniority for lay-off (70 percent), recall (67 percent), and job postings (59 percent). However, seniority applied to only a minority of workers for promotions (48 percent) and transfers (47 percent). Moreover, in the majority of these collective agreements, seniority is not the sole criteria but would be considered in combination with qualifications or merit.

Unions have found it extremely difficult to negotiate employment equity agreements with employers, although there is some experience to draw upon. In 1984 the Canadian Auto Workers (CAW) succeeded in negotiating an affirmative action program with General Motors. Affirmative action committees were established at each plant, each committee including at least one women, and with 12 hours of company paid time per week to carry on its work. At this time women were just 10 percent of the workers at GM and held only 1 percent of the skilled trades jobs. Nonetheless, the company successfully resisted the unions's demands for goals and timetables, which had included a 50 percent hiring quota for women.[24]

The members of the affirmative action committees received four days of training, and undertook a range of activities. All of the committees worked on gathering information on the proportion of women, native people, visible minorities and persons with disabilities both in their communities and in their workplaces, and participated in educating union members in preparation for a company wide questionnaire on affirmative action. In Oshawa a pre-apprenticeship program was established through a local college to give women the skills to apply for trades positions. In St Catharine's 120 members, the majority women, attended an information session on apprenticeship training. In London and St Catherine's the committee members made presentations of their experiences as trades workers at many local schools. Meanwhile, a central affirmative action committee worked with the union's skilled trades committees to modify the eligibility requirements to enter the trades in order to better accommodate women.

In 1987 the union was again unable to make progress on specific targets and timetables, but did negotiate 3 hours of human rights training for every GM employee on company time, involving 45,000 workers at a cost of $5 million to GM (although there followed

Human rights
training at General
Motors Transmission
Plant, Windsor,
Ontario, 1992.

*Courtesy of CAW,
Nick Brancacchio.*

three years of disagreements between the union and the company
over the content of the course). Also included was a literacy
program, teams to work on harassment at each plant and a child
care fund. For this collective agreement the union and GM received
an affirmative action award from the Ontario Women's Directorate.
In the same year the provisions for affirmative action committees
were extended to Chrysler and Ford.

What have been the results of all this activity? Certainly there
has been education and increased awareness of the issue. However, the union has stated: "our efforts have had little impact on
increasing the numbers of women, racial minorities, persons with
disabilities or aboriginal people in our workplaces." The reason
was: "in spite of vigorous attempts to negotiate goals and timetables, the employers have adamantly refused ... In order for our
efforts to be effective there must be mandatory goals and timetables
in place."[25]

The union has had further experience with the reluctance of
employers to concede any control. In the 1990 round of bargaining
with Ford of Canada, the CAW placed on the agenda hiring quotas
with time limits, the goal being "to make the work force representative of the community as a whole with respect to the target
groups."[26] This round of negotiations resulted in a strike. Although
the employment equity demands were still on the table one week
into the strike, the company remained adamant and the union
gained only that the committees would receive statistics on hiring

from the company, in order to monitor the situation. "So we were able to chip a little more away from their exclusive right to hire. We'll go at it again in '93."[27]

The Communications Workers of Canada (CWC) negotiated a joint committee on employment equity with Bell Canada in 1985, but the company bypassed this committee and established a pilot program in 1987 for women working as operators and in dining services to transfer temporarily into the craft and services jobs predominantly held by men. After 6 months in the job the women returned to their original positions, but formed a pool of candidates for any permanent openings. In 1988 the union negotiated the extension of the joint committee and obtained a letter of understanding that the committee would review the pilot program and formulate future projects. As a result the Qualifications Development Program that ran in 1990 and again in 1991 was offered to more women (150 to 200) in a wider geographical area. The only requirements to make the transfer are very basic, such as a valid driver's license, the ability to work aloft and normal colour vision.

Former telephone operators who participated in the program and now have permanent positions as technicians are quoted in the union's pamphlet on the program to encourage other women to apply. One says:

> I'm an Installer II, Residence. I go into customers' homes, put in lines, crawl in awkward spaces to put lines in basements, etc. I put drops on poles — I was terrified the first few times. The key is don't get discouraged, don't give up … I never dreamt that I would be doing this. It is important to be physically fit. There is a lot of lifting and carrying — boxes and ladders. But you learn how to do it."[28]

Although there is not a big increase in pay initially, over time the women who transfer into such positions are likely to earn up to $150 more than the top rate they could earn as telephone operators.

The union argues that the number of women involved is still too limited, given that there are 15,000 technician positions, and wants to negotiate a clause requiring that women from this program be hired into technician positions before Bell hires off the street.

With the Manitoba Telephone System the CWC has participated in an Equal Employment Opportunities Committee that established a pilot program in 1989 to provide pre-apprenticeship training to women. It provides 18 weeks of training over a 12 month period to put women on an equal footing with men in applying for general apprenticeships. This has an interesting link to the community because the program involved twenty women, eight employees of the Manitoba Telephone System and twelve from a provincial government program to assist low income women, called the Core Initiative Program.

Most recently, the union is applying for funding to analyze how workers with disabilities can be integrated into the workplace. Although some sight-impaired workers are employed as operators, the CWC wants to see hearing and mobility impaired workers hired. The union also questions the ghettoization of disabled workers into the operator positions, and wants to consider what needs to be done to enable them to work in some of the better paid jobs.

Employers and unions often take fundamentally different approaches to what constitutes employment equity. Employers resist required quotas and targets, and prefer not to include employment equity plans as part of the collective agreement. Unions have found that voluntary programs do not work and want any plans to be enforceable through the grievance procedure of the negotiated contract. Sometimes the employer's notion of employment equity is to hire a few more of the target groups into management positions, often by hiring off the street. Unions are more concerned about the situation of the general mass of workers, and want not only more hiring of the target group members, but also internal movement for lower paid and ghettoized workers into more skilled positions. Employers tend to focus exclusively on hiring, whereas unions express concern about what happens inside the workplace, including both the need for broader support to help retain people, and education of the current work force to create an environment of acceptance rather than hostility. Unions have stressed the importance of the education and participation of workers in the success of any employment equity plan in order to avoid resentment and hostility, while employers have sometimes by-passed even consultation with the union and preferred to introduce their own programs.

In this context of extreme employer resistance over what are regarded as unassailable management rights, as well as fundamental disagreement over what changes are necessary, legislative support for employment equity is crucial. Advocates of employment equity agree that voluntary programs do not work. At the federal level, legislation that only requires employers to report on the composition of their work force has failed to produce any changes and a Special Committee recently reviewed this legislation and was very critical. Companies that obtain contracts with the federal government are required to sign a Certificate of Commitment to employment equity, but this also has no mandatory requirement for a program or change. When the CWC tried to negotiate an employment equity initiative with an employer who had signed such a certificate, the company refused even to discuss the issue.[29]

In 1979 the New Democratic Party government in Saskatchewan amended the Human Rights Code to give the Commission the authority to approve or order affirmative action programs. The regulations included union involvement in joint committees and the Saskatchewan Federation of Labour endorsed the amendments and hired an affirmative action officer to help affiliates negotiate with their employers. Concerned about the possibility of yet stronger legislation that would actually force employment equity, employers indicated their increased willingness to deal with the issue. Several different unions in both the public and private sectors were successful in initiating analyses of their workplaces. In most cases it was found that while racial minorities and persons with disabilities were under-represented in the workplace, women were present but ghettoized into lower paid office jobs. Unions pressed for more hiring of minorities, paid education leave, and reduced minimum requirements for the more skilled jobs.[30] Before many initiatives could be brought to the test of implementation (and most had already met with problems and interruptions), a Conservative government was elected and the program was abandoned.

In Quebec the Parti Quebecois government in 1982 passed amendments to the Charter of Human Rights and Freedoms that allowed the Human Rights Commission to recommend affirmative action programs or impose them through the courts, including the right to investigate, approve, supervise and monitor programs. As in Saskatchewan, this legal framework has enabled unions in Quebec to negotiate employment equity programs. The Quebec division of the Canadian Union of Public Employees (CUPE) produced a "Union Guide for the Implementation of Affirmative Action Programs" and developed a course on how to negotiate the issue. By 1987 CUPE locals in Quebec representing workers in municipalities, hydro, universities, transportation and social services were involved in negotiating affirmative action programs.[31]

The Fédération des affaires sociales, the largest union in Quebec, established a joint committee that has undertaken the laborious process of analyzing the workplace in detail. Pilot projects have

Employment Equity for Workers with Disabilities

■ OFL/FTO

MAKING IT HAPPEN

*Employment Equity
for Persons with Disabilities —
A Guidebook for Shop Stewards
and Union Personnel*

One of the most effective employment equity models is a series of programs operated by the International Association of Machinists and Aerospace Workers (IAM). Beginning in 1980 in Seattle with the IAM Projects with Industry program, the union began to help persons with disabilities obtain jobs and achieve successful careers.

Since 1980, the union has developed job placements for persons with disabilities, for youths with disabilities making the transition from school to employment, and for persons with disabilities who need supported employment services. The programs are operated by IAM CARES, which is the union's Center for Administering Rehabilitation and Employment Services. In North America, IAM CARES has placed more than 7,500 persons with disabilities in jobs.

In 1989, the national IAM CARES program was established in Canada under the name IAM CARES\AIM CROIT with centers in Vancouver and in Montreal. This program provides on-the-job training, placement and related services to individuals with disabilities for self-sustaining jobs in the private sector. Job placement specialists staff both centers. These specialists help individuals with disabilities satisfy their career needs in accordance with their career goals and preferences.

Achievements of the Canadian program so far confirm its success. After 24 months of operation, more than 623 placements have been made. IAM CARES\AIM CROIT is now negotiating with the federal government to establish similar centers in Ottawa/Hull, Toronto, Winnipeg and Edmonton.

From "Making it Happen: Employment Equity for Persons with Disability," a guidebook produced by the Ontario Federation of Labour.

been set up that have looked at every job title, determined in which titles there might be job discrimination, established an appropriate percentage for the representation of women, considered what female labour is available to fill such positions, and examined what policies have lead to the discrimination. At the time of my interview with this union, the recommendations from the pilot projects had not yet emerged.

In Ontario employment equity legislation had its first reading in June 1992 and is expected to become law in 1993. Bill 79 identified four target groups — aboriginal people, persons with disabilities, members of racial minorities and women. However, gays and lesbians are not included and lobbying from the gay and lesbian community has, thus far, failed to alter this. The proposed legislation requires that employers prepare and implement employment equity plans. These plans are to remove barriers to recruitment, employment and promotion, so that the work force will reflect the presence of the four target groups in the community. Public sector employers will have from twelve to eighteen months to prepare and file a plan, while employers in the private sector will have from eighteen months to three years, depending upon the size of the work force. Where unions exist, the preparation of the plan is to be carried out jointly between the union and the employer, separately from the usual collective bargaining process. Two agencies, an Employment Equity Commission and a Tribunal, will monitor and enforce the legislation, ultimately with fines of up to $50,000. This legislation will be unique in Canada and its impact will be watched closely by other jurisdictions.

The question of seniority has received considerable attention, since it is sometimes viewed as a barrier to groups that have been discriminated against in the past and therefore have not had the opportunity to accumulate seniority. Perhaps the best known example is the "Women Back Into Stelco" campaign. In 1979 the United Steelworkers (USWA) in Hamilton backed five women in their complaints to the Human Rights Commission that Stelco had refused to hire any women since 1961. After six months of campaigning and publicity, Stelco hired the five women complainants and agreed to a 10 percent hiring quota for women. By the summer of 1981 over 200 women were working at Stelco. However, in the recession and general lay-offs that followed almost all these women lost their jobs and few were recalled. "Women were especially hard hit because, as specified in the contract, vulnerability to a layoff depended largely on seniority."[32]

Unions have a long tradition of support for seniority clauses, precisely because they are regarded as a much fairer alternative than relying on the employer's decision (decisions that are often discriminatory, among other problems). In general unions are suspicious of changes that might weaken seniority clauses to the employer's advantage, and they have some cause for concern. For example, when the Human Rights Commission was given additional powers in Saskatchewan, "Employers were openly declaring that affirmative action provided them with a chance to 'get rid of seniority clauses'."[33]

The CAW has argued that it is not fair to place the burden of past discrimination by employers upon the backs of older workers, reducing their opportunities or job security for the benefit of others. Most unions argue that stronger seniority clauses are required, and that they will protect all workers from employer abuse, including those in the target groups. Plant wide, inclusive seniority lists are recommended, so that workers can transfer from one type of job to another without losing their seniority. It has also been recognized that seniority should be negotiated to cover leaves of absence so that certain workers are not disadvantaged, particularly women on maternity leave. In bargaining units of over 500, 50 percent of workers were covered by a collective agreement that provided for the accumulation of seniority during maternity leave, and 41 percent had this provision for adoption leave.[34]

However, modified seniority clauses have been negotiated by a small number of unions. In first contract negotiations at Dona Lake Mine in Ontario, the United Steelworkers of America wanted an employment equity plan for native workers, and under first contract arbitration the plan was included in the collective agreement. It states "In all cases of vacancy, promotion, transfer, layoff and recall from layoff, native employees shall be entitled to preference if they have the ability and physical fitness to perform the work, notwithstanding their seniority." As well as the seniority provision, this agreement also entitles native workers to a three month leave of absence each year for traditional activities, such as hunting and trapping. The Grain Services Union has negotiated with the Saskatchewan Wheat Pool an arrangement that "all designated group members would be credited with years of seniority equal to the average seniority within the classification which could be used for the purposes of bidding, promotion, layoff, or recall."[35] Such agreements are still rare. Out of the 1,235 collective agreements analyzed by Labour Canada, only two had modified seniority clauses for affirmative action groups. The implications of seniority for affirmative action merit further analysis, but it is important to bear in mind that employer resistance is a more serious barrier to change than union seniority clauses.

In March of 1990 over 400 home support workers, members of the British Columbia Government Employee's Union, were on strike because of pay rates as low as $5.10 per hour. They wanted recognition of their role in enabling the elderly, the chronically ill and persons with disabilities to remain at home when they would otherwise need to be institutionalized.

Courtesy of the British Columbia Government Employee's Union.

Table 3-1: Pay and Benefits for Union and Non-union Workers,* 1978.	Union ($)	Non-union ($)	Differential (%)
Total compensation	16,977	12,323	37.8
Pay for time worked	13,192	10,159	29.9
Total fringe benefits	3,786	2,163	75.0
Vacation Pay	889	579	
Paid holidays	597	409	
Sick leave	125	84	
Other paid absences	24	13	
Workers compensation	298	165	
Canada/Quebec pension	165	147	
Other pension plans	650	233	
Life/health insurance	364	152	
Unemployment insurance	216	187	
Other benefit plans	49	15	
Miscellaneous payments	410	180	

*Employers with at least 100 workers.
Source: Statistics Canada, *Employee Compensation 1978*, Cat 72-619,, Ottawa, 1980, p.27, Table X.

Benefits and Working Conditions

What used to be called "fringe benefits" are by no means marginal additions to the pay rate. The last time that Statistics Canada analyzed the issue in 1978, employee benefits averaged $33.97 for every $100 paid in basic wages.[36] Vacations, statutory holidays, long term disability and pension plans, health and life insurance, sick leave, maternity leave and a range of other benefits have become an expected part of the total compensation package for many workers.

Unionization improves not only rates of pay, but also the total compensation package including various benefits.[37] Table 3-1 shows the results of the 1978 study by Statistics Canada mentioned above, which examined benefits by unionization. While unionized workers earned 30 percent more than non-union workers, the differential in benefits was much higher. The union negotiated package of benefits was worth 75 percent more than the benefits for unorganized workers. On everything from paid vacations, holidays and sick leave to pension plans and life and health insurance, unionized workers received better coverage than the non-unionized.

A more recent study of the impact of unionization upon pensions found that a worker employed in a union job was 22 to 25 percent more likely to have pension coverage than if the same worker was employed in a non-union job.[38] Unionization offers to women, as to all workers, the opportunity for an improved and extended package of benefits.

Apart from general benefits for all workers, there are certain issues that affect women particularly. There are three questions to consider here. Have unions had some success in negotiating issues of concern to women, is there an improvement over time in satisfying those needs, and is there further room for progress?

In 1986 Labour Canada started to collect information on major union contract provisions, those that cover over 200 workers in the federal jurisdiction and over 500 workers elsewhere. In 1992 this included 1,235 negotiated contracts covering almost two and a half million workers. This data allows us to examine what has been negotiated into major union contracts, including issues of specific interest to women. It should be noted here that there is a relationship between what unions bargain and legislated provisions. When many union contracts have negotiated a particular provision, it may become a relatively accepted part of the benefits package. At this point pressure may build to provide a similar benefit for the broader work force, contributing to the push for improved legislation.

Table 3-2 shows the proportion of workers covered by contract clauses relating to family responsibilities. The most extensive coverage is for maternity leave with well over three quarters of the workers having some provision. In most jurisdictions, employment standards legislation provides for 17 weeks of leave for maternity, while four jurisdictions provide 18 weeks. Of the workers covered

Table 3-2: Percentage of Workers Covered by Contract Provisions on Parental Responsibilities, January 1992

Maternity Leave - Duration	**78.5**
17 weeks or less	20.8
18-25 weeks	24.0
Over 25 weeks	26.7
Extended Parental Leave	**31.9**
Extended Paternity Leave	**35.4**
Adoption Leave	**63.9**
17 weeks or less	33.3
18-26 weeks	22.2
Over 26 weeks	4.6
Paid Maternity Leave	**49.1**
76-100% salary for 17 weeks	21.4
Income beyond 17 weeks	16.4
Paid Adoption Leave	**22.9**
76-100% salary for 17 weeks	20.2
Income beyond 17 weeks	0.1
Family Illness Leave	**39.8**
Paid Family Illness Leave	29.4
Personal Reasons Leave	**58.0**
Paid Personal Reasons Leave	5.3
Day Care Facilities	**3.0**

Source: Labour Canada, Bureau of Labour Agreement Data Base, January 1992. This data includes 2,434,055 workers in total, covered by 1,235 major collective agreements.

by major contracts, 20 percent receive 17 weeks or less, which is no more than the period provided by legislation, although having it written into the workplace collective agreement may clarify the arrangement and reduce the likelihood of employer resistance. Just over half the workers in this data base are covered by maternity leave of 18 weeks or more, and more than a quarter (27 percent) have over 25 weeks of maternity leave.

Beyond the time required for physical recovery from childbirth, increasing emphasis has been laid upon the need for parental leave, time to care for young children that might be taken by either parent. Thirty two percent of the workers in the data base have extended paternity leave, while 35 percent have extended parental leave. There is no information on the number of weeks involved. Until recently all these arrangements represented advances for workers over legal minimums, since it is only in the last three years that parental leave has been included under employment standards legislation. There is far more variation in provision of parental leave than maternity leave, varying from three jurisdictions that have no parental leave, to several that provide from 12 to 17 weeks for each parent, to Quebec that provides 34 weeks for each parent.

For adoptive leave 63 percent of the workers have some coverage, and 27 percent have bargained for at least 18 weeks of leave. As with parental leave, until recently these were trend-setting arrangements, because adoption leave has appeared in employment standards legislation only within the last three years in most jurisdictions. It is usually equivalent to the number of weeks provided for parental leave, and varies from 6 to 34 weeks for each parent, with no provision in two jurisdictions. It remains to be seen whether unions will now proceed to bargain arrangements beyond the legislated minimums, but it will be difficult to assess give the variation in arrangements from one jurisdiction to another. However, now that there have been legislative advances on the question of leave, it may be more useful for unions to focus upon the more difficult question of pay for parental leave.

The issue of pay for maternity leave has received more attention in recent years, since women may be unable to benefit from the leave provisions if they must sacrifice their income while they are away from work. Under federal unemployment insurance legislation a woman on maternity leave who meets the eligibility requirements faces a two week waiting period with no benefits, followed by 15 weeks of benefits that cannot exceed 60 percent of her usual wages, but are also limited by an established maximum amount which may be below 60 percent of her wages. Since these arrangements constitute a considerable loss of income, some unions have bargained improved coverage. It is harder to bargain pay for maternity leave than the leave itself, because of the direct cost to employers. Nonetheless, there has undoubtedly been some real progress on this issue.

In 1979 the Quebec Common Front first negotiated a break-through arrangement of 20 weeks of paid maternity leave at full pay. This meant that the employer paid the woman's wages for the two week waiting period, topped up the 15 weeks of unemployment benefits to full pay, and paid full wages again for another three weeks. This was followed in 1981 by the Canadian Union of Postal Workers, which negotiated 17 weeks of paid maternity leave after a six week strike and became the first national union in Canada to obtain such a benefit. These initial gains were built upon by other unions, as shown in Table 3-2. By 1992 paid maternity leave had become relatively common, negotiated for almost one-half of the workers covered by major contracts. Twenty-two percent of workers have provision for a top-up of their 15 weeks of unemployment insurance benefits, plus income to cover the two week waiting period. Sixteen percent have bargained for income protection beyond this 17 week limit.

In November 1990 changes to the unemployment legislation allowed eligible parents to obtain another 10 weeks of benefits to be shared or taken by either parent. It is too soon after the legislative changes to assess the impact upon union negotiations, but it opens the possibility for unions to negotiate top up arrangements that would cover this 10 week period, so it may be that unions will be bargaining wage top ups for parental leave as well as maternity leave.

Prior to 1990, adoptive parents were eligible for the same 15 weeks of benefits provided for maternity leave. Twenty three percent of workers in this survey have bargained for paid adoption leave, and 21 percent have obtained salary coverage for up to 17 weeks. However, the 1990 changes in unemployment insurance were negative for adoptive parents, since their benefit period was actually reduced from 15 to 10 weeks. This will probably mean that top-up arrangements already negotiated into collective agreements for adoptive parents will also be reduced to 10 weeks plus the two week waiting period, although unions may continue to press for improved coverage.

Apart from the period surrounding the birth or adoption of a child, there are the ongoing demands of child care that conflict with the requirements of a job. Negotiating leave for family illness is an important support mechanism for parents and 40 percent of workers have managed to obtain this provision. Almost 30 percent of workers have this type of leave with pay, so that their income is protected. Leave for personal reasons can be taken for any purpose, but it gives parents additional flexibility to deal with children's dental appointments, special school events, and so on. Fifty eight percent of workers have obtained this type of leave, although only 5 percent have access to this leave with pay.

Very few unions have negotiated day care facilities. Just 3 percent of workers have collective agreements that include such an arrangement. There is some controversy over the relative advantages and disadvantages of workplace day care, and it is a relatively complicated undertaking requiring space, staff and a suitable schedule for the workers involved.

However, several unions have been involved in establishing workplace child care programs. The B.C. Government Employees' Union was probably the first to introduce a union-funded day care centre in Victoria in 1971.[39] Public sector unions in Quebec and elsewhere in Canada have successfully negotiated the establishment of a number of child care centres with the employer providing some financial subsidy or rent-free space. In 1983 the Canadian Auto Workers was the first union in the private sector to negotiate the inclusion of a day care fund into a collective agreement. The employer at Canadian Fab, Stratford, Ontario, agreed to pay two cents per hour per worker to help finance child care costs for its workers. The union also negotiated a child care fund with Chrysler, Ford and General Motors and in 1989 a group day care centre was opened in the Windsor area to serve workers from all three employers.

An important issue to raise with regard to benefit coverage is that one group of workers, gays and lesbians, have been excluded from coverage for many of the benefits. Although individual gays and lesbians are covered like other workers, the problem arises when they attempt to obtain the benefits provided for the spouses, partners, or families of employees. Many gays and lesbians have relationships no less stable or long term than other workers, and

Table 3-3: Percentage of Workers Covered by Selected Contract Provisions of Interest to Women, January 1992.

Anti-Discrimination	63.1
Sexual Harassment	42.7
Health and Safety - Video Display Terminals	
Additional Rest Period	6.1
Special Eye Examination	6.1
Reassignment (e.g. for pregnancy)	27.3
Varying Hours	
Flextime	11.6
Compressed Work Week	20.3
Job Sharing	6.7
Part-time Workers	
Vacation	40.3
Holidays	39.0
Sick Leave	39.4
Seniority	36.8
Health and Welfare	34.4
Severance Pay	21.5
Pensions	8.0
Ratio of Part-time to Full-time	2.3
Workers with Disabilities	
Right to Transfer/Training	3.4
Employer Willingness to Transfer/Training	34.7
Other (Includes Hiring Disabled Workers)	1.3

Source: Labour Canada, Bureau of Labour Information collective agreement data base, January 1992. This data includes 2,434,055 workers in total, covered by 1,235 major collective agreements.

lesbians in particular may have children from previous relationships. When a spouse or common-law partner is defined as a member of the opposite sex, or a family as consisting of a man, a woman and children, gays and lesbians are not able to obtain the same benefits as other workers. This covers a wide and important range of items, including health insurance, group life insurance, dental and vision plans, compassionate leave, leave for family responsibilities, pension plans, relocation expenses, and sometimes items such as family membership in social/recreational facilities and travel passes. Given the importance of these benefits as part of the overall pay package, it has been suggested that there is "a wage rate based on sexual orientation."[40]

With pressure from the gay and lesbian community, unions have been moving to deal with this issue and negotiate coverage for same-sex spouses. Only anecdotal information is available, but certainly a number of unions have successfully negotiated this arrangement. However, where employers or insurance carriers have refused to include same-sex spouses, lengthy court battles have ensued under various human rights laws in different jurisdictions. Unions have been generally supportive of the need to include same-sex spouses for benefit coverage and have supported these claims and complaints with resources and finances (see Chapter 7 for further details).

Table 3-3 shows the percentage of workers covered by various other contract provisions of importance to women. Almost two-thirds of workers are covered by a general anti-discrimination clause, but there is no information on what grounds are prohibited for discrimination. Race and sex are normally included. However, in some unions lesbians and gay men are still attempting to negotiate that sexual orientation be a prohibited ground for discrimination at the workplace. On sexual harassment, 43 percent of workers have contract language which deals in some way with this issue. There is no information available on the negotiation of racial or personal harassment clauses, although some unions have negotiated these. On sexual harassment, again there has undoubtedly been considerable progress on this issue over time, since it was virtually unheard of in the union movement fifteen years ago.

There has been some action to protect workers, mainly women, who work with video-display terminals (VDTs). Clerical and secretarial workers are particularly vulnerable because VDTs are widely used for word processing, and information storage and retrieval. Thus far only a minority of workers have any protection, 20 percent having obtained protective reassignment and just 6 percent are covered by additional rest periods and special eye examinations. There continues to be controversy around whether these machines have a negative influence on health, and this hampers attempts to negotiate protection. In Quebec pregnant women have the right to reassignment or to withdraw from the workplace, an important precedent not included in legislation elsewhere.

The opportunity to vary the work schedule can be useful for women balancing family responsibilities. Twenty percent of workers covered by this data have provisions to work a compressed week. This means the same number of hours per week, but they are compressed into a four day schedule, or a four day week every two weeks. Twelve percent of workers have access to flexitime, which means that core hours must be worked each day, but there is flexibility around scheduling the remaining hours. Job sharing is when a position is split between two workers, and generally raises many of the same problems as part-time work, such as benefits and seniority. It is quite unusual with only 7 percent of workers having such a provision.

It is not easy to assess the coverage of part-time workers in union contracts since there is no way of knowing how many of the contracts might cover only full-time workers. However, since 40 percent of workers have contracts that provide for vacation, holidays and sick pay for part-time workers, at least that proportion must involve part-time workers. Part-time workers are less often protected by seniority, health and welfare arrangements or severance pay, and only 8 percent of workers are covered by collective agreements that have part-time workers included in pension plans. It is also apparent that it continues to be rare for a union to negotiate limitations on the use of part-time work with a ratio of part to full-time workers.[41] Only 2 percent of workers are covered by such a contract clause.

For workers who are disabled on the job, a considerable number of unions have negotiated that these workers will be transferred to another job, or where necessary trained for different work. However, while 38 percent of workers covered by a major contract have such a provision, only 3 percent have the right to this consideration, the others having a clause that only indicates the

Breakthrough on Negotiation of Harassment Policies

Toronto Hydro workers, members of the Canadian Union of Public Employees, recently negotiated the right to leave work — with full pay — if they are harassed in any way. The provision takes as its model the right to refuse unsafe work from health and safety legislation — discrimination being viewed as a hazard at work, not unlike occupational injury and disease.

Union members facing harassment will be able to leave the workplace immediately and report the incident to a union representative for investigation.

This policy is part of a larger program called "Respect at Work" that includes workshops for both management and workers on what constitutes harassment and how to respond to it.

The types of harassment covered under this new policy include not only race, religion, colour, sexual orientation, gen-

der and disability, but also any "statement or action which undermines a person's dignity or worth."

"Harassed workers win right to leave," *The Leader, Canadian Union of Public Employees* 7: 2, Nov.-Dec.1992, p.1.

employer's willingness to consider such provision. Clearly, this does not require the employer to make accommodation by adjusting the workplace to enable a disabled worker to continue at the same job. Collective agreements that require the hiring of workers with disabilities, that is employment equity, are almost non-existent.

It is apparent that unions have taken some action with regard to negotiating issues of particular concern to women, including racial minority women, disabled women and lesbians. It is also clear that there has been some progress over time, although it is not possible to analyze this statistically. Labour Canada's data base on collective agreements was not complete until 1988, which is therefore the earliest date for comparison. In general there are small improvements on most issues between 1988 and 1992, but since contracts have been renegotiated only once or twice over this period, it is insufficient to assess the changes taking place. However, it will be important for the future to watch the trends in bargaining these provisions, the pace of improvement and the development of new issues.

The question of whether unions have done enough to bargain issues of concern to women is harder to answer. It is impossible to know from analyzing contracts what occurred during the collective bargaining process to reach this final stage. The specific characteristics of both the union and the employer play a part. It is clear that unions in the public sector have been more successful in bargaining these issues than unions in the private sector. On every contract provision discussed above, public sector workers have considerably higher levels of coverage than private sector workers. For example, on paid maternity leave 72 percent of public sector workers included in the database are covered, compared to only 11 percent in the private sector. Forty-three percent of public sector workers have provision for paid family illness leave, but only 7 percent of private sector workers. On sexual harassment, 56 percent of public sector workers have a provision, compared to only 20 percent in the private sector. The higher number of women union members in the public sector would have an influence here, but it may also be that employers in the public sector are less likely to oppose such provisions.

Certain benefits may never arise for discussion, let alone negotiation. For example, in a local with no women workers, or where the women have already completed their families, maternity leave may be ignored. Then, in negotiating with the employer, compromise is always required and some demands are lost. The Ontario Federation of Labour has suggested that "in many workplaces, women's issues are still the first to be dropped at the bargaining table."[42] Where the union does press the point and the employer is opposed, the final pressure is to strike, but very few contracts are settled by strikes, the workers standing to lose so much for uncertain results. The position of the employer is crucial here. If the union is an accepted part of the workplace, the employer is not pressed financially and the workers have been improving the contract at each round of bargaining, the stage is set for some good clauses to appear. However, if the employer is resisting the union at every step and feels that profits are threatened, the negotiating team may be hard pressed to obtain even the most basic pay and benefits package.

Undoubtedly unions have plenty of scope for improvement in bargaining on many of these matters. One-third of workers are not protected by an anti-discrimination clause and the majority of workers are not covered by provisions on sexual harassment. Only a small minority have access to flexible working hours, and part-time and disabled workers need increased protection. Leave with pay for family responsibilities, whether for maternity, adoption, family illness or personal reasons, applies to only a minority of workers. Gay and lesbian workers continue to struggle to be included in benefits relating to family coverage.

Conclusion

In comparison to non-union women workers, most unionized women have increased control over their work situation, have negotiated higher pay as well as pay rates more in line with those of men, and have improved benefits and conditions of work. In negotiations with employers unions have undoubtedly been advantageous for women in the work force. The following chapters consider how women have fared inside the union movement itself.

Monique Simard, Vice-President of the Confédération des syndicats nationaux 1983-1991, being interviewed at an equal pay demonstration in Montreal, May 1989.

Courtesy of Alain Chagnon.

4

Moving Up: Women into Union Leadership

One way to identify the status of women inside the labour movement is to examine their ability to obtain leadership positions. The only Canada-wide information available on the composition of union leadership is for Canadian executive board members. It shows that 25 percent of the executive positions of all unions were held by women in 1989.[1] This means that women were clearly under-represented on union executives, because 39 percent of all union members were women. However, the situation has been improving over time, since women held only 18 percent of these positions in 1980, and only 9 percent in 1970.

This information is available broken down by the three types of unions. International unions have a membership that is 25 percent women, but there was only one woman out of the eighty-four executive board members in 1989 (1 percent). The national unions have a membership that is 46 percent women, while 25 percent of their executive board members were women. Finally, the membership of government unions is 48 percent women, but among their executive board members only 13 percent are women.

This data is of limited value because it relates only to head office union executives. While top executive positions are one aspect of the question, local presidents and executives, union committees, delegates to conventions and union staff also form part of the leadership and all have an impact upon the direction of union policies and activities.

In order to be able to examine the place of women in the broader union leadership, I conducted a series of interviews with the Canadian Labour Congress, the Confédération des syndicats nationaux, the ten provincial Federations of Labour and thirteen selected unions (one having declined to participate). The unions were chosen to reflect the diversity in the labour movement, and

Table 4-1: Executive Board Members by Type of Union, 1989			
Type of Union	**Executive Board Members**	**Women Executive Members**	**% of Women**
International Unions	84	1	1.2
National Unions	2228	557	25.0
Government Unions	156	20	12.8
Total	2312	578	25.0

Source: Statistics Canada, Corporations and Labour Unions Returns Act, unpublished data for 1989.

included both national and international unions, unions that represent workers in different industries and occupations in both the public and private sectors, unions from different regions of the country, and unions with both large and small percentages of women members. The unions are listed in Table 4-2 with information on their membership. In total these thirteen unions represent a 39 percent of all women union members in the country.

All the interviews with both the unions and the central labour organizations were conducted over a six-month period from October 1990 to March 1991, and the information presented here therefore relates to that time period, unless otherwise indicated.

Top Executive Positions

From the interviews conducted for this study information was collected on the number of women in executive positions both for central labour bodies and for the thirteen unions. Looking first at the labour centrals, information on the proportion of women affiliated was available for only three of these organizations, and in each case the representation of women on the executive was lower than that among the membership. The Canadian Labour Congress has an affiliated membership that is 37 percent women,[2] but only 26 percent of women on its larger executive council and only 17 percent on its smaller executive. Women comprise 50 percent of the membership of the Confédération des syndicats nationaux, but 33 percent of the executive. In the Quebec Federation of Labour, women comprise 30 percent of affiliate membership, but only 25 percent of executive positions.

Table 4-2: The Thirteen Unions Interviewed, Size of Membership and Percentage of Women Members, 1989

Union	Total Membership	No. of. Women Members	% of Women Members
Canadian Union of Public Employees (CUPE)	381,845	197,914	51.8
United Food and Commercial Workers International Union (UFCW)	183,823	96.122	46,9
Canadian Auto Workers (CAW)	173,568	35,995	20,7
United Steelworkers of America (USWA)	163,001	21,462	13.2
Public Service Alliance of Canada (PSAC)	144,726	68,032	47.0
Fédération des affaires sociales (FAS)	98,846	67,034	67.8
Communication Workers of Canada (CWC)	39,646	13,569	34.2
British Columbia Government Employees Union (BCGEU)	39,530	21,783	55.1
Ontario Secondary School Teachers Federation (OSSTF)	37,043	15,107	40.8
Office and Professional Employees International Union (OPEIU)	26,554	18,458	69.5
Hotel Employees and Restaurant Employees International Union (HERE)	25,057	14,584	58.2
Newfoundland Association of Provincial Employees (NAPE)	16,352	8,561	52.4
United Nurses of Alberta (UNA)	13,302	13,067	98.2

Source: Statistics Canada, Corporations and Labour Unions Returns Act, unpublished data for 1989.

Considering all of these labour centrals together, three out of the twelve presidents were women at the time of the interviews, while women formed 28 percent of the members of their combined executives. Since women comprise 39 percent of total union membership, women continue to be under-represented in these positions. However, the fact that over one-quarter of executive positions on these labour centrals are held by women represents a dramatic improvement over time.

One important reason for this improvement has undoubtedly been the affirmative action programs implemented by most of these labour centrals. Between 1983 and 1987, all but three established a minimum number of executive positions for women (see Table 4-3).

The programs are implemented in different ways. For example, at the Canadian Labour Congress the affirmative action program provides six general positions for women on the Executive Council, the largest executive body with a total of thirty-eight members. As the seats were added to the existing executive, the women in these positions duplicate the representation from the largest affiliate unions, which are already represented on the Council by the Presidents of those unions. Five of the nine labour centrals with affirmative action programs specify that women will be vice-presidents, a more influential position than a general seat on the executive. The most extensive use of affirmative action is in the B.C. Federation, where thirteen seats have been set aside for women on the larger executive body with thirty-eight members, and four of these are vice-presidents, who would therefore also sit on the smaller executive of fourteen members.

The large number of seats set aside for women in the B.C. Federation is particularly interesting because they were also designated rather than added, meaning that the positions for women did not expand the executive, but were taken by women from among the seats that already existed. Only the B.C. and Manitoba Federations have designated seats. The more usual mechanism of creating additional seats for women means that the men's positions on the executive are unaffected, a more gradual move towards equal representation. In some instances there is concern that women in these added positions might be marginalized as "extras," regarded as duplicating representation that already exists. However, it may be the only alternative, where the election process is unlikely to remove men from their positions, or where the com-

Table 4-3: Women in Executive Positions in Labour Centrals			
Labour Central	**No. of Women/ Total on Executive***	**% of Women**	**Affirmative Action Seats**
Canadian Labour Congress (CLC)	2/12 (10/38)	17 (26)	6
Confédération des syndicats nationaux (CSN)	2/6 (15/46)	33 (33)	-
British Columbia Federation of Labour BCFL)	5/14 (14/38)	36 (36)	13
Alberta Federation of Labour (AFL)	10/25	40	4
Saskatchewan Federation of Labour (SFL)	9/27	33	-
Manitoba Federation of Labour (MFL)	5/18	28	4
Ontario Federation of Labour (OFL)	7/27 (17/70)	26 (24)	5
Quebec Federation of Labour (QFL)	4/16	25	3
New Brunswick Federation of Labour ((NBFL)	3/16	22	1
Nova Scotia Federation of Labour (NSFL)	2/15	13	-
Prince Edward Island Federation of Labour (PEIFL)	3/13	23	1
Newfoundland & Labrador Federation of Labour (NLFL)	3/14	21	2
Total	95/337	28	39

Four organizations have a two-level structure and the larger executive board or council figures are given in brackets. The positions on the smaller executives are included in the larger. The total includes the larger structures.

Source: Interviews conducted by the author.

Quebec Federation of Labour and Confédération des syndicats nationaux

In Quebec there are two major labour centrals. The Quebec Federation of Labour has affiliated unions that represent 475,000 workers in the province and of these 30 percent are women. It is composed largely of unions in the private sector such as steel, auto, chemicals and meat packing, but also has some public sector workers; for example, members of the Canadian Union of Public Employees and postal workers. The affiliates of the Federation include unions that draw their membership from across Canada and also international unions.

The Confédération des syndicats nationaux has affiliates that represent 245,000 workers from Quebec and 50 percent of these are women. Much of its membership is drawn from the public sector, including government employees and social services, but also includes workers from metal, paper, communications and various other businesses. Its affiliates draw their members exclusively from within the province of Quebec.

In recognition of the different situation in Quebec, the Quebec Federation of Labour has a more autonomous relationship with the Canadian Labour Congress (CLC) than the other Federations. For example, while the CLC develops and organizes educational courses for use across the country, the Quebec Federation receives financing to carry out its own education program, related to the specific situation and legislation in that province.

The Quebec Federation has also developed its own procedures for dealing with internal disputes among its affiliates, while other Federations rely upon the CLC to handle disagreements. In general, the Quebec Federation is expected to represent the interests of workers in that province autonomously. For example, in the debate over the Charlottetown constitutional accord the Quebec Federation of Labour recommended a "no" vote, although the CLC was supporting the "yes" campaign.

position of the executive is determined by union and regional representation, and is difficult or inappropriate to change. On the positive side it does mean more women on the executives, and if it is less threatening to men already holding executive positions, it may be easier to obtain.

Of the nine labour centrals that have affirmative action programs, the women's seats are usually elected by all the delegates to the convention, as with other executive positions. However, there are two exceptions. In the Alberta Federation the women's positions are elected by a caucus of women delegates only, and while men may attend this caucus they cannot speak or vote. At the Quebec Federation an all-women caucus elects the women's affirmative action positions, which are then confirmed by a vote of all the Convention delegates. The purpose of this election process is that the women elected to these positions should reflect the needs and concerns of the women members. In interviews with women in other provinces, some considered such a process undemocratic, and were concerned that the elected women might be marginalized as dealing only with narrowly defined women's issues. At the Ontario Federation, for example, a conscious decision was made to have the affirmative action positions appointed by the affiliated unions in order to link the male leadership of those unions more closely with the women on the executive. The purpose was to reduce the isolation of the women and increase the chances of action on women's issues. The difference in approach reflects the on-going tension between women's separate interests and the relationship with the general union movement.

Affirmative action is not universally supported, even among women. Some union women argue that it is undemocratic, and that women should be elected to executive positions in the usual manner. Some believe that women elected to the executive through affirmative action are in a weak position, because they have not been accepted through the usual channels. However, others are convinced that we would wait a long time for women to move up "naturally," and that injustices should be corrected sooner rather than later. Often such programs were established only after considerable organizing and lobbying, and therefore represent a certain victory for women. On the other hand, the necessity for affirmative action is seen by some as a failure, the failure of the union movement to achieve equality without resorting to such programs. One woman activist has written:

> Feminist unionists knew that, if true equality existed in the union movement, affirmative action would never have been needed at all.[3]

Whatever the arguments for and against, affirmative action is an established fact of life in the labour movement and has undoubtedly been very influential in "getting the girls to the top."[4] Of the ninety-five executive seats held by women in these organizations, fully thirty-nine of them (41 percent) are affirmative action positions. Without them, the representation of women on these labour central executives would fall from 28 to 18 percent.[5]

Table 4-4: Women Executive Members, Convention Delegates and Presidents of Locals in Thirteen Unions					
Union	% Women Members	% Women on Executive	No. Women/ Total Executive	% Women Convention Delegates	% Women Local Presidents
UNA	98	95	20/21	94	96
OPEIU	70	45	5/11	60	50
FAS	68	56	14/25	53	54
*HERE	58	-	-	-	5
BCGEU	55	30	6/20	38	33
NAPE	52	42	13/31	37	28
CUPE	52	45	9/20	41	45
PSAC	47	26	8/31	26	34
UFCW	47	10	4/40	17	1
OSSTF	41	14	1/7	38	25
CWC	34	10	1/10	37	22
CAW	21	15	2/13	13	11
*USWA	13	-	-	8	8

*These international unions do not have a Canadian executive and the HERE does not have a Canadian convention.
Source: Interviews conducted by the author.

Turning to consider the thirteen unions, at the time of the interviews there was only one woman holding the top executive position, and this was the President of the United Nurses of Alberta, which has a membership that is 98 percent women. Just prior to the interviews the woman president of the Fédération des affaires sociales resigned, and several months after their completion the Canadian Union of Public Employees elected a woman president, and not for the first time. Nonetheless, it is obvious that women are badly under-represented in the very top leadership positions, even in those unions with a majority of women members, of which there are seven in this study.

Two of the thirteen unions are internationals with a Canadian Director, but no Canadian executive. In the remaining eleven unions, Table 4-4 shows that women are not over-represented on any executive. Two of the unions have executives that are very close to being representative. In the case of the United Nurses of Alberta, the membership is almost exclusively women, while the Canadian Auto Workers has only 21 percent women members and therefore requires only two women on the executive of thirteen to virtually achieve representation. It must be recognized that this is a quite different situation than say the Office and Professional Employees International Union, where seven out of the eleven member executive would need to be women in order to achieve a similar level of representation, therefore requiring a far more radical change.

Three unions have a somewhat larger gap between the proportion of women members and the proportion of women on the executive, between six and twelve percentage points. However, in the six other unions women are poorly represented on the executives, there being a gap of over twenty percentage points between the proportion of women members and the proportion of women on the executive.

Despite the clear under-representation of women in union executive positions, the majority of unions in this study have not implemented affirmative action programs. While most labour centrals have implemented arrangements to ensure a number of women on their executives, only five of the unions in this study have made any such move, only four still have such an arrangement, and two of these were informal understandings. In 1985 the Communication Workers of Canada added two positions specifically for women to the union executive, but this was discontinued in 1988 as part of financial cutbacks.

Since 1982 the Fédération des affaires sociales has had one position on the executive set aside for a woman, a vice-president responsible for women's issues. The Canadian Auto Workers has an informal arrangement that at least one woman will sit on the Canadian Council, which is an important body of rank and file activists, and this woman is then automatically also a member of the National Executive Board. The B.C. Government Employees Union has also had an informal arrangement, begun in 1975. It has been understood that if the president is a man, then the other full-time paid officer position of secretary-treasurer will be a woman, and also that one of the two general vice-presidents will be a woman. However, since the interviews were completed, the May 1991 Convention of the union rejected a resolution to formalize this arrangement, and then proceeded to elect two male vice-presidents, instead of one man and one woman.

The Newfoundland Association of Public Employees has taken the most extensive action to improve the representation of women. The union held local seminars on the issue of affirmative action to educate members in preparation for an Affirmative Action Convention in 1989. The Convention increased the Executive Board from twenty-five to thirty-one positions, creating six affirmative action positions for women. The new positions were added with regard to the existing structure, including one woman general vice-president, a woman representative for each of the two largest occupational components with a majority of women members, plus three area representatives.

Affirmative action has been accepted by the majority of labour centrals as an appropriate method to improve the representation of women on their executives, and while it is much less common among unions, it is gaining ground as a necessary strategy.

Delegates to Conventions

Executive members for unions and labour centrals are elected by delegates to conventions, which also establish general policy for the organization, and make constitutional and financial changes. It is therefore important to consider how many women attend conventions as delegates.

The P.E.I. Federation had not counted the proportion of women delegates at their conventions. At the time of the interviews the Canadian Labour Congress had also not collected this information, but did so for the first time at its 1992 convention, where 25 percent of the delegates were women. The percentage of women delegates at the conventions of the other labour centrals is listed below:

CSN	36 percent	OFL	22 percent
BCFL	35 percent	QFL	27 percent
AFL	32 percent	NBFL	40 percent
SFL	43 percent	NSFL	35 percent
MFL	37 percent	NLFL	28 percent

Assessing this information is not straight forward because the proportion of women members varies from one labour central to another, and only three of these centrals knew the proportion of women represented by their organizations. The membership of the Canadian Labour Congress was 37 percent women in 1989, while women comprised only 25 percent of delegates to its convention. The Quebec Federation of Labour represents 30 percent women, and had 27 percent women delegates at its last convention, very close to representative. The Confédération des syndicats nationaux represents 50 percent women and had 36 percent women delegates at its last convention, a larger gap. The Saskatchewan Federation felt that with 43 percent of women at its last convention it had achieved representation or possibly even over-representation of women. However, most centrals indicated that while there has been a significant increase in the number of women delegates attending convention over the last ten years, and that women are also more active and vocal than in the past, women are not adequately represented as convention delegates.

The labour centrals themselves do not control the delegates. The union affiliates decide their own representatives in their own way and the federations can only educate and encourage. In some cases there are constitutional arrangements for the representation of certain unions and/or certain regions, so that the options are limited.

Of the thirteen unions in this study, the Hotel Employees and Restaurant Employees Union does not have a Canadian convention. Out of the twelve other unions, Table 4-4 shows that in one case, the Communication Workers of Canada, there was a slight over-representation of women as delegates to convention. In four other unions there was a difference of less than ten percentage points between the proportion of women members and the proportion of women delegates. (UNA, OSSTF, CAW, USWA). Five unions had gaps in representation of between ten and twenty percentage points (OPEIU, FAS, BCGEU, NAPE, CUPE), and two had even larger gaps in representation (PSAC, UFCW).

Commonly, delegates arrive at conventions because they have been active at the local level within their union. This is most usually the starting point for all involvement and activity at different levels within the union, and is considered in the following section.

Local Leadership

For all of the unions in this study it was possible to obtain the number of women and men holding the position of local president (see Table 4-4). Women are not over-represented as local presidents in any union, although four have equal or almost equal representation. Two of these are the unions with the smallest proportion of women members, the United Steelworkers and the Canadian Auto Workers. As already mentioned, for these unions, with less than 20 percent women members, it does not require a huge shift to alter the representation significantly. Only a few women as local presidents, or one or two women on the executive will meet the requirements for representation. This is easier to achieve and poses less threat to male leadership than a situation where the majority of the union's members are women, and so the majority of union positions must change from being held by men to being held by women in order to obtain equal representation.

The United Nurses of Alberta, which is almost exclusively women, has women as presidents of almost all its locals. Otherwise, the Canadian Union of Public Employees is the only union in which women comprise more than one-third of the total membership that has managed to get very close to a representative position of women as local presidents. The remaining nine unions have a considerable disparity between the proportion of women members and the proportion of women who have obtained the position of local president. Two unions, the Hotel Employees and Restaurant Employees and the United Food and Commercial Workers Union, have remarkably few women as local presidents.

For this study it was not possible to collect data on local executive positions other than the president. However, some unions have examined the situation, and found that women are more often secretaries, than presidents, vice-presidents or treasurers. For example, in 1989 the National Union of Provincial Government Employees (NUPGE), a federation of provincial government unions, surveyed its component unions. The study found that while women were over half the total membership (56 percent), only one-third of local presidents were women, but two-thirds of the secretaries were women.[6] The Fédération des affaires sociales has also collected this information. This union's membership is 68 percent women, while the presidents of its locals are 54 percent women, treasurers 65 percent, and secretaries 81 percent.[7] In a survey by the Canadian Union of Public Employees in 1988, when the membership of the union was approximately half women, 42 percent of local presidents were women, 46 percent of vice-presidents, 58 percent of secretary-treasurers, and 71 percent of recording secretaries.[8] In all these unions, women more often appear on executives in their traditional secretarial role, but are less often found in the more influential positions.

One study provides an exception to this situation. A 1989 survey by the Quebec Federation of Labour of its member unions, found that women were actually over-represented as presidents of locals, since 30 percent of the members of affiliates were women, while they formed 38 percent of the local presidents. While this is undoubtedly an important step forward, the study pointed out that women were twice as likely to be presidents of the smaller, and therefore less influential, locals.[9] This point was also raised by the unions in this study. For example, the Canadian Auto Workers was aware that while the overall representation of women as local presidents was good, the women were concentrated in the smaller locals within the union.

Committees and Collective Bargaining

Apart from the elected executives, unions appoint committees to advise the executive and assist in carrying out various aspects of the work. Involvement in these committees is commonly an important step towards future advancement within the union.

In its survey of its ten component unions mentioned above, the National Union of Provincial Government Employees (NUPGE) examined the representation of women on the unions' committees, stating: "Membership on these Committees, particularly in the role of Committee Chair, can be an important way for women members to develop leadership skills and gain recognition in a leadership role."[10] The ten unions have a joint female membership of 56 percent of the total, while women formed 33 percent of committee members, and 30 percent of the chairs of committees (excluding women's committees).

However, it should be noted that two of the ten component unions did have a representative percentage of women on the committees. One union, the Newfoundland Association of Public Employees, has carried out a general affirmative action program requiring that each committee be comprised of two men and two women. As well, a staff member services each committee, and across the committees the staff must be half men and half women.

In the Quebec Federation of Labour survey of its affiliated unions, women were also under-represented on union committees. Women are 30 percent of the membership of the Federation, but comprised 26 percent of the members of affiliated union committees (excluding women's committees). This study also gives information on the types of committees. Women formed 28 percent of the union negotiation committees, 25 percent of the health and safety committees and 22 percent of the grievance committees.[11] It was raised in the interviews with both the Quebec Federation and the Confédération des syndicats nationaux, that in Quebec the health and safety committees are traditionally male dominated, and that this needs improvement.

Bargaining committees are especially important, and in my interviews with unions it was stressed repeatedly that this was the route both to higher elected positions, and into many of the staff positions. Negotiating experience is often considered essential. As one person put it: "The key to all the structural things are the bargaining committees. That's where people develop authority and credibility in the union."[12]

It is therefore of particular concern that women are often poorly represented on these committees. The NUPGE study found that women are under-represented on the bargaining committees of its component unions, even those with a high proportion of women members. In fact, only those bargaining units with a small proportion of women members, were likely to have equal representation of women on their bargaining committees, because just one or two women were necessary.[13] In my study, although the actual figures were not always available, those interviewed generally commented that women were not found on bargaining committees, or were harder to keep on these committees. For example, in the Ontario Secondary School Teachers' Federation women are 41 percent of the membership, but of the chief negotiators for the union only 21 percent are women. Over half the members of the B.C. Government Employees Union are women, but on the public sector bargaining committee, which covers the majority of its members, only one third of the committee members are women.

However, there were some exceptions. The Fédération des affaires sociales has a central negotiating committee, with elected representatives of occupational groups, and there had been no difficulty in getting women involved, even though some have to move to Montreal for the negotiations. In the Newfoundland

The 1983 convention of the Ontario Federation of Labour established an affirmative action program. The five new women vice-presidents being congratulated by OFL President Cliff Pilkey were (left to right): Carol Anne Sceviour (Steelworkers), Evelyn Sammons (Ontario Public Service Employees' Union), Edith Johnston (United Automobile Workers), Jean Robertson (United Food and Commercial Workers), and Julie Griffin (Canadian Union of Public Employees).

Courtesy of the Ontario Federation of Labour.

Association of Public Employees, before the last round of negotiations for the government services component, there was a struggle to get equal representation on the negotiation committee, four men and four women, and this was achieved. The United Nurses of Alberta has a central negotiation team for hospitals that includes one nurse per district plus a chief negotiator. It has not been difficult to involve women and it is considered an honour.

There is some discussion about the difficulty of involving women in collective bargaining, and a number of factors suggested to explain why it is often unattractive to women. If holding union position and responsibility is intimidating for some, then the collective bargaining process, upon which so much depends, is the most alarming. It requires dedication of time and effort over an indeterminate period of time and, in the case of centralized bargaining, sometimes moving to another city for the duration. It may mean living in a hotel room during the most intense parts of the process and possibly meeting up to 24 hours a day. It not only represents an important responsibility, but is also a confrontation between the union and management. In some situations it involves considerable displays of aggression and anger. Two questions are being asked: are women comfortable participating in this process, and can it be changed?

Clearly, it is not easy for women with domestic responsibilities to undertake the requirements of collective bargaining. Even in the United Nurses of Alberta, where women participate fully in the process, few women who take on the job have young children; they have "either very supportive husbands or minimal responsibility."[14] Some women argued that for at least a good part of the negotiating procedure it could be handled more rationally, on a nine to five basis, and without the aggressive "eyeball to eyeball" approach. They question whether it is advantageous for the union negotiators to be exhausted by the process. Others disagreed:

> It's not a nine to five job, it's a vocation. When you're into it, you're into it and nothing else matters. It can't. Management careers are on the line, companies go under if management doesn't do things properly. To expect that they're going to change that is just not realistic in a capitalistic society.[15]

Apart from the aggressive approach towards management, but related to it, is the issue of what is described as "a male culture of negotiation," which extends from being tough at the table to the way issues are discussed among the negotiators, to drinking in the bar. At another level men may simply feel more at ease with other men in this situation, because it is what they are used to. The culture suggests that you have to be tough and strong to handle negotiations, and that men are more likely to fulfil these requirements. All this makes it hard for women to break in, or even to want to.

Staff Positions

Apart from elected positions and committees, unions also hire staff to service their members, often, although not exclusively, drawn from the ranks of the membership. This is another kind of leadership position, and involves giving advice in negotiations, helping with grievances and other complaints, forming education and research programs, and generally being in contact with the membership over the full range of union issues. I therefore asked in my interviews about the proportion of women in staff positions, excluding administrative and clerical staff. Here and there efforts have been made to hire more men into these positions, but generally they remain in unions, as elsewhere, over 90 percent women. The following discussion relates only to specialized staff and regional representatives.

In the labour centrals the number of staff varied according to the size of the province, and two federations of labour had no staff

Table 4-5: Women Service Staff in Thirteen Unions			
Union	% Women Members	% Women Staff	No. Women/ Total Staff
UNA	98	80	8/10
OPEIU	70	50	15/30
FAS	68	22	12/55
HERE	58	30	14/46
BCGEU	55	44	28/63
NAPE	52	25	3/12
CUPE	52	27	76/286
PSAC	47	35	48/138
UFCW	47	12	4/33
OSSTF	41	28	8/29
CWC	34	21	9/43
CAW	21	13	11/84
USWA	13	7	7/105

Source: Interviews conducted by the author.

(P.E.I. and Newfoundland and Labrador). The Nova Scotia and New Brunswick Federations had only one staff person each, and both were men. The Saskatchewan Federation had two staff, and Manitoba had three, all men. At the Alberta Federation there was one woman out of four staff positions. Interestingly, both the Ontario and B.C. Federations had a majority of women on staff, five women out of nine in Ontario and four women out of six staff in B.C. The Quebec Federation of Labour had carried out a survey in 1989 when 18 percent of the permanent staff were women, while the affiliated membership is 30 percent women. The Canadian Labour Congress employs seventy-two staff, of which nineteen are women, that is 26 percent, compared to the affiliate membership of the Congress which is 37 percent women.[16] Thus, with the two exceptions of the Ontario and B.C. Federations, women were under-represented in the staff positions of these labour centrals.

Turning to the unions, women are not over-represented on the staff of any union in this study, although four had representative or close to representative numbers of women on staff (see Table 4-5). Two of these were the unions with a small proportion of women (CAW and USWA), so that a relatively small proportion of women were needed in order to be representative. Nonetheless, they have accomplished this. The B.C. Government Employees Union and the Ontario Secondary School Teachers Federation also did not have a large gap between the women membership and the proportion of women on staff. However, the remaining seven unions have not hired many women on staff, compared to the number of women members. Three unions had very large gaps (30 to 50 percentage points) between the percentage of women members and the percentage of women on staff (FAS, HERE, UFCW).

Apart from the under-representation of women in staff positions, more women are hired into positions at head office than in the field. This is important because the field staff (often called bargaining reps or business agents) work directly with locals and members, and they are in a position to encourage or discourage women and women's issues at the local level. Where bargaining is decentralized they advise on bargaining demands and are available to help in the bargaining process. For example, in the Canadian Union of Public Employees women are 27 percent of the total staff, but this breaks down into 47 percent at head office and only 22 percent in the field. At the Public Service Alliance 35 percent of all the staff are women, but at the national office women are 41 percent of the staff, while women are only 27 percent of the regional staff. At the Canadian Auto Workers women among the servicing staff in the field were described as "virtually non-existent." The same situation held in unions with small staffs. For example, at the Newfoundland Association of Public Employees, the three women out of a staff of twelve were all at the head office, and all four service staff in the regions were men.

One problem is that the field jobs usually require collective bargaining experience, and women are often absent from bargaining committees, as already discussed above. It is easier to hire women into education, research or even organizing positions at head office, than to meet the requirements for bargaining experience for field positions. As one union staff member explained: "If there is an opening in organizing you have more freedom (to hire women) because you don't have to pick someone with bargaining experience."[17]

At the Public Service Alliance with its large staff, it was possible to analyze the types of jobs held by women at head office, and the same problem with bargaining experience was reflected there. In some departments the number of men and women were equal or nearly so, such as the equal pay and classification division, where six women were employed out of a staff of twelve. But women were heavily concentrated in the social and occupational rights section (eight out of nine), and virtually absent in the negotiations department, where only one woman worked in a total staff of eleven.

While women are still under-represented in staff positions, several unions have taken important steps to improve the situation. The Office and Professional Employees International Union has had an affirmative action program in place since the early 1980s that gives preference to hiring women, where there is equal ability to do the job, and the number of women hired has increased as a result. This union, as is common with international unions, has very little centralized structure, and only one appointed staff person is employed at the national level. Therefore, the fifteen women on staff out of a total of thirty for this union are all working at the local and regional levels, servicing members.

The Canadian Union of Public Employees established a training program in 1986 to train members for staff rep positions in the field, and with a mandate that at least half the trainees should be women. The fourteen week training program consists of six weeks of education and two months experience in the field. It provides alternative training to the collective bargaining route, as well as increased confidence to apply for positions. After the training, participants form a pool of candidates for staff rep jobs that become vacant. The program has been offered three times, nineteen women out of a total of thirty-three members have been involved, and the majority are now working as reps for the union.

The Ontario Secondary Schools Teachers Federation passed an affirmative action program in 1987 which included hiring staff. The goal was "to achieve proportional representation of women at all levels in all areas of the Federation organization and activity within five years."[18] This is the union with one of the most representative rates of women on staff.

The collective agreement that covers the staff of the Confédération des syndicats nationaux and its affiliated federations, including the Fédération des affaires sociales, contains an affirmative action program that was negotiated in 1989. It established a joint committee (with a majority of women members) to fix numerical objectives for certain jobs and to examine what other steps need to be taken. It also sets aside seniority for every second position posted, so that women can be hired where possible. However, there have been problems recruiting women into these positions, because few women are interested and sometimes none apply for the posted vacancies. Consequently, the training process is being examined, as well as support mechanisms such as a buddy system, that might help women to deal with the heavy workload. At the time of my interview, the Fédération des affaires sociales had a very low level of representation of women on staff, at 22 percent, given that women comprise 68 percent of the overall membership of the union. For the Confédération des syndicats nationaux and all its member federations combined, only 18 percent of the permanent staff were women, although women constitute 50 percent of the membership.

In some instances action has been spurred by specific complaints. At the last convention of the Communication Workers there was a heated discussion on affirmative action, because of complaints that in one of the regions a rep position had been filled by a relatively unknown man, while two active women members had been overlooked. It was decided that an affirmative action policy would be drafted for discussion at the following convention.

In response to problems raised by women staff members, the Public Service Alliance has taken a number of initiatives to improve the position of women working in the union. A meeting was held of all women regional representatives across the country to discuss their concerns and propose solutions. It is now policy that one member of every staffing board, which hires staff, must be from a target group. Experience in women's issues has been incorporated as an area of expertise in assessing candidates. As well, training on gender relations has been provided to all regional representatives. An affirmative action program was being negotiated into the staff collective agreement, and meantime the number of women hired into regional positions had increased.

There is no doubt that more women are being hired into staff positions in the union movement, although women are still under-represented, especially in the regional or field positions away from head office. In some unions affirmative action programs have been negotiated by union staff to improve the situation.

Summary and Conclusion

The information presented in this chapter may be summarized as follows:

- Women hold 28 percent of the executive seats at the labour centrals in this study, and 41 percent of these are affirmative action positions.

- In only one union out of the thirteen in this study was the top position held by a woman, and women were proportionately represented on only four union executives.

- Four out of the thirteen unions had some form of affirmative action program for central executive positions, two of them informal arrangements, one of them very extensive.

- A minority of the labour centrals and unions had a representative number of women delegates at their most recent convention.

- As presidents of locals, women are representative or close to representative in only four of the thirteen unions. In other local executive positions women are more likely to be secretaries than to hold more influential posts.

- The evidence suggests that in most cases women are under-represented on union advisory committees, and particularly on the important negotiation committees.

- In staff positions, women are under-represented in the majority of labour centrals and unions, especially in the field positions outside of head office.

Over the last ten to fifteen years there is no doubt that the position of women inside the labour movement has improved considerably. Women are more often found at the microphones of union conventions, sitting in elected positions and taking staff positions. There are now examples where women are fully represented on staff or executives. While this is cause for some congratulation, the analysis in this chapter leaves no doubt that much remains to be accomplished. In most cases, women continue to be under-represented on central and local executives, in committees, at conventions and in staff positions.

Affirmative action programs have been an important mechanism for improving the situation, but they have not been adopted by all labour centrals, nor by many unions, and they are most often limited to certain executive positions. The evidence presented here suggests that, where implemented, affirmative action programs have had a substantial impact. One way for the union movement to improve the participation of women would be to expand these programs into those centrals and unions where they do not now exist, and also to apply the same principles to other areas than just central executive positions, including local executives, advisory committees and staff positions.

The Ontario Federation of Labour's first women's conference, Bargaining for Equality, held in April 1979 in Toronto, spanned generations of trade union women. Leta Ziler, a member of the United Steelworkers of America smiles with her granddaughter Pat Van Petter from ACTWUA Local 1826 as they display "Equal Pay For Women," a major theme at the conference.

Courtesy of Calm Photo

5

Women's Activities and Issues Inside Unions

While any union activity or issue may be of concern to union women, there are those that have been particularly geared to changing and improving the status of women inside unions. Women's committees and conferences have been the means for women to organize within unions and they are examined first in this chapter. How extensive are women's committees within the union movement, how are they structured in relationship to the unions that they work within, and how does this affect their work? Then, given space limitations, three issues of particular concern to women have been selected for examination — child care and family responsibilities, sexual and personal harassment, and union education. Unions have passed and implemented policies to improve the situation for women in each of these areas. How extensive have those policies been and what are the current problems?

The following discussion continues to draw upon material obtained from interviews conducted for this study with twelve labour centrals and thirteen unions, as described in Chapter 4.

Women's Committees

Women's committees are the critical base of women's activity inside the union movement. They are the major way in which women raise their issues, press for change, and get their demands onto both the convention floor and the negotiating table.

The activities of women's committees have been extraordinarily diverse, geared to changes within unions themselves, obtaining benefits through the bargaining process, and working for broader social change. These activities have included organizing conferences and meetings, producing educational information on issues, lobbying government and writing briefs on a broad range of women's issues, working with women's groups outside of the labour movement, organizing for special events including International Women's Day, researching and presenting policies for the organization's approval and pressing for their acceptance, lobbying for affirmative action, pressing issues of concern to women in collective bargaining, encouraging the development of more women's committees, and organizing caucuses at conventions. One woman said:

> Everything that has evolved on women's issues has come from the women's committee, including internal union policies and contract negotiation suggestions.[1]

The Extent of Women's Committees

Every one of the twelve labour centrals interviewed for this study has a women's committee. As Table 5-1 shows, the earliest was the Ontario Federation of Labour, which first set up a women's committee in 1961. However, it disappeared in 1968 when two women from the Women's Committee "merged" with the all-male, six-member Human Rights Committee. A women's committee was not re-established until 1978. In the early 1970s, the B.C. Federation was the first to establish a women's committee in 1970, followed by the Quebec Federation in 1972, and the Canadian Labour Congress and the Confédération des syndicats nationaux in 1974. The Saskatchewan, Nova Scotia and Manitoba Federations instituted their women's committees later in the 1970s, and they were established in all labour centrals by 1987.

The only union in this study without any women's committee is the United Nurses of Alberta, which has a membership that is 98 percent women, and has not felt the need for a specifically women's committee. However, in the other twelve unions the level and type of women's committee varies considerably. Some unions, most commonly the internationals, are not centralized, and committees on any topic generally do not exist at the national or head office level. Therefore, women's committees are formed at the regional or local level. Thus, in the United Steelworkers, there are three districts in Canada, of which the two largest (Ontario and Quebec) have women's committees, but the third does not. The Office and Professional Employees Union has no structure above the local level, and the three largest locals (Quebec, Vancouver, and Ontario) have women's committees, although the one in Vancouver is currently inactive. The Hotel Employees and Restau-

Table 5-1: The Establishment of Women's Committees in Twelve Labour Centrals and Thirteen Unions

Labour Centrals		Unions	
Ontario Federation of Labour	1961-1968 1978	B.C. Government Employees Union	1975
B.C. Federation of Labour	1970	Newfoundland Association of Public Employees	1975
Québec Federation of Labour	1972	Public Service Alliance of Canada	1976
Canadian Labour Congress	1974	Office and Professional Employees International Union	1978
Confédération des syndicats nationaux	1974	Fédération des affairs sociales	1980
Saskatchewan Federation of Labour	1977	Canadian Union of Public Employees	1981
Manitoba Federation of Labour	1978	Ontario Secondary Schools Teachers Federation	1981
Nova Scotia Federation of Labour	1978	Canadian Auto Workers	1981
New Brunswick Federation of Labour	1980	Hotel Employees and Restaurant Employees International Union	1985
Newfoundland and Labrador Federation of Labour	1980	United Steel Workers of America	1986/88*
Alberta Federation of Labour	1983	Communication Workers of Canada	1986/90*
P.E.I.. Federation of Labour	1987	United food and Commercial Workers Union	1990
		United Nurses of Alberta	-

* In these unions women's committees were established at the regional level at different times.
Source: Interviews conducted by the author.

rant Employees Union also has no structure above the local level, and only the Toronto local, representing one-fifth of the union's membership, has a women's committee. The Communication Workers, although not an international, also does not have a women's committee at the national level, but three of its four regions have women's committees.

Table 5-1 gives the dates that women's committees were established at the highest level within the union, given the structural variations. The B.C. Government Employees Union and the Newfoundland Association of Public Employees were the first to establish women's committees in 1975, followed by the Public Service Alliance in 1976. By the end of 1981 all the public sector unions in this study had initiated women's committees. In the private sector the Office and Professional Employees Union had its first women's committee in a large local in 1978. The Canadian Auto Workers established a women's committee at the Canadian Council level in 1981, although its predecessor, the United Auto Workers, had a women's advisory committee and different forms of a women's department at the international level since the early 1940s. Other unions in the private sector established women's committees somewhat later, between 1985 and 1990.

Most unions have women's committees at more than one level. According to the union structure there may be committees at the local, component, regional, provincial, and national or head office levels. For example, the Canadian Union of Public Employees set up its women's committee at the national level in 1981, but there are also regional committees at the provincial level and many local committees.

At the local level, it is generally difficult to know how many locals within a union have established women's committees, since no count is made. Some unions indicated that they were almost non-existent, while in others they were common, and a few unions were actively encouraging the development of more local women's committees. In only one union were women's committees mandated as part of the local structure, and that was in the Canadian Auto Workers. Consequently, in this union most of the locals had women's committees and the question is not whether they exist or not, but how well they are functioning. In international unions with only a local structure, and where women's committees exist only in the larger locals, women in the smaller locals have no access to any alternative structure for activity around women's issues.

Twenty years ago women's committees were virtually non-existent, while now they are the norm, found in all the labour centrals and most of the unions in this study. It would be inaccurate to say that women's committees are no longer questioned as part of the labour movement's structure, but they have obviously attained a considerable degree of acceptance and recognition.

The Structure of Women's Committees

Since women's committees have become a regular feature of the union landscape, more attention is being focused on how they are structured in relationship to what they are meant to accomplish.

In the labour centrals, the affiliated unions determine the membership of the women's committees, by putting forward their representatives who are then confirmed by the executive. How the affiliate union chooses their representative is their own concern; it may be by election or just by appointment of an active woman, and sometimes it is a woman member of staff. Often the women's committees themselves may identify likely candidates.

Women's committees inside unions take many different forms, relating as they do to different union structures. For example, in the Canadian Auto Workers it is not easy for a woman to join the central women's committee, because she must first be elected as a general delegate to the Canadian Council. This is an important decision-making body between Conventions, comprised of 350 to 400 delegates, and competition for the places is often intense. Only as a Council delegate can a woman then volunteer to join the central women's committee. It is not an open arrangement, and a woman needs a high profile in the union in order to be elected as a Council delegate from her local. On the other hand, the women on the committee are well-connected and experienced, and can therefore exert considerable influence within the union.

At the opposite end of the scale, the women's committee of the Ontario Secondary School Teachers Federation is composed of members who need only volunteer to be on the committee, and then be confirmed by the Executive. While this means that the process is open to any woman who is reasonably active, the committee has been regarded as having relatively low status within the union. For example, if a woman is moving ahead in the union, she becomes a local president or joins the negotiation committee, rather than belong to the women's committee.

The women's committee of the Fédération des affaires sociales falls between these two. Members represent eleven regions in Quebec and are elected in their regions, but they are elected specifically to the women's committee, and do not hold general positions as in the Canadian Auto Workers.

Sometimes women reach the same women's committee in different ways. The women's committee of the B.C. Government Employees Union has representatives from each of ten components representing different occupational groups. Some of the members are elected by their components, but others are appointed. In the United Food and Commercial Workers, the representatives to the women's committee are based on the regional membership of the union. Where a provincial council exists, it chooses the representative, but otherwise the locals within a region decide among themselves upon the representative.

Within the same union, the structure of women's committees often varies from one region to another, or from one level to another. In the United Steelworkers the Ontario district office initiated the women's committee by calling a meeting of active women, which is now loosely advisory to the district director. However, in the same union in Quebec, the women's committee is formed of representatives of the different regions. In the Canadian Union of Public Employees, members of the committee at the national level represent the ten provinces and the airline and broadcasting divisions of the union. They are appointed by the national executive in consultation with the region or division, and are usually the chairs of the regional women's committees where these committees exist. At the regional level, women's committees may be formally constituted in the by-laws or established on an ad hoc basis.

Usually the membership of women's committees is all women, but this is not always the case. In a study by the National Union of Provincial Government Employees of its components, three out of the nine women's committees had male members.[2] The Quebec Federation of Labour reported in its 1989 survey of its affiliates that 91 percent of the members of women's committees were women.[3] This continues to be cause for discussion for some unions. The affirmative action program of the Newfoundland Association of Public Employees included that all committees would comprise two men and two women, and this was applied also to the women's committee. However, at the Fédération des affaires sociales, when a man was elected from his region to the women's committee, this was protested and he never took his seat.

With one exception, which will be discussed below, women's committees are advisory to the general union executive or its equivalent. Like committees on other subjects, they report to the executive and can make recommendations. In some cases they have their own budget, in others they must apply to the executive for approval where expenditure is involved. Where controversial issues are raised, committee members can lobby the executive for a positive response. There have been fierce battles over particular issues, affirmative action and funding among them. The outcome in such a conflict will depend upon many factors, including the political climate in the organization and the influence of the women's committee.

Some women's committees have developed to the point where it would be politically inadvisable for the executive to ignore or deny their recommendations. They carry out many activities within the union movement, are supported by the membership, and regarded as an important aspect of the work. However, some women also spoke of a backlash against women's committees and issues; a situation in which it was becoming harder rather than easier to obtain support for women's concerns.

Women's Conferences

Women's conferences provide a forum for women to meet together, and they are also educational. Like women's committees, conferences have become a regular part of union activity, held by the majority of labour centrals and unions. All of the labour centrals hold regular annual or biennial women's conferences, except the Manitoba and Saskatchewan Federations, where they have been held less regularly, and Alberta where none has been held as yet.

Among the unions, the United Nurses of Alberta has never held a women's conference, and again this union is in a different position given that its membership is 98 percent women. The Fédération des affaires sociales does not hold women's conferences because in its structure the central Confédération des syndicats nationaux organizes such events and not the individual federations. Two other unions have never held any women's conferences (OPEIU and HERE). The Communications Workers' and the United Steelworkers have organized conferences in their Ontario regions, but not in other regions or at the national level.

The United Food and Commercial Workers Union held its first Canadian women's conference in 1989. Six unions hold regular conferences every year or two years (BCGEU, CUPE, NAPE, PSAC, OSSTF, CAW). In the B.C. Government Employees Union, conferences are held in every region rather than one central conference, in order to involve more women. The Public Service Alliance and the Canadian Union of Public Employees hold both regional and central women's conferences.

The conferences are generally educational in nature, covering a wide range of issues of concern to women. They are provided as a service to women members and open to all to attend. They are an important means of bringing women together to discuss issues, although there is rarely any formal process. In most cases they do not receive a report from the women's committee, discuss policies or priorities, nor establish a program for women within the union. Nonetheless, women's conferences may still influence the direction of union policy and action. For example, the women's conferences held by the Quebec Federation of Labour send a report on their deliberations forward to the Convention as well as a political statement, so that although the conferences do not pass resolutions, neither are they only educational. In some unions and labour centrals informal recommendations arise from workshops, and strong support for issues may be expressed. Women's committees then have a base of support in their work that the union cannot simply ignore. There is one exception to the usual informal process, the Public Service Alliance, and it is worth considering in detail.

The Public Service Alliance of Canada

In this union the women's committees and conference are not just advisory, but play a more direct role in formulating union policy. Most important, the women's conference can send resolutions direct to the floor of the union's Triennial Convention. This means that the women's conference, as a political body, is formally structured with representative delegates. The union structure has eighteen components that represent the workers in different government departments, rather than by occupation or region. Each of the components sends nine delegates to the women's conference, plus one additional delegate for every 500 women members. This is an interesting example of a structure to represent women specifically, rather than all union members. Also important

is that each of the union's regional women's committees may send two delegates to the women's conference, giving them a direct link to the process of forming resolutions for the National Convention.

These regional women's committees are themselves organized differently than in most unions, since they do not relate directly to the mainstream union structure. They are not advisory to the union's executive bodies, but are set up as autonomous committees that relate formally only to the national head office and to the women's conference. They can be established wherever there are representatives from three components. This means that they cut across the cumbersome component structure of the union, but they are also independent of the regional offices of the union, since they receive their funding from the national office. There are other women's committees at the national and component levels that are advisory to the executives at those levels, and that work within the traditional component structure. However, the regional women's committees are independent.

How did this situation arise? The Alliance held its first women's conference in 1985, an educational conference that was open to all. However, later that same year at the Triennial Convention of the union, a resolution was passed that future Conventions would "review the report of the Triennial National Women's Conference and vote on recommendations adopted at the conference." This phrase meant that the women's conference would be able to send resolutions direct to the Convention. Some Alliance women believe

Panel at the Canadian Labour Congress Women's Conference, November 1991: (left to right) Nancy Riche, Executive Vice-President, CLC; Penny Richmond, Women's Bureau, CLC; Shirley Carr, President, CLC; Judy Darcy, Secretary-Treasurer, Canadian Union of Public Employees; Dick Martin, Executive Vice-President, CLC; Louisette Hinton, Executive Council, CLC; Huguette Plamondon, Executive, United Food and Commercial Workers union; Grace Hartmann, past-president Canadian Union of Public Employees.

Courtesy of Photo Features Ltd. Murray Mosher.

that its implications were not fully understood by many of the delegates, and were themselves surprised when the resolution passed.

As a result of this resolution, the next women's conference was political, able to pass resolutions to be sent to the Convention, and it was therefore formally structured with delegates. A round of regional women's conferences were held before the national women's conference, allowing many issues to be discussed at a more local level before the national conference. At the women's conference in 1988, workshops were geared to formulating resolutions to be voted on in plenary sessions, which were conducted according to formal rules of order.

Sixty-two resolutions went forward from the women's conference to the 1988 National Convention of the union. They included resolutions calling for affirmative action on the national executive, for representation of women on bargaining teams, and for seats at the Convention for twenty women from the women's conference. Of those that came to the floor, only two passed. The first was to increase the funding for the regional women's conferences, and the second provided for funding from the national office to establish regional women's committees. Both were considered to be relatively "mild" resolutions, but again the ramifications were greater than expected.

The increased money for the regional women's conferences doubled the participation of women in the lead up to the next national women's conference. More important, the regional women's committees proved remarkably popular and by the end of 1990, thirty-five of them had been established. These women's committees sent delegates to the next women's conference in 1990. This conference concentrated on producing fewer, but stronger, resolutions, and sent twenty-three forward to the 1991 National Convention. However, much of this Convention was consumed with financial problems and none of the resolutions were dealt with, so they were referred to the National Board of Directors.

The Board has proceeded to adopt certain resolutions, particularly those dealing with drafting policies, organizing campaigns or lobbying government on issues such as sexual harassment, abortion, sexual orientation, health and safety issues, violence and equal pay. However, the resolutions defeated by the Board include all those that called for change in the structure of the union, such as proportional representation of women at National Conventions, one delegate from each regional women's committee to Convention, equal representation of women on negotiation teams, and the election of three women representatives from the women's conference to sit on each pre-Convention committee. A resolution that affirmative action should be negotiated for all staff levels and all target groups was also defeated. Increased funding for women's committees and conferences has also been rejected, as well as a proposal to fund race relations committees in all regions.

What has been the overall impact of this structure for the regional women's committees and the women's conferences? Women within the Alliance have a clear motivation to discuss desired changes in detail in order to formulate resolutions for Convention. This has meant moving beyond articulation of the problems to consider actual modifications to the union to achieve improvements. The debates in women's committees and at regional and national women's conferences have produced a series of extensive resolutions that express specific alternatives for the union structure and operation.

Secondly, the women's committees have become an important element of rank and file activity within the union. Some would say that they constitute the most dynamic part of the union. Many of the committees have developed their programs of activity and are working well. However, for a few the autonomy of the structure is a mixed blessing. Establishing a committee is an easy process and they are not limited by local or component executive decisions, but they have to be self-initiating since they are not automatically part of the on-going union structure.

Thus far, the impact of the women's conferences has been limited, because out of all the resolutions put forward to Convention, only two have been passed. However, if the women's committees continue to develop and influence the union, and if the resolutions continue to propose innovations, the pressure for change may become irresistible. At the same time there are informal influences created by a conference of 400 active women members demanding change. A process for change has been initiated and it will be important to watch its development.

Questions for Women's Committees

It is neither possible nor useful to suggest that one form of organization for women's committees is better or more effective than another. The variations are rooted in the history and politics of specific unions and different labour centrals. However, during the interviews several concerns were raised about how women's committees operate.

Formal Structures

Sometimes questions are raised about the wisdom of formally structuring women's committees. Women may come together to set up committees in a spontaneous way and may not wish to formalize the arrangement and attach themselves to the regular union structure, at least initially. Is it better to provide a structure for women to organize, or even mandate the existence of women's committees like the Canadian Auto Workers at the local level, or is it preferable to allow women to come together first and formulate their own structures? Some argue that women's committees are supposed to provide an alternative to the bureaucracy of the union, not replicate it. There is concern about becoming too thoroughly entrenched in union structures that may need to be changed. These arguments have some validity, especially at the local level and where women have just begun to organize.

However, there are two compelling reasons why most women's committees quickly need some structure. First, if women's committees are to receive funding, which they will need for activities, and even for meetings above the local level, they must be formally constituted. Secondly, it is difficult to influence an organization without connecting to its decision-making processes. Part of the purpose of women's committees is to represent women's interests inside the union movement, and formal links are commonly the way to accomplish that.

Representing Women

The process by which women become members of a women's committee determines who can join, how influential they are and who is represented. Where members of women's committees are simply appointed, criticisms are made of favouritism, lack of democracy and the tendency of male-dominated executives to appoint less "troublesome," non-feminist women. For example, a women's committee that is appointed, that brings together women in different parts of the country who are flown in for two or three meetings a year, and that lacks any connection to the women members in the union, may have little claim to represent anyone and therefore very limited influence.

Elections are the more democratic process, making the representative accountable to the union membership. Elected representatives have a connection to the members in taking positions, and a claim to some influence given that they represent more than just themselves. However, where elections do take place, the members of women's committees do not usually represent women per se, but are in the position of being elected by the general membership, both male and female, from their regions or components or locals to represent women's concerns. While this makes them less accountable to women members, it may make them a more influential force for change.

Dependency

Women's committees are dependent upon the mainstream union movement, for funding and for changes that affect women's welfare. It has been noted elsewhere that it is extremely difficult, if not impossible, to sustain a women's committee if the union executive is hostile.[4] In a major local of one of the unions in this study, an active women's committee had developed. Monthly supper meetings with child care were established, educational courses and assertiveness training were offered, speakers were invited and skills workshops developed. Following elections, the new president of the local spear-headed a backlash against women's issues, including cutting off the funding. The women's committee has now ceased all activity.

On the other hand, where the executive is supportive they have sometimes initiated women's committees. This was true in the Ontario district of the United Steelworkers mentioned above. Another example was in one of the components of the B.C. Government Employees Union, where the male president of a majority-male component helped to establish a women's committee and has encouraged women to attend executive meetings to learn more about the union.

It seems there are two lines of defense against the negative consequences of such dependence. One is a political response, building support for women's committees and women's issues within the organization, so that any backlash is itself subject to disapproval. The other is to institutionalize women's committees and conferences and their funding, so that they cannot be easily dislodged. The women's committee then becomes enshrined within the union by-laws or constitution, and a certain level of funding is automatic rather than subject to executive decision.

Time for Two Structures

It takes time to relate to two structures, both the women's network and the main union organization. This is more than just the problem of reporting in two directions, although that in itself can be time-consuming. Working only within the women's committee structure does not necessarily produce results within the general union. It is important to be connected to the broader union structure, and to be well connected. For example, at the labour centrals, members of the women's committees who are also members of their own union's executive will usually have more contacts and influence when it comes to pressing for change. In several union interviews it was mentioned that, to be effective, members of the women's committees also needed to be active in other parts of the union structure. Issues raised through work in the women's committees must be channelled into the mainstream union. This double duty within the union movement takes the commodity that women seem least able to spare — time.

Between Women's Committees

With the mushrooming of women's committees at different levels inside unions, questions arise about the inter-relationship between women's committees within the same union. Since women's committees are most commonly organized in relationship to the existing structure of the union at whatever level, they rarely have any relationship among themselves, at least not formally. As a rule there is no direct connection from local women's committees, to the regional and head office levels. Each functions autonomously at its own level, relating to the main union structure, and each may be structured in a different way, as outlined above. There is rarely any formal method to funnel issues up from the concerns of women in local committees to the higher decision-making levels of the union.

There are informal connections. Women meet at union functions, at meetings, courses and conventions. Women's conferences bring women together to discuss issues, although again the expression of concerns and possible initiatives is usually indirect rather than through formal resolutions or recommendations. If strategies are co-ordinated it is because of informal networks and discussion.

In some cases this is changing, or attempts are being made to establish links. In the Canadian Union of Public Employees, as regional women's committees have developed, it has become the norm for the chairs of those committees to be appointed to the national Equal Opportunities Committee, providing a link between the two levels. At the Confédération des syndicats nationaux, it is formally established that four times a year, all those responsible for the status of women throughout the organization and in the affiliated unions, meet to discuss and co-ordinate activities. Less formally, at the Fédération des affaires sociales a conscious attempt was being made to raise the profile of the central women's committee members in the regions that they represent, and make them available as resource people. At the Canadian Auto Workers, the members of the central women's committee are there because they have been elected to the Canadian Council and not because of any necessary connection to women's committees or women's issues. However, these women's committee members are starting to play a more active role at women's conferences and forums, so that they become better known and connected to women in the union.

In their work women's committees face many contradictions or tensions. They attempt to represent women's interests within union structures created to represent all union members. They are critical of union structures and processes, but must have a relationship to them in order to make changes, and so they challenge union structures while working within them. They often work autonomously, although they are ultimately dependent upon the mainstream union movement. At the same time they are grappling with their own forms of organization and structure.

The following discussion moves on to consider three of the issues of concern to women that women's committees have raised and pressed forward within the union movement.

Child Care and Family Responsibilities

Several studies have found that child care responsibilities may preclude union involvement for women. In a 1980–81 survey of union activists by the Confédération des syndicats nationaux, 82 percent of the women said that having children limited their involvement in the union, compared to 33 percent of men. Women activists were less likely to have children than women members in general, and the higher the position in the union the fewer the number of women with children. This negative impact was not apparent for men, who tended to be more likely to have children in the higher positions of responsibility.[5] In 1985 Chaison and

The Barriers within Unions

It is not easy for a woman to be labeled shrill and strident and even hysterical for speaking forcefully on a convention floor when her brothers, who say exactly the same thing and bellow as if they ate megaphones for breakfast, are heartily congratulated for their fire and brimstone speeches.

It is not easy to be told by a higher up male trade union official, as I was quite a few years ago, that when I cried a little in a very emotional strike meeting which I was chairing, when we were voting to go back to work under wage controls, that I was not displaying "leadership qualities" and also to be told that "you have to be real tough to be a union leader you know!"

It is not easy for women to endure the double standards that exist around social life within our union. If you like to drink, dance and party "like the guys," the rumours and innuendoes can be quite incredible. On the other hand, if you avoid the social scene, the drinking, the hospitality suites and so on, then you get an opposite kind of label — which is almost as hurtful and harmful. You are "workaholic," you are "too serious," you should "loosen up," "be one of the guys," etc, etc ...

If you spend your days and nights and weekends in meetings or conferences, and if you seem able (for a while) to pull off twenty million responsibilities without flinching, you are considered a social oddity and teased incessantly for not living a "normal life" like everybody else. On the other hand, if you do have children or family responsibilities and you try to distribute the workload or plead periodically for time off to lead a "normal life," too many people will still imply that this means you are simply not up to the job and that union leaders must be able to devote themselves full-time to the job ...

If you take your four month old son to the CLC convention with you, as I did a couple of months ago because I didn't want to be separated from him for a week when he was so young, some will still say to you, despite affirmative action and child-care and all of the other policies being debated on the floor, that you should "get your priorities straight." And that it really is not very cost-effective to provide child care at conventions when not many kids are registered.

No matter how right you feel about the choices that you are making or the different roles that you are trying to combine, the guilt is still overwhelming. Half the time you feel guilty for being a "lousy mother," for "selfishly" staying involved in your union to the detriment of your children. The other half of the time the guilt is because you are not being a good enough trade unionist, you are not working night and day for the cause no matter what toll it might take.

Judy Darcy, "The Barriers Within — How Unions Have to Change," in *Strong Women, Strong Unions: Speeches by Union Women*, (Toronto: Participatory Research Group and the Canadian Employment and Immigration Union, January 1985) pp. 36–37. Judy Darcy was elected President of the Canadian Union of Public Employees in 1991.

Andiappan surveyed 352 officers of local unions, and 59 percent of the women indicated that child care was an important barrier to union participation, compared to 39 percent of the men.[6]

Children are not the only problem. An early study of the Fédération des affaires sociales in 1977 found that 78 percent of women in local executive positions were unmarried, compared to only 45 percent of women members in general.[7] The 1980–81 survey already mentioned above, also found that women activists were less likely to be married than working women in general, although again this was not the case for men. It concluded: "Women activists ... more frequently live without a husband, male friend or children than rank and file women."[8]

Union work means long hours, evening and weekend work and sometimes travel away from home. It is demanding and often stressful. In 1989 the Confédération des syndicats nationaux conducted another survey of 223 women who were either local presidents or holding higher union positions. Seventy percent of these women held six or more union responsibilities, while 28 percent held more than ten union duties. These would include such tasks as being a member of the executive, sitting on various committees and acting as a representative to other organizations. Involvement in women's committees and activities is often an additional responsibility for women. These obligations consumed 11 hours a week on top of normal working hours for local presidents, and 16 hours per week for women in higher union positions.[9] Since a full-time job requires 32 to 40 hours per week, and women activists spend between 29 and 34 hours per week on domestic tasks,[10] their triple burden amounted to between 72 and 90 hours of work per week.

Given these conditions, it is not surprising to find that women active in their unions suffer from work-related problems. The same study reported that 75 percent of women activists had personal, physical or psychological problems related to their union role. More than one-third (36 percent) of these women were considering leaving their union positions, because of the burden of union tasks (56 percent), psychological pressure (29 percent), family pressure (27 percent) and health problems (29 percent).[11] The high turnover among women in union positions has been noted elsewhere,[12] but no study has been conducted to compare men and women in this regard.

In 1990 the Canadian Union of Public Employees undertook a detailed analysis of the workload of its staff. It found that service staff work between 51 and 57 hours per week including frequent evening and weekend work, spend five to six nights per month travelling away from home, and typically work on four of their statutory holidays and nine of their vacation days. Between 80 and 90 percent of the service staff felt that their workload was too much to handle. Among this large majority that complained of a heavy workload, 60 percent felt burned out, 64 percent had experienced work-related health problems in the previous year, and 70 percent complained that the demands of their jobs conflicted with family needs.[13]

The Union Response — Child Care

To encourage the participation of women with children, the majority of the labour centrals and unions in this study had developed some kind of child care policy. Three Federations of Labour (QFL, NSFL, NLFL) and two unions (UFCW, USWA) had no policy on child care. The locals of the Hotel Employees and Restaurant Employees Union set their own arrangements, and one of the two largest locals had a policy while the other did not.

Most commonly child care services are offered for conventions and conferences, provided at the location of the event. While this may be useful for women with young pre-school children, and women who live nearby, it has serious limitations. Parents must pay the cost of transporting children to the event, including air fares for children over the age of two years. The union activities, both formal and informal, are not confined to regular nine-to-five hours, although the child care provision may be. Sometimes the quality of the child care is excellent, but there has also been criticism, and parents question the wisdom of bringing children if they are to spend many hours confined to a hotel room. Children must be left with an unknown care-giver, which some tolerate but others do not. For these reasons, on-site child care is now almost universally described as unpopular, used by only a few delegates, if any. On-site child care must continue to be offered for the participants who do need it, although it is often cancelled when no-one requests it. The Ontario Public Service Employees Union is contemplating paying the travel costs for children to attend such events with their parents, which would deal with one major barrier. This is a new approach, mentioned by none of the centrals or unions in my interviews.

Reimbursement for child care is a more popular arrangement, where the union member makes their own arrangement for child care and the cost is reimbursed by the union. Seven of the twelve labour centrals in this study, and all of the unions with a child care policy, provide some kind of reimbursement. However, the conditions under which it can be obtained vary. Sometimes only national conventions and conferences are covered, but not committee meetings prior to convention or other union meetings. Often the policy may cover central or national events, while regions and locals make their own arrangements, if any. As a result the first level of activity within a union, in the local, often does not provide for child care costs. In some cases delegates are covered, but union staff are not.

The amount of the reimbursement provided is a major problem. Commonly daytime care is reimbursed at around $15 per day, while 24 hour care will be $35 per day. Both rates are far below the actual cost of obtaining child care. Some unions provide up to $60 a day, which is a great improvement, but still may not cover the full costs. Only a small minority of unions or centrals provide for the actual cost of the child care.

In general the union movement has been reluctant to finance the full costs of child care for all union activities, and yet there is a far more difficult challenge to meet. Providing child care for union events does not resolve the problem of the general commitment of time demanded from union activists.

The Union Response — Time and Workload

The United Nurses of Alberta is unique in having a policy that no meetings or union activities are to be held on week-ends. Annual meetings and workshops must be held during the week and lost wages are paid by the union. Local meetings are kept to one and a half hours, held during the week and immediately after the day shift, so that additional travelling is kept to a minimum. One reason for this arrangement is that nurses commonly work alternate weekends, and are rarely prepared to give up their free weekends for union activities. But also:

> There is a fairly good recognition within the union now that the roles that our members play are multi-faceted and we don't want the union to be a burden in terms of participation.[14]

In one other union a Never-on-a-Sunday policy for union meetings had been raised by the women's committee, but met with a distinct lack of enthusiasm from the executive.

The cost of covering lost wages is a major expense, so unions continue to hold various union activities during their members' "spare time." There are few exceptions, especially at the local level. The B.C. Government Employees Union has negotiated two local meetings a year on the employer's time into the collective agreements of some colleges. The meetings start two hours before work finishes, and everyone attends since it is paid and at the workplace. "It makes a huge difference in attendance."[15] Such an arrangement is extremely unusual, although negotiating local union meetings during working hours has been proposed for many years.

Above the local level, negotiated arrangements are only slightly more common. For example, the Fédération des affaires sociales has negotiated paid leave from work for union meetings above the local level, and the locals pay for any transportation or accommodation involved. The Canadian Union of Public Employees has more than 2,000 collective agreements and, as of the end of 1990, only 18 percent provided paid leave for union functions such as seminars, conferences and conventions.[16] Unions themselves pay lost wages for members to attend union education courses and conventions held during normal working hours, but not for regular union meetings.

Apart from the timing of union meetings and other functions, there is also the problem of overwork for union activists and staff. This not only prevents the participation of women, it leads to high divorce rates among union activists, and mental and physical breakdown. It means the loss of good unionists who leave the movement, as well as the exclusion of those who refuse to become involved.

Other criticisms were made during the course of my interviews. Staff are overworked, it was suggested, because there is too much reliance upon "union experts" and not enough help and encouragement so that members at the local level could handle more problems themselves. Some feel that the crisis mentality prevalent in many union offices indicates a lack of direction. Staff and activists work frenetically on one crisis after another, but without an overall plan initiated and established by the union, that would provide a focus for the work and help to establish priorities.

This is not an easy issue to resolve. Most union locals operate on the basis of volunteer labour, provided after members have put in their full-time working hours for pay. It is difficult for paid union staff and officials to limit their hours to 40 per week in this context.

The members place heavy demands on the union, and often crisis situations require immediate attention. Hiring more staff to handle the load may not be an option financially. In the study by the Canadian Union of Public Employees, the staff made many recommendations for improvements, and while hiring more staff was one proposal there were others that did not involve increased expenditure. They included increased self-servicing by locals and the training to help them do that, and reduced expectations from locals for services; improved organization and planning of work with advance notice of deadlines; clearer goals and priorities for union work; improved communication and co-ordination between different parts of the union; improved staff training; and better use of computer technology. For union activists not on paid staff, other suggestions for change have been made, including sharing union positions to share the workload, rotating responsibilities, and limiting the time spent in official positions.

While these issues are being tentatively discussed in a few unions, and particularly among women, in general there does not yet exist the commitment and creative thinking that would be necessary to find solutions and make these types of changes. Part of the problem is that union activists are too busy to spend time considering how to do things differently. Perhaps also, as one woman commented tersely: "Families are not a priority."[17]

Sexual and Personal Harassment

Sexism within unions is no more resolved than it is within society generally. During my interviews many examples were given of incidents involving sexism and harassment. Women complain of not being taken seriously, of their contributions being disregarded, that women's issues are considered unimportant, and that there is a lack of accommodation for women's other responsibilities. There are also more serious incidents. It is important to give such examples, because unionists, both men and women, still argue that these kinds of events do not occur in the union movement:

- Two women staff members quit their jobs at a regional office, unable to deal with the level of harassment, including the negative remarks suggesting that they were lesbian.

- The only woman on a negotiating team goes back to the hotel room for a break with her colleagues, who proceed to watch a pornographic movie, cheering on the action.

- A woman staff rep works out of her own home because she cannot work in the office where the otherwise all male staff are openly hostile.

- At a week long educational school for unionists, the men decide to go to a bar with a wet-T shirt contest as part of their evening entertainment.

- A woman staff member is receiving threatening telephone calls from her former partner, a man who is in a more powerful position within the union movement.

Apart from such incidents that take place at union events or involve union staff, unions also have to deal with worker to worker harassment on the job. This raises complications because both the person who complains of sexual harassment and the alleged harasser are members of the same union.

Most unions and labour centrals have taken action to attempt to deal with sexual harassment. Policies opposing sexual harassment are now relatively common, and are increasingly often read out at the beginning of union events, sometimes including a mechanism for dealing with complaints. Various courses on sexual harassment have been developed, sometimes provided for men and women separately and sometimes presented as part of other training courses so that more union members are reached. Written policies, articles and videos on the topic have been prepared and distributed. In some cases extensive mechanisms have been elaborated for dealing with cases of harassment between union members, and have been negotiated into collective agreements.

In recent years other forms of harassment have been recognized, particularly the problem of racial harassment. The United Steelworkers passed a policy on sexual harassment in 1987, followed in 1989 by a policy on racial harassment. The Canadian Auto Workers has produced a kit called "Confronting Harassment in the Workplace," which includes both sexual and racial harassment. The Ontario Federation of Labour prepared a document called "Challenging Harassment," which included sexual, racial and personal harassment, the last covering "unwanted remarks, jokes, innuendoes or taunting about a person's abilities, political belief, marital and family status, religion, record of offence, receipt of social assistance, sexual orientation and union activities."[18] There has been a shift from policies solely on sexual harassment to include other forms of harassment as well. Most recently, the Public Service

Alliance has produced a video that covers not only sexual and racial harassment, but also harassment because of sexual orientation and disability.

Despite considerable action on the issue over a number of years, satisfactory solutions seem hard to find and harassment between union members continues to be a difficult and controversial issue within the union movement. There are specific reasons for this.

Unlike other issues that unite union members against the employer, harassment between union members raises the uncomfortable picture of union members mistreating other members, when they are supposed to work together for common goals. It undermines the central notion of union solidarity. It may be difficult to discuss sexual harassment, for example, without men feeling accused and becoming defensive. While it is certainly no longer acceptable to laugh and jeer about the issue, at least not at union conventions, the Ontario Federation of Labour has recently commented:

> The debate is not over. Only 18 percent of collective agreements in Ontario include language on sexual harassment (this information is not available for other types of harassment). Today, activists may meet silence rather than discussion. Resistance to this issue has gone underground. This makes education and change harder to achieve.[19]

Unions were established to represent members against employers and are bound by law to represent all their members, leading to confusion when two members are in dispute. The victim wants union protection, but so does the alleged harasser. Perplexing situations can arise. In one case an employer fired a harasser, who appealed it through the union as an unjust dismissal and was re-instated, leaving the victim of the harassment angry and frustrated. In another situation the victims of harassment complained to the employer, the harasser was disciplined and the victims found themselves in trouble with the local union for "wronging a brother." Some unions represent both sides, while others claim the right to refuse to represent following investigation of the complaint.

The United Steelworkers attempts to recognize the problem, while still protecting workers' rights with regard to the employer:

> Our policy ... is based upon a desire to mediate resolutions between co-workers in an amicable and non-adversarial manner. Because the workers involved are both members of our union, emphasis will be placed on resolving the complaint without the intervention of the employer, government agencies or the courts.[20]

Educational Poster

Women in unions are raising many issues beyond those discussed in this chapter. Recently, violence against women has emerged as a concern in some unions, and this educational poster was produced by the Canadian Auto Workers.

EVERYONE TOUCHED BY VIOLENCE SUFFERS.

OFTEN SILENTLY.
THE SHAME.
THE UNSPOKEN.

In the labour movement we speak out against injustice. In all its forms.

Even when it is inside our own families. Our own union.

CAW women and men are working together for social justice and human dignity.

Violence. First we must name it. Then, together, we can work to stop the suffering.

If you or your child are being hurt or intimidated, or you know of someone who's in that position, break the silence!

For assistance call your local Wife Assault Helpline, shelter or sexual assault centre.

Contact your local union women's committee for more information.

VIOLENCE: BREAK THE SILENCE.

CAW TCA

Union officials in each District are designated as Racial or Sexual Harassment Complaints Counsellors, available to mediate confidentially in cases of racial or sexual harassment. If this fails, the union policy proposes application to a human rights tribunal, and only as a third option would a complaint be passed to an employer. The policy states that complaints must be resolved where possible "without putting any workers in a vulnerable position vis-a-vis the employer." If an employer disciplines a worker for harassment, the union commits itself to handle grievances arising from such situations just like any others.

The Public Service Alliance of Canada takes a very different position, which is that the employer is responsible for maintaining a work environment free of harassment. This was the decision of the Supreme Court of Canada in the Bonnie Robichaud case. She was a worker for the federal government and was harassed by a manager, but the employer claimed that it was not responsible for the actions of its employees. Eight years later in 1987 the Supreme Court disagreed, finding that the employer was responsible for the work environment. On this basis the Alliance advises its members to take grievances against the employer in cases of harassment, even if the harasser is a co-worker, because of the employer's responsibility to maintain a harassment-free environment. The employer then investigates the case and determines any disciplinary action. A union member who has been disciplined for harassment may wish to grieve the discipline, but the union takes the position that it will only support such a grievance if it considers that the discipline has been unfair.

The Public Service Alliance is not the only union that reserves the right to refuse to represent the harasser. Both the Canadian Auto Workers and the Fédération des affaires sociales have policies that, following investigation of the case, the union has the right to refuse to represent a member in grieving disciplinary action taken as a result of harassment. In the case of the B.C. Government Employees Union, a specific mechanism is laid down involving the union and the employer, and where discipline is imposed as a result, the harasser does not have the right to take a grievance.

The B.C. Government Employees Union has negotiated a two-level mechanism. First, representatives of both the union and the employer investigate the complaint, and the Deputy Minister resolves the issue and determines any disciplinary action. The agreement states that the disciplined harasser does not have the right to take a grievance. Second, if either side is dissatisfied, the situation may be reviewed by a panel including union and employer representatives, with a mutually agreed upon chair. This arrangement has produced difficulties in the public sector, because the employer has caused inordinate delays (despite stated time limits), by rejecting all proposals for chairs of panels and taking months to come to decisions. The employer has also on occasion failed to follow the mechanism in the collective agreement, taken harsh disciplinary action unilaterally, and placed the union in the position of grieving the case of the alleged harasser. The union is now looking at a policy that would involve external people being available to arbitrate, without the direct involvement of the employer.

The Canadian Union of Public Employees has not developed a standard approach to harassment and a variety of mechanisms have been used. Investigations have been undertaken by union and management representatives together, by an Equal Opportunity Officer from the union, by the management human relations person, or by a lawyer hired for the purpose. In some cases one staff person has represented the complainant, while another from a different area has represented the alleged harasser. In one case a man was fired by the employer, regained his job with representation from the union, and then was given a one month suspension and required to take sensitivity training. The union has recognised the need for a standard mechanism and is still considering what that should be.

Undoubtedly the union movement has taken up the problem of sexual harassment, and more recently other forms of harassment, in a way that was inconceivable ten years ago. Union education on the subject is quite extensive and real attempts are being made to handle the situation both inside the union movement and at the workplace. However, the issue is complex and there continues to be considerable difficulty in producing and implementing a satisfactory policy to deal with complaints. At the same time not all unions are committed to action in this area, and the policies passed at union conventions are not necessarily respected at all levels or by all members of the union.

Union Education

Most unions run their own training sessions to develop basic skills, such as stewards' training, negotiating and handling grievances. Larger unions often also run a variety of other courses on broader topics, such as health and safety, human rights and economic issues. The Canadian Labour Congress provides education in week-long regional schools for members of its affiliates outside Quebec, and is primarily responsible for an eight week residential labour college once a year. In Quebec, both the Quebec Federation of Labour and the Confédération des syndicats nationaux organize education for their respective affiliates.

Activists and potential activists take union courses to develop their skills, and to advance within the union movement, so it is important to consider how many women are attending these courses. However, not all unions and labour centrals track course participants by sex, so the information available is somewhat limited.

The Canadian Labour Congress provides scholarships to cover lost wages and expenses for participants at their week-long courses in different parts of the country. It is estimated that these scholarships cover at least one third of the course participants, the others obtaining financing from their own unions. I was able to carry out a manual count of the number of men and women receiving these scholarships in the year from April 1990 to March 1991. Names that could not be identified as male or female were relatively few (4 percent) and not clustered by region or type of course, so they have been excluded from the following discussion. The results show that 1,226 union members received scholarships during the year and that almost 36 percent of these were women. If the women's courses are excluded, this figure drops to 30 percent. As of 1989 women comprised 37 percent of the membership affiliated to the Congress,[21] so the proportion of women receiving scholarships for all courses was equivalent to the representation of women in affiliates.

Table 5-2 shows the numbers of men and women receiving scholarships by the major courses attended. The Women in the Work Force course was the fifth largest in terms of the number of Congress scholarships and involved 101 women, demonstrating a considerable investment of money and energy by the union movement. Among the other courses, the lowest level of participation by women is in the Health and Safety and Collective Bargaining courses. This reinforces the concern expressed in union interviews that women are poorly represented on health and safety committees, and on collective bargaining committees. (See Com-

Table 5-2: Canadian Labour Congress Scholarships for Week-long Courses, April 1990 to March 1991

Type of Course	Total	No. of Women	% Women
Collective Bargaining	223	56	25.1
Stewards' Training	165	48	29.1
Leadership Skills	152	51	33.6
Facing Management	117	39	33.3
Women in the Work Force	101	101	100.0
Health and Safety/ Workers' Compensation	80	17	21.3
Union Counselling	69	24	34.8
Public Speaking	67	19	28.4
Labour Law	67	18	26.9
Arbitration	43	16	37.2
International Affairs	29	11	37.9
Other Courses	113	37	32.7
All Courses	1226	437	35.6

Source: File count of course participants by author.

mittees and Collective Bargaining, Chapter 4). Labour Law, Public Speaking and Stewards' Training courses also have a participation rate by women of less than 30 percent.

The Canadian Labour Congress is also primarily responsible for the annual Canadian Labour College, an eight week residential course that is the pinnacle of union educational opportunities in English Canada. It involves a broad range of education in economics, politics, sociology, history and labour law, geared to the needs of union activists. After considerable efforts to recruit more women, in 1991 women were for the first time just over half the total number of students.

The Quebec Federation of Labour maintains data not only on its own courses but also those given by its affiliates. For the year 1990 to 1991 over 11,000 unionists participated in all these courses and 30 percent were women. This is equivalent to the representation of women within the Federation, which is also 30 percent. A number of specialized courses are provided by the Quebec Federation of Labour itself, and of the 1,324 participants in these courses between 1990 and 1991, women comprised 25 percent. This shows some improvement over time, since for the two years from 1989 to 1990 women comprised just 18 percent of the participants in these courses.

I attempted to obtain information on the educational programs of the four largest unions in the study. However, in the United Food and Commercial Workers Union, education is handled at the local level and no information was available for the union as a whole. The Canadian Union of Public Employees was also unable to provide access to the information.

The Public Service Alliance held weekend courses for 1,293 members in 1991. Excluding the 5 percent of unknown gender, women comprised 48 percent of the participants in these courses, equivalent to the 47 percent of women members in the union. The lowest participation of women was on courses for the members of Health and Safety committees (32 percent) and those to receive training on Competitions and Appeals (38 percent), while the highest was on the course called Men and Women Talking (73 percent) and on Technological Change (63 percent). As well, the Alliance runs week-long residential courses, which also have a very good participation level for women. In 1990, 570 members took these courses and 53 percent were women. If the course on Women and Work, run for women only, is excluded, women still constituted 42 percent of the participants of all other courses. Looking over a three year period, these rates of participation have remained relatively steady.

The Canadian Auto Workers has a much lower proportion of women in the union at 21 percent, but has had the struggle of involving women in a union that remains predominantly male, industrial workers. The union does not maintain figures on the numerous weekend courses offered in its area schools across the country, but does track the participants in its Paid Education Leave program. This involves a four week course that runs for one week a month for four months, and covers the history of the union, media and communications, basic economics, legislation and politics. The most recent figures, for 1989, show that of the 287 participants, 22 percent were women. In 1988 it was 25 percent women and in 1987 18 percent. For graduates of the four week program, the union offers a course called "Economics and Society" twice a year, and here the participation of women is lower and has fluctuated more. Between 1981 and 1989 215 members have taken this course and 16 percent were women overall.

It has been recognized that women should not only attend courses, but also teach them. The Canadian Labour Congress has encouraged women to become instructors. Over the two years of 1990 and 1991 courses to train instructors were given in all four regions to a total of 131 unionists. Forty-nine of these trainee instructors were women, which is 37 percent of the total, and therefore the same as the proportion of women unionists represented by the Congress. In Quebec, women comprised 26 percent of the 262 participants in instructor training courses given by the Quebec Federation of Labour between 1990 and 1991. This is just slightly below the proportion of women members among the Federation's affiliates, which is 30 percent. The participation by women had improved from 24 percent the previous year.

Among unions, the Public Service Alliance runs an instructor program for members and over the two years 1989 and 1990, thirty-seven men and thirty-seven women have taken the course. The Canadian Union of Public Employees has developed the Occasional Instructor Program, which since 1986 has provided training to 300 men and women who then form a pool of instructors. One man and a woman are taught as a team and then teach as a team, with equal responsibility. The Canadian Auto Workers has a week long training program to develop Local Union Discussion Leaders (LUDLs), who then form a pool of instructors and teach virtually all of the union's courses at all levels. At the last LUDL training session held in 1991, only women, visible minorities and members from outside of Ontario could attend, these groups having been identified as necessary additions to the pool of instructors. There are now a total of 53 LUDLs and 16 are women.

Union education has been extended to include topics of particular concern to women. Courses on women and work, sexual harassment, human rights, assertiveness training, and equal pay appear among those offered by labour centrals and the larger unions. Some courses have been developed for women only. For example, the Public Service Alliance has run a 6 day residential course for women only since 1984, and also runs weekend courses just for women. The Ontario District of the United Steelworkers has developed a course called "Women of Steel" to encourage women to take on leadership positions within the union. In the summer of 1992 the Canadian Auto Workers held two new leadership courses for the first time, one for women and one for workers of colour. The Canadian Labour Congress offers a week long course on women and work for women only. Other courses are designed to help men and women discuss together the problems women face. The one at the Alliance is called "Men and Women Talking," and that offered by the United Steelworkers is called "Equal Partners."

Another approach to education on women's issues has been to develop shorter modules that can be slotted into general courses and thereby provide instruction to a broader group of unionists than just those who sign up for the courses on specifically women's issues. Probably the most common example would be a module on harassment that can be added to any general union training course. Finally, information on matters of concern to women has been integrated into other courses, so that for example a health and safety course includes the problems of video-display terminals and repetitive strain injuries, as well as factory and construction accidents.

There is no doubt that over the last decade union training programs have made considerable progress in both involving women in union courses and developing materials related to women's concerns. Nonetheless, certain problems were raised in my interviews. There is still considerable negative feeling about material on women's issues. Where it is presented separately it is criticized as divisive; where it is presented as part of other courses, it is sometimes considered irrelevant and unnecessary. The resistance and even hostility to education on women's issues creates tension among course participants, especially on residential courses. This is sometimes part of a another problem at residential courses, where a culture of drinking and parties makes some women feel out of place and uncomfortable.

Union education raises again the problem of time for women. Many of the shorter one and two day courses are held on weekends, while the longer, residential courses involve a week or more away from home. Some attempts have been made to handle the problems this may cause. For example, in Alberta women were not signing up for the week long residential course offered through the Canadian Labour Congress. As a result, in 1991 the course was held on a non-residential nine to five basis in Edmonton. Women could go to the course as they would go to work, returning to their homes in the evening, an arrangement that proved to be more popular.

The Canadian Auto Workers runs an important four week course for its members, an intensive training for union leaders. This is funded through the union's negotiated Paid Education Leave plan, so the members do not lose wages or their vacation time. To reduce the problems with family, the four weeks are divided into one week at a time rather than held as a block. Also, spouses and partners are involved in a pre-session weekend to explain the course and its purpose, and develop a commitment to the four week process.

Another problem raised in my interviews is how members are chosen to attend courses. Locals usually send their choice, and sometimes it is seen as a perk for union involvement rather than a way to educate more people. As a result the same local officials return to take courses year after year, the "repeat attenders," thereby excluding other members. Unions concerned about this make attempts to track the names of past participants and encourage new faces. Sometimes courses are laddered, so that one course follows another. The Canadian Auto Workers has developed two day courses specifically for new bargaining units and new local executive officers, to ensure their involvement.

The cost of sending members to courses is always an issue. This is why so many courses are held on weekends, so that lost wages need not be paid. Locals have limited budgets for financing members on courses, and must cover training in basic union skills, such as shops stewards' training and grievances. In smaller locals this may leave very little for any of the broader courses, including those on women's issues. Good courses may be rarely used or under-used because of this problem. Some unions try to deal with this by providing some central funding for members from smaller locals. It is sometimes suggested that these central scholarships should be more extensive since it would also mean shared control with the locals over who attends the courses.

Children at the child care centre while their parents attend classes at the Canadian Labour Congress Summer School during "family week," United Auto Workers Education Centre, Port Elgin, Ontario, 1980.

Courtesy of the Canadian Labour Congress

During my research I found examples of a different style of union education, courses that involved other members of the family. The Ontario region of the Canadian Labour Congress holds a "family week" each year at the Canadian Auto Workers' Port Elgin centre. From 80 to 100 union members, their spouses and older children participate in union education and activities, while child care is provided for the young children.

The United Steelworkers runs weekend residential courses for the family, and union members attend with their partners and older children. The sessions provide information on the goals and operation of the union, and time to discuss the difficulties raised by union activism.

> We have frequently found that whether our activists are men or women, that usually the spouse has no idea what the work involves, or why the spouse is as involved as they are.[22]

These courses have also provided services such as investment training on a low income, and retirement counselling. The participants have been very enthusiastic.

The Canadian Auto Workers runs a summer program for the whole family. The union provides the cost of transportation and accommodation at its Port Elgin education centre. Families use two weeks of their vacation time for a program that is a mixture of recreation and union education. The adults and older children are divided into "locals" and work up to a mock convention in the second week. In 1989 240 families were involved. In 1990 110 families participated, including the families of twenty-one women members (19 percent).

In Saskatchewan a new program is providing union education for the children of union members. With the support of its affiliates and the Canadian Labour Congress, the Saskatchewan Federation of Labour is running a week long residential school in the summer for teenagers aged 13 to 16 years old. It covers five themes — the purpose of unions, racism, international solidarity, women's issues and the media. The idea is to provide union education for children that they would not receive elsewhere, and also to deal with some of the resentment that children of activists can feel toward their parents. One young woman who participated commented that before the course she had just seen the union as taking her father away and had never understood the purpose of his involvement. Sixteen children were involved in 1989, the first year, and there were 31 participants in 1990. The only requirement is that one parent be a union member. Staff for the camp come from the affiliate unions and their wages are paid by their union, so the cost of the camp is kept very low.

From the information available it seems that unions have achieved a good overall representation of women on union courses. This is especially encouraging because it suggests that an increasing number of trained women unionists will be active in the union movement. There still needs to be some encouragement for women to enter certain courses where they are not yet well represented, especially health and safety and collective bargaining. New courses have been developed to meet the specific interests of women, and there are a few initiatives to provide family education programs.

Among the industries with the lowest rates of organization, trade and personal/business services are of particular concern, since between them they employ 34 percent of all workers, and 40 percent of all women workers. Overall less than 12 percent of workers in the personal/business services belong to unions.

Photos courtesy of D. Hemingway and Canadian Labour (bottom left).

6

Unorganized Women

Women cannot benefit from union protection if they do not belong to unions, and two-thirds of employed women are not unionized. While the proportion of unionized women has increased significantly over the last 20 years, still the large majority remain outside unions. While the gap in unionization between men and women has narrowed over the same period, still more men than women are union members. Moreover, recent developments do not bode well for the continued unionization of women workers. This chapter examines the level of unionization both in general and specifically among women, considers what makes it difficult to organize more workers, and looks at what unions are doing about it.

Recent Trends in Unionization

The third wave of unionization, among public sector workers in the 1960s and 1970s, lead to a massive increase in the number of women union members, as described in Chapter 2. As this wave of organization tailed off in the late 1970s, the pace at which women joined unions slowed down, although it continued to more than keep pace with the growing number of women working for pay. However, this changed in the 1980s, when organization among women barely kept pace with the growing number of women workers. For five years between 1983 and 1988 the rate of unionization among women in the paid labour force stagnated at around 28 percent, although there was an increase again for 1989 to 29 percent.

Meanwhile, despite fluctuations, there has been an overall decline in unionization among men. In the late 1960s the rate of unionization among men hovered around 40 percent, and this has fallen to 38 in the late 1980s. The combination of the decline in unionization among men and the stagnation among women has lead to a fall in the overall rate of unionization in the 1980s. In

1983 35 percent of paid workers were unionized, falling to 33 percent by 1987. By 1989 there was a recovery to 34 percent, still lower than the 1983 level.[1] Thus, while women continue to unionize and to do so at a faster rate than men, it may be of little comfort to find that their influence is expanding in a labour movement that is stagnant or declining.

This fall and stagnation in the proportion of unionized workers is caused by several factors. Unionization in the public sector slowed once the majority of workers there belonged to unions. Attempts to unionize workers in other industrial sectors have been largely unsuccessful, so that the trend to increased unionization has faltered. In particular the private service sector has proved resistant to organizing efforts. Campaigns to organize bank workers in the finance industry and sales workers in department stores in the retail trade industry have largely failed, leaving these industries virtually untouched by unionization.[2]

The severe recession of the early 1980s took its toll in jobs, and therefore union members. In 1982 there was a decline, not just in the rate of unionization, but in the actual number of union members. This is the only absolute decline in the number of union members recorded since the data was first collected in the 1960s, and ten of the sixteen largest unions in Canada saw a decline in membership. By the late 1980s eight of these unions had not managed to recoup their losses, especially internationals representing the traditional skilled trades and manufacturing sectors, including the United Steelworkers, the International Woodworkers, the International Brotherhood of Electrical Workers, and the Canadian Paper Workers Union.[3]

Apart from the recession, more fundamental economic changes are taking place. Shifts in the composition of the labour force are working to erode jobs and therefore union members in the traditionally well-organized manufacturing industry.[4] This is partly the result of technology making human involvement redundant, and partly the result of increased competitiveness and free trade, leading businesses into bankruptcy or out of the country. Service industries have been growing faster than the goods-producing industries throughout this century, but the speed of the shift has accelerated dramatically. Service jobs are no longer just increasing faster than goods-producing jobs; between 1981 and 1986 all new jobs created were in the service industries.[5] Many of these new jobs are in the private service sectors that have resisted unionization.

There is a shift in employment taking place not only between industries, but also within industries. In general middle wage jobs are being lost and there is an increase in both lower and higher paid work, a polarization between the "good jobs" and the "bad jobs."[6] Moreover, a large proportion of new jobs are non-standard, that is part-time, temporary and small-scale self-employment. They are generally low paid and insecure jobs, held particularly by women, young workers, recent immigrants and visible minorities. Between 1981 and 1986, half of all new jobs created were these "non-standard" types of jobs.[7] Employers are insisting upon a cheaper and more flexible work force, including more part-time, casual and contract work, all harder to unionize than regular full-time workers. The increase in non-standard types of employment is occurring not only in the little-unionized private service sector, but across industrial sectors generally, causing a loss of unionized jobs.

Unionization in the private sector declined from 26 to 21 percent over the 10 years from 1975 to 1985,[8] and if this trend continues it is estimated that the rate of unionization among workers in the private sector will fall as low as 17 percent by the turn of the century.[9] Meanwhile, the union strongholds in the public service have also been threatened. Federal and provincial governments have introduced policies of deregulation, privatization, restraint and cutbacks, resulting in a loss of jobs. Consequently, between 1986 and 1988 the number of unionized government workers declined by 23,000, although there was a recovery of 5,000 members by 1989.[10] New circumstances have been created for the union movement by a combination of industrial restructuring, technological change, economic recession, increased international competition and free trade.

Where are the Unorganized?

The following discussion examines where the unorganized are located and why they do not belong to unions. This analysis is made possible by relatively new data from the Labour Market Activity Survey (LMAS) conducted by Statistics Canada. This material allows a detailed examination of unionization, by sex, by industry and many other factors. The most recent data available for this study was for 1989, and the following information is for that year unless otherwise stated. Appendix II provides a more detailed discussion of the data and how it is used in this chapter.

It should be noted that the historical discussion to this point is drawn from a different source, and therefore differs from the data that follows.

For the sake of simplicity, three industries — agriculture, other primary and construction — have been separated in the tables and generally excluded from the analysis. They each have rather unique patterns of employment, and for the most part function within a different legal framework. It does not seem relevant to explore these particularities in detail, since less than 4 percent of all employed women work in these three industries combined.

Unionization by Industry

In 1989, 38 percent of all paid workers in Canada belonged to unions, and 62 percent did not. Figure 6-1 shows how this large percentage of non-union workers were distributed across different industries.

There is a high degree of variation in rates of unionization from one industry to another. First, the two public sector industries, public administration and education/health services, are the most highly organized, at 70 and 67 percent respectively. These industries have sometimes been referred to as "saturated" as far as union membership is concerned. The implication is that no further advances can be made in these industries, because most of those who can be unionized have been, the remainder being management exclusions or other groups either impossible or difficult to organize.

The other two industries with above average levels of unionization are the more male dominated transportation and manufacturing industries. Transportation is actually a mixed industry including both parapublic sectors such as the Post Office, public hydro companies, Via Rail and the Canadian Broadcasting Corporation, as well as entirely private companies such as telephone companies, gas companies and trucking businesses. In this industry 60 percent of the workers are organized. Manufacturing has a relatively long tradition of unionization, and has often been perceived as the "heart" of union organizing, given the struggles of the 1940s for industrial unionism, and the prominent place of the large auto and steel unions in the labour movement. However, although the rate of unionization is above average at 45 percent, the majority of workers in this industry do not belong to unions.

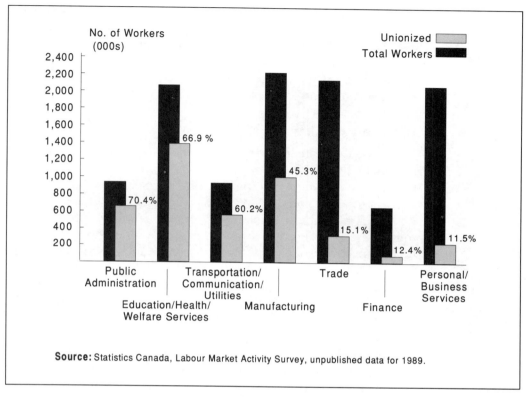

Figure 6-1:

Unionization by Industry, 1989

The three private sector service industries of trade, finance and personal/business services have very low rates of union members, 15 percent or less. In trade, only supermarkets and warehouses have any degree of unionization, while the enormous number of independent and chain retail outlets, as well as department stores, remain predominantly non-union. The finance industry includes insurance and real estate companies as well as the banks. As already mentioned above, recent attempts to organize workers in department stores and banks have met with almost total failure.

Finally, the personal/business services industry has the lowest rate of unionization and is comprised of two quite different parts. The personal services include restaurants, hotels, bars, hairdressers, dry cleaners, cinemas and theatres, clearly employing many unskilled and low paid workers. Some hotels have been successfully organized, and actors and musicians may be unionized, but otherwise unions have had little impact. The business services include employment agencies, security and collection services, but also highly qualified and professional business consultants, such as accountants, architects, computer programmers, scientists, engineers and lawyers. Overall less than 12 percent of workers in the personal/business services belong to unions.

Where are the Unorganized Women?

Among the industries with the lowest rates of organization, trade and personal/business services are of particular concern, since between them they employ 34 percent of all workers, and 40 percent of all women workers. As can be seen in Figure 6-2, over half of all non-union women workers are employed in these two industries. Any serious attempt to organize women workers must focus upon the situation in personal/business services and in trade.

Although the finance industry also has a very low rate of unionization, it also employs a relatively small proportion of the work force (5 percent). Ten percent of unorganized women are employed in this industry, fewer than the number in either education/health services or manufacturing. Despite its very high rate of unionization, education/health services contains 14 percent of all unorganized women workers. Although manufacturing has a long tradition of unionization, more than one out of every ten unorganized women is working in this industry.

Unionization of Women and Men

The overall rate of unionization for all workers is 38 percent, but this does not apply equally to women and men. Only 34 percent of employed women belong to unions, compared to 41 percent of men. How important is this difference? If women were organized at the same rate as men, another 413,700 women would belong to unions. To give some indication of the significance of the issue, this is more women than the total number of unorganized women in the finance industry.

In every industry women are less often unionized than men. By far the largest gap is in manufacturing where 50 percent of men are unionized compared to only 33 percent of women. The next largest gap is in education/health services with 72 percent of men organized compared to 65 percent of women. In the other industries the difference in unionization between men and women varies

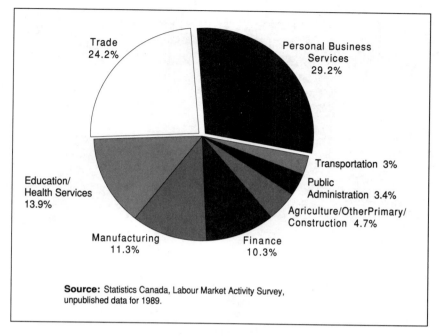

Figure 6-2:

Unorganized Women Workers by Industy, 1989

from two to four percentage points. The reasons for the lower rates of unionization in some industries and among women are explored in the discussion that follows.

Unionization of Racial Minorities

The LMAS asks about ethnic background, making it possible for the first time to examine the unionization of visible minority and native workers. However, included in the survey as visible minorities are blacks, Arabs, Asians and Latin Americans, and also aboriginal people. It is not possible to consider these groups separately because of the sample size, and I therefore refer to these combined groups as racial minorities.

The data reveals that racial minority workers are less likely to be unionized than other workers. In 1989 32 percent of native and visible minority workers belonged to unions, compared to just over 38 percent of non-racial minority workers. The 271,700 racial minority workers who belonged to unions constituted 5.8 percent of all union members.

Table 6-1: Distribution of Paid Workers by Industry, Sex and Racial Minority Status, 1989

	Racial Minority Women	Racial Non-Minority Women	Racial Minority Men	Non-Racial Minority Men
Public Administration	5.3	7.2	4.2	8.5
Education Health/Welfare Services	20.3	26.7	8.5	8.7
Transportation/ Communication/Utilities	5.9	4.5	7.0	10.5
Manufacturing	15.7	10.8	27.3	24.2
Trade	18.5	18.2	14.4	17.0
Finance	9.7	7.5	4.3	3.3
Personal/Business Services	23.3	21.3	27.7	11.9
*Agriculture and Non-Agricultural Primary	1.3	1.9	2.5	5.7
Construction		1.7	4.1	10.1
All Industries	100.0	99.9	100.0	99.9

* Combined due to size of sample.
Source: Statistics Canada, Labour Market Activity Survey, unpublished data for 1989.

When women and men racial minority workers are examined separately, there are significant differences. Racial minority women are more likely to be unionized than racial minority men, 34 percent compared to 30 percent. This is different than the situation among non-racial minority workers, where the women are less often unionized than men, 34 percent compared to 42 percent. This means that white men are most likely to be unionized, followed by both racial minority and white women, with racial minority men the least likely to belong to unions.

Looking at where visible minority and native workers are employed by industry helps to explain this situation. Table 6–1 shows that the patterns of employment for racial minority and white women are quite similar, although white women are some-what more likely to work in education/health services while racial minority women are more likely to work in manufacturing. It is clear, however, that racial minority men have very different patterns of employment than do white men. Most significant is the heavy concentration of racial minority men in personal/business services, the industry with the lowest rate of unionization. Only 12 percent of white men work in this industry compared to 21 percent of white women, 23 percent of racial minority women and 28 percent of racial minority men. However, while both groups of women are also concentrated in the highly unionized education/health services sector, which would increase their rates of unionization, men of either group are far less likely to work in this industry. White men more often than racial minority men work in public administration, transportation, construction and the other primary industries, which all have above average rates of unionization.

One consequence of this situation is that among racial minority workers 138,800 women are unionized, compared to 132,900 men. Therefore women constitute just over half (51 percent) of the total number of racial minority workers that belong to unions. This is different than the situation of women in the union movement as a whole, who are still in the minority.[11]

Why are They Unorganized?

Why are the rates of unionization lower in some industries and among women and racial minorities? The reasons explored below are the size of the workplace, part-time and part-year work, clerical work, employer opposition and labour relations legislation.

Size of Workplace

The size of workplace has a profound impact upon unionization. The policy to certify by individual workplace makes the cost of organizing small workplaces prohibitive, particularly when any form of employer opposition drags out the legal delays and expenses. The close contact between workers and management makes employer resistance harder to withstand and the workers more vulnerable since concealment of union activity is difficult. Moreover a small workplace does not necessarily imply a small employer, since large companies often operate many small work sites, banks and retail chains being obvious examples. In this situation a few workers may face the resistance of a powerful business. Once organized, the chances of losing those members is increased by the low survival rate among small workplaces. Of the

Table 6-2: Rate of Unionization and Distribution of Workers, by Sex and by Size of Firm, 1989

Size of Firm	Rate of Unionization	Distribution of all Workers	Distribution of Women Workers	Distribution of Men Workers
0-19	12.6	27.9	30.8	25.3
20-99	32.1	20.9	20.0	21.7
100-499	50.1	15.6	14.6	16.5
500+	55.9	35.6	34.6	36.5
All firms	37.9	100.0	100.0	100.0

Source: Statistics Canada, Labour Market Activity Survey, unpublished data for 1989.

firms with fewer than 20 workers in 1978, only 50 percent survived until 1986, compared to 67 percent for firms of 20–99 and 72 percent of firms with over 100 workers.[12]

The smallest workplaces with less than 20 workers have a particularly low rate of unionization. Only 13 percent of these workers belong to unions, compared to the overall rate of 38 percent. The proportion of unionization rises in step as the size of firm increases: in firms with 20–99 workers 32 percent belong to unions; in workplaces of 100–499, 50 percent are organized; and finally in the largest firms of over 500 workers, 56 percent of the workers belong to unions (see Table 6-2).

This situation would be of little significance if few workers were employed in small firms, but over one-quarter (28 percent) of all workers are employed in the smallest workplaces of less than twenty workers. Almost half (49 percent) of all workers are employed in workplaces with less than 100 workers. Moreover there is evidence that the number of small workplaces is growing. In Ontario between 1978 and 1986 the percentage of workplaces with fewer than twenty workers increased from 16 to 24 percent of the total number of workplaces.[13]

As one would expect, industries with a low rate of unionization have a large proportion of small workplaces. In personal/business services fully 70 percent of workers are in firms with less than 100 workers, and in trade the figure is 60 percent. The reverse also holds true. Public administration, education/health services, transportation and manufacturing are all industries with relatively high rates of unionization and the majority of the jobs in these industries, between 63 and 71 percent of them, are concentrated in firms with more than 100 workers.

However, there is one exception to this pattern. Very few workers are organized in the finance industry, and yet the majority are employed in large workplaces. Sixty one percent of the workers in this industry are found in workplaces with more than 100 workers, and over half (51 percent) are employed in the largest firms with more than 500 workers. There has been a focus of attention upon the real difficulty of organizing small bank branches,[14] but in fact the majority of workers in finance are employed in large offices.

For women, the overall impact of small workplaces upon their lower rate of unionization is somewhat mixed. There is a significant difference in the proportion of men and women in the smallest workplaces with fewer than twenty workers. In these firms are employed almost 31 percent of women workers, compared to 25 percent of men, and this would have a negative impact on the rate of unionization among women. However, it is also the case that slightly more men than women are employed in workplaces of 20–99 workers, which have rate of unionization somewhat below the average. In the larger firms there are slightly more men than women, but the differences are very small (Table 6-2).

However, there are important industrial variations. In education/health services, manufacturing and personal/business services, women are clearly concentrated into the small workplaces, while men dominate the larger workplaces. This would help to explain the differential rates of unionization for men and women within these three industries. However, the same pattern does not hold in other industries, where the differences by sex in terms of size of firm are either negligible, or inconsistent.

Part-time and Part-year Work

Part-time and temporary workers are harder to organize than full-time permanent employees. Because of their limited and varied working hours, they are harder to identify and contact than full-time workers, and where they have no job security they are more vulnerable to intimidation and retaliation by employers. In Ontario the practice of separating full and part-time workers into separate bargaining units has not helped the process of organizing part-timers, and casual workers are prohibited from joining unions in several laws covering government workers.

The LMAS data allows us to examine the rates of unionization for both part-time and part-year workers. Part-time workers are employed for less than 30 hours per week, while part-year workers are employed full-time but for less than 12 months (see Appendix I for more detailed definitions). While the overall proportion of workers who belong to unions is 38 percent, the rate falls to only 27 percent among part-time workers and to 21 percent among workers employed part-year. For part-time workers who also worked less than 12 months, the rate of unionization drops to only 12 percent.

These non-standard types of employment form a major segment of the labour market. Nineteen percent of all workers are employed part-time and a further 10 percent of workers are employed full-time but only for part of the year. Thus the total proportion of workers in these non-standard types of jobs, and therefore with low rates of unionization, constitutes 30 percent of all workers. Almost one out of every three workers in 1989 was employed part-time or part-year (see Table 6-3).

More women than men are employed in part-time jobs, while men are more likely to work in the part-year occupations.[15] When part-time and part-year are combined, the larger number of part-time workers and the very heavy concentration of women in part-time work produces a concentration of women in these non-standard jobs overall. Thirty-seven percent of women workers hold either part-time or part-year jobs compared to 23 percent of men.

Part-time and part-year employment is found in all industries, although the highest proportions are found in personal/business services, trade and education/health services. Thus, the three industries with the largest numbers of unorganized women workers also have the highest proportions of non-standard jobs. Personal/business services has a remarkable 44 percent of its workers in part-time and part-year work. Trade is not far behind at 37 percent, while even education/health services has almost one-third of its workforce in non-standard jobs (32 percent). The finance industry again proves to be an exception, with a low rate of unionization and also a below average level of non-standard jobs (19 percent).

Table 6-3: Percentage of Workers Employed Part-Time and Part-Year, by Sex, by industry, 1989

Industry	% of Part-time Workers	% of Part-year Workers	% of Part-time and Part-year Workers	% of Women Part-time and Part-year	% of Men Part-time and Part-year
Public Administration	10.1	9.4	19.5	25.0	15.3
Education/ Health/ Welfare Services	28.4	3.9	32.3	37.0	19.7
Transportation/ Communication/ Utilities	12.0	7.2	19.2	25.0	16.9
Manufacturing	5.2	9.2	14.3	21.6	11.4
Trade	27.8	8.8	36.6	47.2	26.5
Finance	14.1	4.9	19.0	21.4	14.1
Personal/ Business Services	30.3	13.4	43.7	47.6	38.2
Non-Agricultural Primary	5.4	23.3	28.7	47.7	25.2
Construction	8.9	27.5	36.4	45.8	35.0
Agriculture	22.3	31.4	53.7	56.8	51.7
All Industries	19.2	10.3	29.5	37.3	22.6

Source: Statistics Canada, Labour Market Activity Survey, unpublished data for 1989.

In all industries women more often hold part-year and part-time jobs combined than do men, so that this would have an impact on women's lower rate of unionization in every sector. In two industries, trade and education/health services, there is a particularly strong concentration of women into non-standard jobs. In trade 47 percent of women are employed part-time or part-year compared to only 27 percent of men, and in education/health services the figure is 37 percent of women compared to 20 percent of men.

Clerical workers

Clerical work cuts right across industrial sectors, since clerical workers are found in all industries.[16] It is important to consider this occupational category in some detail, since almost one-third (32 percent) of all women in paid jobs are clerical workers. By comparison only 7 percent of men are employed in clerical occupations. There are two and one quarter million clerical workers and 80 percent of them are women. If unions are unable or unwilling to organize clerical workers within an industry, even where other workers are unionized, this will have a negative influence upon the rate of unionization among women. The organization of clerical workers has been hampered by the practice of certifying office workers into separate bargaining units from factory workers in the same industry, and likewise placing inside and outside workers into separate units. In some cases, especially small workplaces, clerical workers are considered too close to management and excluded from the bargaining unit.

Thirty-two percent of all clerical workers belong to unions, somewhat lower than the overall rate of unionization of 38 percent. However, there are important industrial variations. The LMAS data allows us to examine the unionization of clerical workers in different industries (see Table 6-4).

There are two industries where there is a very considerable gap between the overall rate of unionization and that for clerical workers. In manufacturing the unionization of clerical workers is much lower than the general rate of unionization; only 26 percent of clerical workers are organized compared to the overall rate of 45 percent. Unions in the manufacturing industry have tended to focus on organizing the industrial rather than the clerical workers. It is perhaps more surprising to find the same situation in education/health services, where unionization of clerical workers is only 48 percent compared to 67 percent for the sector overall. The lack of unionization among clerical workers would help to explain the lower rates of unionization among women than men in these two industries.

In other industries there is little difference. In the three industries where the overall rates of unionization are low (trade, personal/business service, and finance), there is little distinction between clerical and other workers, since the rate of unionization for all is very low. The transportation/communication industry is unusual because clerical jobs are more highly organized than the

Table 6-4: Rate of Unionization of Clerical Workers, by Industry, 1989		
Industry	**Overall Rate of Unionization**	**Rate of Unionization of Clerical Workers**
Public Administration	70.4	72.0
Education/ Health/ Welfare Services	66.9	47.9
Transportation/ Communication/ Utilities	60.2	68.5
Manufacturing	45.3	26.2
Trade	15.2	18.8
Finance	12.4	14.2
Personal/ Business Services	11.5	11.7
Non-Agricultural Primary	34.8	14.6
Construction	34.3	10.3
Agriculture	10.6	2.0
All Industries	37.9	31.8

Source: Statistics Canada, Labour Market Activity Survey, unpublished data for 1989.

industry in general (69 percent compared to 60 percent). This is probably due to the high rate of unionization among communication workers, particularly postal workers, who are included in this data as clerical workers. In public administration unionization of clerical workers is also slightly higher than that of other workers, attributable to the high level of unionization among clerical workers employed by the federal and provincial governments.

Employer Opposition

Unionization normally entails more leverage for workers in obtaining improved pay and conditions of work, more control and more protection in the workplace. Employers therefore have every reason to oppose organizing campaigns, particularly in resisting the entrance of unions into industrial sectors that are generally non-union. In the 1930s and 1940s employers in manufacturing

Bank Violations of Canadian Labour Law

During the attempts to unionize bank workers in the late 1970s, before the Canada Labour Relations Board, banks were found to be in violation of the law on all the following points:

- firing staff for union activities
- transferring workers involved in a union to a different branch
- denying promotion to an employee due to union activity
- hiring additional workers at a branch in order to undermine the majority of union members required to form a union

- holding individual and group meetings during working hours ("captive audience" meetings) to apply pressure to workers to prevent them from unionizing
- requiring workers at unionized branches to make up cash shortages at the end of the day out of their own pay, while this was not required at non-union branches
- withholding regular annual pay increases only from unionized branches.

Source: Julie White, *Women and Unions* (Ottawa: Canadian Advisory Council on the Status of Women, 1980, p.45.

and mines staunchly refused to recognize industrial unions, and the resulting disruptions ultimately produced legislation to regulate labour relations. More recently, the successful opposition of employers in the finance and trade industries has been well-documented.[17]

Employer opposition is often most effective in small workplaces where workers are placed in a close relationship to management and it is therefore more difficult both to conceal union involvement and to resist hostility and intimidation. Likewise part-time and part-year workers are particularly vulnerable to employer resistance and retaliation where they do not have any security of employment. These factors may combine to create an effective barrier to organizing efforts.

There is a clear difference in regard to employer opposition between the private and public sectors. In the public sector the antagonism has been less virulent, in part because governments at all levels are more constrained in being seen to obey the law. While many restrictions are placed upon the rights of public sector workers, basic recognition has been far easier to obtain in the public sector than in many private sector industries. In 1985, while the rate of unionization was only 21 percent in the private sector, in the public sector 66 percent of all workers belonged to unions.[18]

In the current economic context, employers are stressing the necessity of controlling labour costs to meet international competition, and are moving to increase their use of various forms of cheap labour, including women, racial minorities and immigrants, part-time and casual workers. Employers express strong opposition to any attempts to improve the pay and conditions of the lowest paid workers, whether by unionization or by legislation. For example, in Ontario there was intense resistance to equal pay legislation in the private sector and forceful lobbying to weaken the impact of the law.[19] More recently, employer reaction to suggested changes in Ontario labour relations legislation have been remarkably virulent. (See discussion below.)

However, this opposition has been overcome in other countries where a much larger proportion of the work force is unionized, including in industries such as banking and the retail trade. In their resistance to unionization, employers in Canada have been aided and abetted by labour relations legislation.

Legislation

Theoretically, of course, none of the factors outlined above should affect the fundamental right of workers to join a union. Women, racial minorities, part-time and part-year workers and those employed in small workplaces are supposedly guaranteed by law the same right to join a union as any other workers. Why has the legislation failed to enable these workers to organize?

In Canada, labour relations are subject to extensive legislation. A group of workers may not simply contact a union, become members and obtain representation, as is possible in other countries. A union applies to the Labour Relations Board, established to administer the law, for certification, that is the legal right to represent a particular group of workers. In order to be certified, the union must prove that the majority of the workers within a workplace wish to join. It is the Board that determines the appropriate bargaining unit, that is who is eligible to join the union, and also whether the union has sufficient support to be certified to represent that group of workers. To this end the Board considers the number of signed union cards, examines evidence presented at hearings, and may order a vote.

Many criticisms of this system have been raised in recent years, as the difficulty of organizing in the expanding private service sector has become increasingly apparent. While the legislation varies from one jurisdiction to another, many of the basic features are the same and pose the same problems.

Certain workers are denied the right to unionize, those excluded varying from one jurisdiction to another. Three provinces exclude domestic workers, and four exclude professionals, such as doctors, dentists, lawyers and architects. Those who perform the management functions of hiring and firing are generally excluded, because of the likely conflict of interest. However, in all but four jurisdictions this restriction prohibits all supervisory workers from belonging to unions, even though they have no ultimate control over hiring or firing. Likewise, office staff, particularly secretaries, are considered to have a close relationship to management and are regularly excluded from the bargaining unit if they are considered to do work related to labour relations determined to be confidential to management. In several jurisdictions civil service legislation denies casual workers the right to unionize. In some cases the Labour Relations Boards practise exclusionary policies. The Ontario Board separates full and part-time workers into different bargaining units at the request of the employer or the union, weakening both the chances of organizing and the bargaining strength of part-time workers.[20]

During an organizing drive the union must rely upon the workers for information on the number of workers employed and how to contact them. Where the workers have little communication among each other, where part-time, casual and call-in workers are used, or where turnover is high, the union may have real difficulty obtaining accurate information. This is crucial at the certification hearing where the union needs a certain percentage of workers signed up for immediate certification, or to obtain a vote. The union tries to organize, not knowing the exact size of the bargaining unit or what a majority will require. Unions are not permitted access to the workplace to obtain information or contact workers, union materials cannot be distributed at work, and no discussions of the union drive may take place during working hours. If workers are to be able to exercise their right to unionize, it has been proposed that unions should be supplied with a list of workers' names and addresses, and should be able to organize at the workplace in non-work areas such as cafeterias and parking lots.

Once an application for certification is filed, the employer is notified and therefore aware of the organizing campaign. The period between filing the application and the Board's hearing of the case can be one of open warfare between the union and the employer. The reason is that the workers' intentions are not accepted as of the date of application, but any "changes of heart" may be taken into account until the final certification hearing. For employers opposed to unions, this is an invitation to use this time period to influence the workers' decision. The employer is not prohibited from involvement in the union campaign, although it is illegal to coerce or intimidate workers. During the campaign to organize the Eaton Centre in Toronto in the 1980s, an employer-supported group called Stop the Union Now was allowed to hand out materials in the workplace and the Board upheld the employer's right to send letters on the subject to every worker. Meanwhile, union organizers attempting to distribute materials at the entrances to the store were evicted from the shopping mall.[21] It is extremely difficult to prove where expressing an opinion ends and intimidation begins, and critics have called for a system in which the employer would remain silent during a unionization campaign.

Where the employer oversteps the line and is found to have interfered in the workers' right to unionize, the penalties are mild to non-existent. In one unfair labour practice complaint involving a bank, the union requested from the Board an order to force the bank to stop captive audience meetings, end worker interrogations and cease disseminating anti-union literature, plus a public apology, damages and immediate certification. The bank was found to be in violation of the law, but was required only to send to every worker the Board's decision to that effect — 41 pages of legal argument. The union obtained no remedy and the bank received no punishment.[22] In another case La Banque Nationale closed a branch due to a unionization drive and was ordered to pay $144,000 into a trust fund for organizing, and send a letter to all workers stating its support of collective bargaining. The bank appealed to the Supreme Court, where the penalties were described as "extreme" and "totalitarian," and overturned.[23] Huge fines and jail terms have been imposed upon unionists found to be on strike illegally, while employers who violate workers' right to unionize face no deterrent.

In virtually every unionization drive that encounters employer opposition, a major problem has been delays in obtaining Board decisions. Delays work to the advantage of the employer, providing more time for anti-union activity, and raising doubt about the union's effectiveness. If a worker is fired for union activity and not reinstated by the Board until months later, other workers are

effectively intimidated and the organizing campaign is under-
mined, if not killed outright. In Ontario the Board takes an average
of six months to reach a decision on a complaint of unfair dismissal
for union activity.[24] In workplaces with a high turnover, workers
who have joined the union may leave and then more workers must
be signed up to ensure a majority. In Quebec the Confédération
des syndicats nationaux has experienced many cases of not
months, but years, of delays as decisions are appealed and
appealed again to higher courts. Meanwhile the employers are
provided with the opportunity to establish company unions, rather
than those that truly represent the workers' interests.[25]

The legal contortions, technicalities and delays are very costly
for unions. Since every workplace has to be separately certified,
the same process must be repeated whether there are 5 or 500
workers involved. The financial burden of fighting the banks was
one of the primary reasons for the demise of the Service and Office
Workers Union of Canada (SORWUC), a small feminist union in
B.C. that was successful for a period in organizing a number of
bank branches.[26] It is a difficult issue for unions, which are
accountable for spending their members' dues and have to determine whether the costs involved in organizing small workplaces
are defensible, given the results.

The organizing process is not completed when certification is
obtained, because negotiating the first contract presents another
opportunity for employers to resist unionization. If the union is
unable to improve working conditions through bargaining, support
for the union may be lost. Employers therefore continue their
tactics of delay and obstruction into the negotiation procedure.
One common strategy has been to insist upon bargaining for every
unit separately. In Vancouver, the Banks of Nova Scotia, Montreal
and Commerce all insisted on separate negotiations for every
certified branch.[27] Eaton's refused the union's request to bargain
for all the certified units together, refusing even to negotiate jointly
for full and part-time workers in the same store. At the same time
the process was carried on so slowly that only four bargaining
sessions were held in three months. Although the union complained of bad faith bargaining, this was not upheld by the Board.[28]
These tactics isolate and weaken the workers, lengthen the negotiation process, and exhaust union resources.

In the case of Eaton's the situation was pushed to a strike which
lasted for six months. The impact of the strike was restricted,

because the stores were able to hire replacement workers, given that the basic job is relatively unskilled. Also, picketing was not allowed at store entrances inside shopping malls, but only at the entrances to the malls or the parking lots. The workers were unable to close the stores and although a boycott was organized, its effect was limited. Finally, the workers signed a contract because they reached the six month limit, after which they were not guaranteed of their jobs at the end of the strike. The contract gave only minimal improvements and all of the Eaton's bargaining units later decertified.[29]

The fundamental problem with negotiating a first contract is that the unit required to obtain certification is not necessarily the most effective for bargaining. Often it is easier to organize smaller units of a large company individually. For example, in Nova Scotia, a 1979 decision that the Michelin company had to be unionized on a regional basis effectively squashed any chance of organizing the geographically scattered company.[30] In the case of the banks, the Board decision to organize branch by branch was hailed as a victory. However, negotiating branch by branch proved to be a nightmare. Unions can request joint negotiations for a number of bargaining units, but the employer can refuse, and under the law the issue must not be pressed to a strike.

One attempt to resolve this situation has been the introduction of first contract arbitration. This means that the union can apply to have a first contract imposed, where it seems impossible to obtain a collective agreement through bargaining. This provision exists in five jurisdictions, and the results have been mixed. In some cases it has been difficult to actually obtain first contract arbitration, because in some jurisdictions the union must prove that the employer has bargained in bad faith, and this can be extremely difficult. Sometimes the imposed contract is weak, reducing both faith in the bargaining process and support for the union. Most important, in a small bargaining unit that did not have the power to negotiate a first contract, nothing has changed when the time comes to negotiate a second contract. Consequently, decertifications still occur in cases where a first contract has been imposed, although some do succeed in negotiating a second contract.[31]

In Ontario the introduction of first contract arbitration in 1986 had two effects. Knowing that a contract could be imposed, employers are more likely to negotiate in good faith with a certified union and reach an agreement.[32] However, since the employer's opportunity to resist unionization over a first contract was reduced, the battle around certification intensified. Immediately following the introduction of first contract arbitration, challenges to certifications increased and employers turned to anti-union petitions to convince the Board that workers do not want to organize.[33] Such petitions are signed by workers after the certification application, and often by workers who have also signed union cards, because the employer will know who has and has not signed the petition. The petition throws doubt upon the validity of the signed union cards, delays the certification, gives the employer time to mount further opposition, and can cause a vote to be held even where a majority of workers signed union cards at the point of application.

For all these barriers to unionization, various corrective measures have been proposed, including extending the right to unionize to those now excluded, allowing unions access to workplaces and information for the purpose of organizing, prohibiting employer involvement of any kind, accelerating the Labour Board process with time limits, and strengthening first contract arbitration. While such changes would undoubtedly improve the chances of unionization campaigns, it has also been argued that even these improvements would not resolve the basic problem of organizing under the current system, especially in small workplaces.

The fundamental issue is that the legislation is based upon bargaining at the level of the individual workplace. At a large factory or plant the workers may carry some bargaining power, but in workplaces with 5 or 10 or 20 workers, there is insufficient strength vis à vis the employer to insist upon real negotiations. The inequality is too great to achieve a collective bargaining relationship. Only sectoral or regional bargaining, combining significant groups of small workplaces, could wield the necessary leverage to ensure serious bargaining, and there is no stable mechanism for this under the law. Unions cannot decide to bargain for larger groups of workers, unless the employer gives consent, which is not forthcoming in any situation advantageous to the unions. Under current labour relations legislation, unions do not determine their own bargaining structure, but are subject to the decisions of the Boards with regard to the size and type of bargaining units.

John O'Grady, former Research Director with the Ontario Federation of Labour, has argued that Canada's collective bargaining system, modelled on the Wagner Act in the United States, was never

In 1991 Local 502 of the United Food Commercial Workers Union successfully organized 250 workers at this Bay store in Anjou and has since organized a second Bay store in Rosemere, both in the Montreal area. The union also represents workers at Bay stores in Victoria, B.C. and Marathon, Ontario, although the majority of Bay workers across the country remain unorganized.

Courtesy of the United Food Commercial Workers Union.

meant to "have much currency outside of the large industrial employers."[34] It was introduced in response to industrial unrest in the manufacturing and resource sectors, and has worked reasonably well in large workplaces, factories, plants and mines, but was never designed for small workplaces. O'Grady concludes: "The unavoidable fact is that the Wagner Act model simply does not work in small establishments."[35]

As Judy Fudge has argued, the legislation is also based upon a gendered version of the labour force.[36] Labour relations laws were designed for blue collar men, employed full-time in large plants and factories. The new reality of part-time and women workers, employed in small workplaces in the service industries was never part of the picture. It has left many women outside of the collective bargaining process, and it has become obsolete given the changing structure of the labour force.

If these arguments are accepted then it is not sufficient to improve the working of the current legislation, because it needs to be more fundamentally changed. There has to be a system that includes broader based bargaining of some kind, allowing negotiations to take place on a much more centralized basis, instead of by individual workplace. There are examples of voluntary agreements to bargain more broadly, but they can be and have been changed where employers decide against them. Unions have no capacity to force employers to bargain on a broader basis.

The exception to this situation is in Quebec, where a union can request that the Minister of Labour issue a decree to extend a collective agreement to cover other, non-unionized workers performing the same type of work. This decree system, as it is commonly called, applies mainly to workers in small workplaces, including garages, hairdressers, the clothing industry, some services such as security guards and some other small industries like furniture making. In 1991, 140,000 workers were covered by decrees, less than 5 percent of employed workers in Quebec.[37] It is not clear that this system has a positive impact upon rates of unionization. Both unions and women's organizations in Quebec have argued for years that it is necessary to permit multi-employer bargaining units and negotiations in Quebec.[38] This would, for example, allow all the workers in a shopping centre, or employed in businesses located on the same street, or in the same industrial park, to unionize and to negotiate jointly with a council to represent the different employers. The Beaudry Commission in that province reviewed the impact of labour relations law in the private sector and recommended this type of legislative change, but no action has been taken.

Union Responses

It was not only the legislation of the 1940s that was geared to organizing male full-time industrial workers, but also the union movement itself. While several unions have organized office and service workers in the private sector, the labour movement has not begun to make organizing in these areas a priority until very recently. In manufacturing, unions organized the plant workers without considering the office workers employed by the same company. Unions did not unambiguously welcome women into the union movement and have not always been prepared to organize part-time workers.

Unions geared to organizing among industrial workers are not necessarily attuned to the needs and attitudes of other workers. Service workers, for example, may have concerns about union involvement because of the impact of possible strike situations upon clients of the service. Office workers in small workplaces may have a very different relationship to management than factory workers in a large plant. The needs of part-time workers may differ sometimes from those of full-time workers, and may even conflict in certain circumstances. Women may not feel at their most comfortable being approached by male organizers. New immigrants may require more detailed explanations of how the system works, and Canadians speaking other first languages than English or French may require translations. The specific concerns of the workers need to be taken into account, and unions geared to white, full-time, male, industrial workers may not be aware of the issues.

Organizing drives are costly, especially given that those most in need of unionization are often low paid, precarious workers in small workplaces. In some cases the dues received would not cover the cost of servicing the local, let alone organizing in the first place. As a result some unions have informal policies not to organize the smallest workplaces, or to assess the situation according to the financial strength of the union. While decisions have to be made about the valid expenditure of members dues, there may also need to be some redistribution of funds within the union movement towards workers with lower pay, who cannot afford to organize, and need to be subsidized.

Unions themselves have been moulded by the legislation, and reflect in their own structures and constitutions the fragmentation inherent in the legal system. Local autonomy is protected and defended. Bargaining on a regional or national basis is exceptional, and may be opposed by union locals concerned to retain control as much as by employers. Union constitutions, structures, staff and legal experts are all in place to deal with the legislation as it stands. Fundamental changes in the law would mean fundamental changes for many unions, and entrenched structures in any organization are usually resistant to change.

As Judy Fudge has pointed out, under the current system, the Boards mediate jurisdictional rivalries between unions by determining which union shall represent a specific group of workers.[39] Jurisdictional lines have always been somewhat hazy, but this is particularly true in industries that are largely unorganized, where unions with no traditional relationship are now trying to organize. Broader based bargaining raises the problem of which unions will bargain for which workers and the possibility that unions will have to determine this among themselves. How this would be achieved is unclear, and could potentially be quite destructive if decisions were hard to reach. In the attempts to organize the banks, the scramble among unions, the rivalries and the inability to mount a co-ordinated campaign did not advance the cause.[40]

Unions that have not lost members thus far in the restructuring process, or that have been able to keep up their member numbers and dues base through mergers rather than new organizing, do not yet face an imperative need to confront these realities. Given the many challenges facing unions on a daily basis, such as wages, job security and new technology, there are many other calls upon their time and resources, which appear more immediate and pressing than the long haul of lobbying for fundamental legislative change.

However, there are also pressures for change. The decrease in the number of union members that occurred in the early 1980s, and the failure of a number of unions to recoup their losses, sent shock waves through the union movement. The warning has been emphasized by the example of the United States immediately to the south, where the rate of unionization has been falling drastically, so that only 15 percent of workers in that country belong to unions. There has been continual speculation about whether Canadian unions will follow in the same disastrous direction.[41] As one review of the situation concluded:

> Unless unions succeed in organizing workers in trade, finance and services, and take steps to make unionization more attractive to women, youth and professionals, the future vitality of the union movement may be at stake.[42]

As a result, unions have a renewed concern with organizing the unorganized, and with responding to the changing nature of the labour force. A 1988 study found this issue to be the foremost concern of union leaders.[43]

Both labour centrals and individual unions have re-emphasized the importance of organizing, and several conventions have passed resolutions to make this issue a priority. Unions have held seminars and workshops to discuss organizing strategies, and have expanded their efforts to unionize into new areas. The United Steelworkers has moved beyond workers in mining and manufacturing to organize hotels and restaurants, security guards, taxi drivers and banks, and in 1990 held a training session on organizing exclusively for women in order to encourage their involvement. The Canadian Auto Workers has moved into airlines, fishing and railways. In some cases unions are following their members as their work is contracted out and privatized. The Public Service Alliance is to produce a policy paper to propose areas where the union could organize, in order to "renew efforts to spread collective bargaining rights to workers who are moved out of federal jurisdiction as a result of contracting out, privatization and devolution."[44] Unions have also been organizing more part-time workers.[45]

Some parts of the union movement are also reviewing their own structures with a view to necessary changes. The Canadian Labour Congress established a task force to make recommendations for structural changes, and adopted those recommendations at its 1992 Convention. The National Union of Provincial Government Employees produced a document recognizing the need to make unions more relevant, including re-evaluation of traditional approaches to collective bargaining and an examination of union structures. It called for a new style of social unionism, involving more members, working with coalitions and putting social and environmental issues into the collective bargaining process. It also has a committee on its structure to report in 1992. The Canadian Union of Public Employees produced a ten point policy paper that suggests co-ordination of collective bargaining with other unions, the development of larger locals through mergers and transfers, plus an examination of its own structure. The United Food and Commercial Workers has developed a new structure in recent years that provides more Canadian autonomy, including a Canadian director and convention. It has therefore been able to establish a national women's committee. As much of this book has discussed, unions are accommodating to the needs of women workers in different ways.

The union movement has also developed a more social approach to its work over the last ten years, moving beyond the task of collective bargaining to participate in a range of issues and struggles.[46] This began through contact with the women's movement and the development of coalitions on day care and equal pay, but has broadened to include a wide variety of contacts and issues. Through the Action Canada Network and numerous specific coalitions, unions are working with many different organizations, including groups concerned with the environment, peace, social services, rural issues, and the rights of racial minorities, persons with disabilities, and gays and lesbians. The union movement is now adding its voice in support of many issues beyond traditional workplace problems. This has meant a new understanding of union members as whole people, affected not only by their workplace lives. It has also meant reaching out to people beyond the narrow limits of representing only union members, which is both necessary in itself and also increases the possibility of organizing other groups of workers.

The problems have been recognized and the union movement is responding. Whether these efforts will prove sufficient to the task ahead remains to be seen. There follows three examples of responses by the union movement to the need to organize, to illustrate some of the problems outlined above and bring to life the meaning of the various barriers discussed. The first example describes the attempts being made by two unions to deal with the increasing use of homework; the second considers a difficult campaign to organize cleaners; and the third looks at the push towards a new legal framework for labour relations in Ontario.

Organizing Homeworkers: The International Ladies Garment Workers Union and the Public Service Alliance of Canada

Only 20 percent of workers in the clothing industry are unionized today, compared to almost 80 percent 30 years ago.[47] One of the reasons for this decline has been the increased use of homeworkers, women workers who collect their sewing from the employer and work at home. The exploitation of these workers is extreme, including rates of pay often well below the minimum wage, the absence of benefits or health and safety protection, and very long hours of work.[48] They are outside of the scope of unionization because they work alone and labour relations laws specify that there must be more than one worker in order to form a union. Employment standards legislation is not enforced, because the isolation and invisibility of these workers means that they have neither the information nor the power to lay complaints. Employers of homeworkers are supposed to register the names and addresses of these workers, but in Ontario only seventy homeworkers are registered for the whole province, while a conservative estimate is that 3,000 are employed in Toronto alone.

The International Ladies Garment Workers Union (ILGWU) has seen a dramatic decline in its membership, due in part to the increasing number of homeworkers. The union was moved to action both by the knowledge that homeworkers undercut the wages of union members, and the more social view that home-workers are an increasing segment of the work force and must receive some protection. With financial support from the Ontario government, the union carried out a study of homeworkers in Toronto. The results were worse than the union expected, with women earning as little as $1 and $2 an hour. The women involved in homework in Toronto are primarily Chinese and Vietnamese, as well as some Portuguese.

The union felt that some action had to be taken and, given a New Democratic Party government in the province, there was the possibility of legislative reform. A coalition was established including the ILGWU, the Workers' Information and Action Centre, the Parkdale Community Legal Clinic, the National Action Committee on the Status of Women, the Ontario Coalition for Better Child Care, and the Metro Toronto Labour Council. This Coalition for Fair Wages and Working Conditions for Homeworkers held a press conference in November 1991 to release the results of the union's study. They have lobbied the Minister of Labour for legislative reform and continued to try to keep the issue before the public.

Meanwhile the union decided that something more direct needed to be done for homeworkers, and early in 1992 Local 12 came into existence, a local for homeworkers. In the United States the union has an associate member structure, developed primarily for organizing activists who cannot formally belong to the union, because their workplaces are not certified. The union determined that this structure could be adapted to enable homeworkers to become associate members. It has the usual local structure, but no collective agreement. The usual union dues are $16 a month, while these associate members pay $12 a year.

What can the union offer to these women, who are not actual union members and do not have a contract? As associate members they receive $1,000 free life insurance, and the union is looking at health and drug benefits that are part of associate membership in the United States, but must be adapted for Canada. A benefit specialist has been hired to design a plan for individual members. Individuals would have to pay a fee for participation, but would benefit from the union's existing benefit fund. It is impossible for

Experiences Sewing at Home

- The usual rate is $1 to $1.50 for each completed dress. It was higher when I started with this firm last year, but they reduced the rate after a few months. I think they pay us half what they pay the workers in the factory. And in the factory, they get pay increases … We get no benefits. I pay the income tax, but I get no benefits. I asked the employer to pay the Canada Pension Plan. He said: "I don't want to be bothered with that, it's your problem." Sometimes when I am working by myself I think about the fact that I am getting older and older, and that when I get old, I will have no pension.

- The most difficult fabrics are the velours. The nap comes off, and gets all over everything in the house, and the air is filled with it. The dust from this fabric is very fine — the consistency of flour. If I am sewing with blue velour fabric, my nose begins to run blue. My doctor says it's no good for me to sew this material even though I am taking allergy shots, but I need the money. Now I usually tie a handkerchief mask over my nose and mouth when I am sewing with velours.

- My cousin's children were still very young — two and four. Her doctor finally ordered her to stop sewing at home because it was causing too much stress for her, and her stomach suffered. She would try to do everything. She would jump up from the machine, feed the baby, quick sew in a zipper, stir the pot on the stove, rush back to her machine, rush back to change the baby and keep on sewing. She would eat her own sandwich while she kept sewing. The doctor told her she would get an ulcer if she kept it up. He said that if you work in a factory you only do one thing at a time — and you take time *off* to eat your lunch.

- Sometimes I just have him sitting up on the sewing machine while I work. Sometimes, though, he sits there saying "No sew." He doesn't want me to do anything, he just wants some attention.

- Of course when my children are older I would like to work outside my home. It is not healthy to stay inside and never breathe fresh air. I wake up and begin sewing by 7 am. I stay inside the house all day. I don't see other people and don't make any friends.

Laura C. Johnson and Robert E. Johnson, *The Seam Allowance: Industrial Home Sewing in Canada*, (Toronto: Women's Educational Press, 1982) pp. 61–62, 78, 80, 90–91.

individual workers to obtain certain benefits because of the expense. Sickness benefits are being examined, since these workers are not covered by unemployment insurance and receive nothing when they are ill. Whereas the union would normally negotiate such a plan with the employer, in this case it would be entirely run by the union. The worker would present the medical certificate to the union and receive a flat rate, perhaps $150 per week, not a large amount but better than nothing.

Meanwhile, the Ontario region of the union received an additional $20,000 from the union's headquarters to hire someone to work on the homeworkers campaign. In March 1992 a woman was hired who is of Chinese descent and speaks both Chinese and Vietnamese. She is available to the members of Local 12 for advice on any problem that might arise, such as a problem with an employer, how to apply for a day care subsidy, or help to write a letter. Since the union's provincial office is close to the Chinese community, women have begun to come to the office seeking help from their union representative. The union feels it may be appropriate to consider running educational seminars on income tax and possibly immigration, once it is established what topics would be most useful.

The hardest part of this new initiative is to make contact with the workers. The union started with the women who were interviewed for the study, who formed the founding members of Local 12. Word of mouth is important. Waiting outside clothing factories to see who comes to drop and collect large bundles of clothing, sometimes produces results. The union also found that many homeworkers have very little opportunity to go out with their children, and has therefore organized two bus trips for homeworkers and their families to a sugar bush and to the Niagara Blossom Festival. The cost is very low, with an even lower price for Local 12 members, and the trips are advertised in the Chinese newspapers. These have been very popular, with 80 people filling two buses for the second trip. The family outings have a value in themselves, but also allow the union organizer to meet more homeworkers and inform them about Local 12.

The Coalition continues to meet and has held sessions with Local 12 to consider what needs to be done. One idea being floated is the need to educate about the negative role played by employer such as the Hudson's Bay Company in using and exploiting homeworkers, possibly a campaign around a "clean clothes code,"

and what it would mean to treat clothing workers with more justice.
There are also plans for a weekend retreat in the summer of 1992
for members Local 12, executive members and stewards from other
locals of the union and Coalition members outside of the union to
examine the situation, and consider in depth what other steps need
to be taken. For some there is still the need to break through the
traditional opinion that organizing homework condones it, and that
it should just be made illegal. The problem with this approach is
that prohibiting homework does not lead to its demise, but only
makes the workers involved even less visible and more easily
intimidated and subject to exploitation.

The ILGWU recognizes that the homeworkers it is organizing
cannot pay for the union's services, either now or in the future.
This is especially difficult in a union where the majority of the
workers are low paid, and therefore cannot subsidize the homeworkers. Apart from the $20,000 received from U.S. head office,
the union's solution has been to fund raise. The Coalition has
obtained a grant from the Ontario government to support its
activities. A fund raising package has been prepared and sent to
other unions and organizations, and donations have begun to
arrive. It is understood that the fund raising will have to continue.
"This is not a money-making project, it never can be."[49]

As of the fall of 1992, Local 12 had 35 members. Although it is
a small group, there are two good reasons for examining this
organizing attempt. First, it is an example of a union attempting to
organize under the most difficult circumstances, faced with legal
and technical and cultural barriers, using new methods and
approaches. Second, homeworkers are not only going to expand
in numbers and into other industrial sectors, they also represent
the new style of worker, that is workers who are flexible, who
create no overhead costs, who require no obligation from the
employer in terms of hours or benefits or even a workplace, who
are cheap even by comparison with Mexican workers, who are
women, recent immigrants and visible minorities. Homeworkers
are the ultimate fulfilment of the newly emphasized "cheap and
flexible" business philosophy of the 1990s. In the future there will
be more homeworkers, but there will also be increased pressure
upon other workers to conform to the same employer demands.

A recent example of such trends is the federal government's
interest in offering homework to its workers. A management

working group was established in 1990 to examine the implications and in March 1992 the Treasury Board published "Working at Home: A Guide to Implementation." This document outlines how to establish homeworking arrangements and, for interested workers, the government is prepared to provide computers, modems and electronic mail facilities for employment at home. Many jobs are considered appropriate for potential homeworking, including "computer programming and analysis, word processing, translating, proofreading, editing, writing, telephoning, accounting, financial analysis and book-keeping."[50] Meanwhile, even before the Guide appeared, some government departments had already introduced homework. Consumer and Corporate Affairs, for example, has advertised the success of their arrangement for a dozen workers now employed in their own homes.[51] Homeworking for federal government workers is not just an abstract idea for the future; Treasury Board is attempting to regulate a practice already underway.

The union representing federal government workers is the Public Service Alliance of Canada (PSAC). Having discovered an enormous expenditure of federal government money on lap-top computers, the union has undertaken its own study of homework, and is in the process of surveying 320 locals.[52] A weekend course in May 1992 was held with people from selected locals, both to gather information and to discuss the impact of homeworking,

Homeworkers from Toronto travelled with friends and relatives to Niagara Falls for a social outing organized by the ILGWU, 1992.

Courtesy of the International Ladies Garment Workers Union.

sometimes called teleworking in this context. The union is also participating in talks with management concerning the implementation and regulation of homework.

The Treasury Board maintains that homework will be voluntary, that homeworkers will continue to be employees of the government and covered by the collective agreement, and that it offers a positive option for workers wanting to combine home and work life in a more flexible manner. The main advantage for the employer is higher productivity, the result of reduced absenteeism and the elimination of breaks, interruptions, and socializing. There is also the possibility of reducing office space and the consequent overhead costs. One enthusiastic supervisor has concluded: "We're balancing babies and briefcases and we're increasing production."[53]

The union is concerned that this rosy picture may not tell the whole truth about working at home. It is suspected that homework will have a differential effect upon men than women. Men will be professional and technical employees, working independently at high salaries and supplied with lap-top computers for greater efficiency and autonomy. Women will be lower paid clerical workers, their productivity monitored by the computer, working simultaneously at paid employment and domestic labour, their career advancement blocked by their isolation and invisibility. A recent study of a small number of women doing clerical work at home in Toronto, revealed that their incomes were lower than when they were employed outside the home, their benefits were reduced, they took on increased responsibility for child care and housework, and their autonomy was limited both by the deadlines and fluctuations of their paid work, and by the schedules and needs of their families.[54] Working at home allowed more flexibility regarding when the work was done, and this was appreciated by the women involved, but it did not reduce the amount of work nor eliminate the conflict between paid work and domestic work.

The Treasury Board document refers to "the misconception that working at home is a primarily a woman's issue, rather than one which is intended to be gender-neutral," and states that homework should not be regarded as a substitute for child care.[55] However, it also notes that "the majority of employees who choose to work at home are young parents,"[56] undoubtedly predominantly mothers. If homework is to be a real choice, then other options have to make it possible for women to balance family and paid work while remaining in their offices. This would entail sharing domestic work, subsidized child care arrangements, extended paid parental leave and more paid leave for family responsibilities, none of which are generally available at this point. Without these alternatives, homework looks suspiciously like an easy option for employers rather than for women workers.

As well as the possible negative impact upon women, there is also the impact upon the union. The PSAC is concerned that homework might reduce a collective orientation fostered at the workplace with a more individualistic approach that would weaken interest in the union and collective action. Homeworkers would be more difficult to contact, and perhaps less available for meetings and union events. It is also not clear what would happen to such employees in a strike situation.

Some apprehensions are yet more fundamental. If, as the Treasury Board has suggested, one potential advantage of homework is reduced office space, how could homeworkers terminate the arrangement and return to their offices at any time, which is also part of management's outline of options. The Treasury Board maintains that the usual employee relationship, complete with collective agreement, would be maintained with no loss of pay or benefits for government workers employed in their own homes. However, the union is concerned that it would be a short step from employees working at home to individual contracts, especially in this period of staff layoffs and increased use of casual workers. Workers on individual contracts become self-employed and may face the same problems as the garment workers discussed above, who cannot be unionized and receive little other protection.

With this prospect in mind, the ILGWU, the PSAC and the Homeworkers' Coalition are planning a joint conference in the fall of 1992 to examine the role of homework, both old and new, and to consider how unions should respond. Despite the problems, homework meets certain short term needs for women, who therefore find it desirable. Thus, while the PSAC is very cautious about the government's proposals, it may be difficult to convince union members of the negative potential. The labour movement in general may learn from the efforts of these unions, because garment and government workers are not alone. IBM has thirty employees in Ottawa working at home with a claimed productivity jump of 20 percent, as well as an estimated saving of $5.7 million over seven years from the reduction of downtown office space. The Bank of Montreal started a homework project in Toronto with

25 workers in early 1991, to be expanded to 500 workers within two years.[57] If homework is the "big wave" of the future, as some anticipate, then it is already rolling in.

Organizing Cleaners: The Canadian Union of Postal Workers

Cleaners are low paid, insecure service workers, and many are women, recent immigrants and people of different ethnic groups. The pay, conditions and insecurity are at their worst when the work is contracted out. This means that office and factory employers do not hire their own cleaners, but pay a private contractor to keep the physical space clean. Cleaning companies tender a bid for the work, sign a contract and provide the staff and materials. The workers are therefore employed by the cleaning company, rather than by the same employer as other workers at their workplace. At best they are vulnerable to low rates of pay and poor conditions because of the tendering and bidding process. At worst they risk losing their jobs each time the cleaning contract is renewed, because a new company with its own workers may bid and obtain the contract. If a business is sold the workers and their union have "successor rights," meaning that the new owner must continue to respect the prior agreement, but this does not apply to changes of contract.

A study of two contract cleaning situations found that because the work is regarded as entirely unskilled, new workers often receive no training or even information. They work with hazardous materials, including chemical solvents and strong soaps, but are not provided with rubber gloves for protection. Equipment that is broken or inadequate, including heavy carts, is not replaced and no health and safety information is provided.

> The daily grind of bending and lifting, stooping and picking up garbage, pushing and pulling, takes its own wear and tear. Swollen ankles, sore backs and arms, and sometimes hospitalization result. Falls and bruises are very common.[58]

Ghost cleaning is a common practice, and means either not providing extra staff to cover for illness or absence, or simply hiring fewer cleaners to do the job than stipulated in the contract. Either way the cleaners have to cover the additional work. The work is normally divided into "light" and "heavy" or the workers divided into "cleaners" and "janitors." Whichever the arrangement, women are exclusively employed in the lower paid category. Despite the many problems, fear of losing the job and cultural and linguistic barriers, often prevent these workers from lodging formal complaints against their employers.

The Canadian Union of Postal Workers (CUPW) is a relatively large national union, representing 46,000 postal workers who sort and deliver the mail for a single employer, the Canadian Post Office. The union has a high profile, a militant history and a reputation for not backing down easily. As a result it has made some breakthroughs in negotiations of its collective agreement on paid maternity leave, technological change and in obtaining equal pay and benefits for part-time workers. It has stressed the importance of social justice and successfully pressed a solidaristic wage policy, reducing differentials between the highest and lowest paid workers.[59] This is an account of what happened when the CUPW decided to organize cleaners.[60]

Until 1986 many of the workers who cleaned the smaller Post Office buildings across the country were employed by the federal government in the Department of Public Works and therefore members of the Public Service Alliance of Canada. Then the Post Office decided to contract out its cleaning work to private companies in each location. The cleaners had been earning $6–10 an hour, and were replaced by workers earning $4 an hour with private contractors. The Post Office estimated it would save $3 million a year.[61] Two hundred and forty cleaners lost their jobs, and were asked to train their replacements. After a series of walkouts, negotiations with the Alliance produced improved severance pay and pension protection, or the right to be re-allocated to comparable jobs elsewhere in the Department.

Postal workers had refused to cross the cleaners' picket lines during their walkouts, causing the closing of postal plants in some instances. Despite the reallocations, the CUPW was struck by the obvious injustice. The work previously done by unionized workers for a federal government department was now performed by non-union cleaners at half the pay rate. Meanwhile a small union, the Food and Service Workers of Canada (FASWOC), was organizing cleaners in Toronto and had organized the cleaners at the large Gateway postal plant. This union approached the CUPW, believing that it was more appropriate for the cleaners to be represented by the same union as the other workers at the plant. As a result cards were signed with the CUPW and the union obtained its first certification for cleaners.

The union then decided to organize cleaners across the country, motivated by its sense of social justice. The non-union cleaners were paid very low wages to clean buildings where the unionized and relatively well-paid postal workers were employed, and the union with its philosophy of equal pay found this unacceptable. The union also wanted to pressure the Post Office to contract in the work, that is to hire the cleaners directly like other workers. The union had some confidence that this goal could be accomplished through negotiations.

The CUPW had little experience unionizing new groups of workers, and no experience with the provincial labour laws. A new staff member was hired who had organized cleaners in FASWOC. Seminars on organizing were provided for local activists, who could then return to their locals to organize. Articles, bulletins and updates were distributed to publicize the campaign, encourage the locals to participate and keep them informed. In most cases the union had no difficulty signing up the cleaners and obtaining certifications. The cleaners were at the same workplace and had every reason to want to improve their conditions. Between 1986 and 1987, cleaners joined the CUPW in Toronto (Gateway and South Central), Scarborough, Ottawa, Kitchener, Quebec City, Halifax, and St John.

The major problems came with negotiating first contracts and then maintaining them. Nine cleaners at the Scarborough plant were among the first to organize and a collective agreement was signed with Pritchard Building Services Limited. Their pay rates increased from $4-$5 an hour to $7-$7.25 an hour, and they gained seniority rights, sick leave and a grievance procedure. One week later the contract was given to Modern Building Services, which refused to accept either the cleaners or their collective agreement. A one week strike resulted and the CUPW President, J.C. Parrot, threatened national disruptions of the postal service if the issue was not resolved. However, Canada Post threatened severe retaliation if postal workers did not report for work, and the first day six workers were under threat of dismissal by the employer. This was not the traditional strike situation for the CUPW. Although the cleaners were in a legal position to strike, the postal workers were not and therefore liable to retaliation by the employer. Most postal workers crossed the picket line. Finally the union settled that the new company would rehire the workers at a pay rate of $6 an hour, to be increased to $7 after a year.

Cleaners at the South Central postal plant in Toronto were on strike for five and a half months for improved pay and conditions, 1987.

Courtesy of the Canadian Union of Postal Workers.

Similar problems arose at the South Central plant in Toronto, where twenty-eight cleaners were earning $4.50 to $4.65 an hour with no benefits. They joined the CUPW, but negotiations for a first contract stalled for months. The cleaners finally walked out in January 1987, beginning a strike that was to last for five and a half months. On the first day ninety-eight truck drivers refused to cross the picket line and received suspensions of three to six days as a result. Thirteen inside postal workers were fired for refusing to cross the picket line and the Post Office made it clear that more heavy discipline would follow. Despite the urging of the union leadership, postal workers crossed the picket line. Replacement cleaners were used throughout the strike and paid $6 an hour, while the company offered less than $6 to its regular workers. Meanwhile, the union was demanding $10 an hour, regarded by some in the union as unrealistic and part of the reason for the protracted strike. Finally, the agreement reached provided wages of $6.25 and $7.25, as well as paid sick leave, increased vacation time and health and safety protection.

Similar situations occurred with variations across the country. In Halifax eight cleaners were fired when they joined the CUPW, and the union filed a complaint of unfair labour practice and set up information pickets at the Post Office and other locations where the company held cleaning contracts. The company relented and agreed to recognize the union, and a contract was negotiated and signed in February 1987. However, three months later the cleaning contract was awarded to a new company, which refused to recognize the union or the agreement, stating that the costs were too high and that it had a previous city wide agreement with the Teamsters Union. The CUPW involved the New Democratic Party in questioning this situation and in calling for successor rights for contractors, and as a result the Deputy Minister of Labour became involved in mediating the dispute. The agreement reached was to allow the transfer of the bargaining rights, but the collective agreement obtained was basically the same as the Teamsters' with few improvements. As nine of the twelve cleaners did not wish to work under this contract because of the increased night and weekend work, the CUPW decided not to pursue the transfer of bargaining rights.

In Quebec City the situation should have been different because at the time contract situations were also covered by successor rights under the law, although this has since changed because of a Supreme Court decision. Fifteen cleaners joined the union and a collective agreement was negotiated that gave them $8.30 to $8.55 an hour. Four months later a new contractor was hired, and the collective agreement should have been respected. However, the contractor fired the workers and contracted every floor of the building to a separate cleaner, so that they became self-employed.

As locals struggled with cleaning contractors that changed every few months, the lack of successor rights and the downward pressure on wages and benefits exerted by the contracting out system, the national office attempted to negotiate contracting in for cleaning work. This also proved more difficult than anticipated. In the 1987 round of negotiations the union went on strike, was legislated back to work and a contract was arbitrated. To the union's credit, the demand that cleaning work be contracted in remained on the agenda throughout the process. However, the arbitrator refused to consider the issue seriously, so no progress was made. By the 1989 negotiations other issues had taken precedence, although the same pattern was repeated: strike, back to work legislation, and compulsory arbitration.

As of 1992 the CUPW represents fewer than sixty cleaners at just two postal plants, Gateway and South Central in Toronto. The campaign to organize cleaners across the country failed, as did the intention to contract in the work. The union was overconfident that its size and militancy gave it the power necessary to deal with the situation, without fully recognizing the difficulties. At the same time, the strength of the union was contained not only by the legal loophole for contractors, but also by the illegality of postal workers supporting cleaners on the picket lines, and by back to work legislation which undercut the union's negotiating power. The Post Office decision to contract out cleaning was part of larger plans for privatization and cutbacks, and their ability to impose those plans was strengthened by the legal framework.

In Ontario, changes in labour relations legislation in January 1993 will protect the bargaining rights, collective agreement, wages and benefits of workers when contracts change hands. This reform was included in the amendments to the legislation in large part because of the efforts of the CUPW and other unions, social and women's groups that formed the Committee for Cleaners' Rights in 1986. This Committee worked to publicize the vulnerability of cleaners working for contracting companies, supported the struggles of cleaners in several different workplaces, and lobbied for legislative reform.[62] Although the Committee no longer exists, the work of its members was critical in raising awareness of the issue and having it placed on the agenda for change.

However, obtaining successor rights is by no means the whole answer. First, it will apply only in Ontario and, for a national union such as the CUPW, the cleaners who work in post offices elsewhere will not benefit. Second, although it brings increased stability to negotiations, still the employer may change regularly and there continues to be a downward pressure on wages and conditions because of competition between different cleaning companies which bid for the cleaning contract. As well, the cleaners would continue to be employed by a different employer than the other workers in the workplace, limiting their bargaining strength and therefore their ability to obtain decent pay and conditions.

> For the CUPW the preferred solution to this problem would be the introduction of a broad-based decree system in which unions and employers would engage in broader-based bargaining and then the terms of these settlements would be imposed throughout the industry.[63]

Contracting-in the work and moving away from the use of cleaning contractors would also be preferable in many circumstances, but both suggestions run counter to the cheap and flexible philosophy of privatization and contracting-out.

Taking on the Legal Challenge: The Ontario Federation of Labour

Until recently, labour relations legislation in Ontario was among the most restrictive of any jurisdiction. The labour movement in that province identified many problems with the Labour Relations Act and, following the election of an New Democratic Party government, took the opportunity to lobby strongly for reform of the law. The Ontario Federation of Labour (OFL) proposed reforms that cover some of the issues outlined above and worked to educate its members and muster support for reform. Seven hundred unionists attended a one-day workshop in the summer of 1991, where the proposed revisions were explained and information provided on how to lobby the government. The Federation organized a tour of fifteen cities to hear briefs, collect information and promote support for legislative change. In the spring of 1992 a demonstration in support of labour legislation reform was held at Queen's Park in Toronto. The OFL and individual unions responded to government discussion papers, prepared briefs and attended consultations on the issue.

At the same time a coalition of women's groups came together called Women for Labour Law Reform, including the following groups: the Campaign for Fair Wages and Working Conditions for Homeworkers, the Chinese Canadian National Council Women's Issues Committee, the Equal Pay Coalition, Intercede — Toronto Organization for Domestic Workers' Rights, the National Action Committee on the Status of Women, the Older Women's Network, the Ontario Coalition for Better Child Care and the Ontario Women's Action Coalition. The coalition held a one day workshop for almost 100 women in January 1992 to discuss the implications of labour law reform for women, and the group then continued to produce information for its members and react to the government's proposals. Concern has been expressed particularly for domestic workers, who are be technically able to unionize under the new legislation, but need special mechanisms if that right is to be exercised in reality, and also for agricultural workers, many of them women, who may still be denied the right to unionize.

Meanwhile, the reaction of business to the suggested reforms was vitriolic. Three business coalitions were formed to oppose the legislative changes, Project Economic Growth, the More Jobs Coalition and the All Business Coalition, the latter being an umbrella organization for sixty-two business groups representing

Steelworkers' Poster on Labour Reform

**LOATHED BY ITS CRITICS
THE #1 THRILLER**

SEE THE SOCIALIST HORDES
drag labour law kicking and screaming into the 21st century.

GAG IN HORROR
as the NDP makes it easier for women and immigrants in low-paid jobs to join unions.

SCREAM
at losing the right to hire scabs to steal jobs from striking workers.

LABOUR REFORM FROM HELL!

LIE AWAKE IN TERROR
at the thought of part-time workers, domestic workers and security guards joining unions.

RECOIL IN SHOCK
as fair play insidiously invades your company.

COMING SOON TO A WORKPLACE NEAR YOU!

A satirical look at big business reaction to Ontario's labour law proposals
Produced by the United Steelworkers of America District 6
Harry Hynd Director

three quarters of Ontario's organized private industry and trade. Loss of companies and jobs was threatened. Specifically the All Business Coalition warned that 480,000 jobs and $20 billion in investment would leave the province if the proposed changes were made.[64] General Motors, Ford and Chrysler, the Big Three auto makers, made public remarks that the legislative changes would harm Ontario's investment prospects.[65] Much of the opposition revolved around the "no-scab" proposal, to deny employers the right to hire replacement workers during a strike. Although 95 percent of all negotiations are settled without a strike and replacement workers are rarely used during strikes, employers in Ontario have descried such a change as a fundamental shift of power in favour of unions. The provision has existed for more than a decade in Quebec with no very dramatic results. However, the force of the employer lobby had an impact in cutting back on the strength of the government's proposals. The Premier made it clear that compromise had to be made.

As of January 1, 1993, amendments to the Ontario Labour Relations Act will come into effect, including:

- Professionals and domestic workers will have the right to organize, and a task force will be established to consider the particular problems of domestic workers in exercising this right. Separate legislation is planned for agricultural workers.

- Access to third party property, such as shopping malls, will be permitted for organizing activities and pickets.

- Complaints of illegal discipline or dismissal during an organizing drive will be given faster hearings under strict time limits.

- Anti-union petitions will be prohibited after a union has applied for certification.

- Unions will have easier access to automatic certification in cases of extreme unfair labour practices on the part of the employer.

- Full- and part-time workers will be placed in the same bargaining unit where the union has overall majority support.

- Access to first contract arbitration will be automatic after 30 days of a strike or a lock-out.

- The Board will have the power to combine bargaining units (such as two branches of the same retail company) where the same union represents both groups of workers.

- The use of replacement workers will be prohibited during a strike, although managers and workers not in the same bargaining unit may perform the work and it may be moved to a different location.

Despite the reaction of business, virtually all of these changes already exist in other jurisdictions in Canada. Most of the reforms are technical improvements that will make it somewhat easier to organize workers. The most far reaching are the limitations on the use of replacement workers and the opportunity to consolidate bargaining units represented by the same union and with the same employer. Both of these will give workers more bargaining leverage in relation to employers, and therefore improve the chances of organizing. Under such a system, for example, Eaton's would have been forced to negotiate for all its bargaining units together instead of one by one, giving the workers more strength to obtain a decent first contract and retain their certifications. In the strike that occurred the employer would not have been able to replace the striking workers, and would therefore have been under more pressure to settle the dispute.

Although consolidated units offer a small step towards bargaining for larger groups of workers for the same employer, it does not resolve the problem of the fragmentation of workers employed by different employees, or represented by different unions. It offers no mechanism to cover either broad sectors of workers or regions. Although they will have some impact on improving the success of organizing campaigns, taken together the reforms are too limited to halt the decline in union membership in the private sector, let alone stimulate an increase. The OFL itself refers to the likely results as "a minor improvement."[66]

However, the Federation has not limited itself to these revisions within the current framework of the law, but has promoted serious consideration of a more fundamental transformation. The OFL has strongly recommended a Task Force to study the question of broader based bargaining, meaning more fundamental changes to the legislation that would permit unionization and collective bargaining either by sector or by region. Although the possibility of such a Task Force was raised in an earlier government document, it was absent from a later Discussion Paper. In response the OFL stated:

It remains a priority for the Ontario Federation of Labour to develop, through the necessary social investigation and consultative process, sectoral mechanisms wherein the collective bargaining parties could fashion structures appropriate for a rapidly restructuring economy ... We call on the government to establish a bipartisan, credible Task Force on Broader Based Bargaining without delay.[67]

Such a Task Force would be able not only to examine the situation in Ontario, but also consider arrangements in other jurisdictions. The OFL also commissioned a study of the Quebec decree system, to examine whether some similar mechanism could be adapted for use in Ontario. The Secretary-Treasurer of the Federation addressed a conference on broader based bargaining, and stressed its potential in reaching the two-thirds of the work force that lacks union protection, especially in small workplaces.[68]

Women for Labour Law Reform, the coalition mentioned above, has also endorsed the need for a Task Force to examine broader based bargaining. The group has called the new changes to the legislation "modest reforms" and has stated that it will continue to be difficult to unionize those most in need of protection. The group has said: "There will be little to console the great majority of women if you and your government do not also take steps to improve the organizing situation for the most exploited women."[69]

However, whether the union movement in Ontario will rally to the OFL in its struggle on this issue is unclear. While legislative change within the current framework was widely supported, a more fundamental transformation raises the difficult issues of structural change within unions and inter-union rivalry, as already outlined above. At the time of writing the union movement has yet to develop its own agenda for what would constitute broader based bargaining.

Conclusion

The restructuring of the economy and of the labour force pose a serious threat to the labour movement. If unions cannot organize in the private service sector, in small workplaces and among part-time workers, women and different ethnic groups, the decline in union membership will continue. Such a decline will in turn weaken the union movement in its attempts to mediate the impact of the economic changes occurring, even upon those workers who are union members. There needs to be what has been called "a fourth wave" of unionization, equivalent to the industrial organizing of the 1930s, or the public sector unionization of the 1960s, but this time in the private service sector.

In order to meet this challenge, the labour movement needs not only to build support and pressure for fundamental changes in labour relations legislation, but must also face the necessary transformation of the union movement itself.

Members of the Public Service Alliance on the picket line in Kamloops, British Columbia, after the federal government refused any pay increase for two years, September 1991.

Courtesy of the Public Service Alliance of Canada. (Kamloops Daily News).

7

Racial Minorities, Persons with Disabilities, and Gays and Lesbians

During the 1980s groups other than women within the union movement have raised their voices and their concerns, insisting that unions deal with the particular problems that they face in the workplace. Increasingly it has been recognized that the term "women" is not homogeneous, but signifies a variety of backgrounds and concerns. People of colour have begun to assert the need to deal with racism at work, and women of colour have criticized the women's movement for failing to recognize their specific experiences and the additional difficulties they face. People with physical and mental disabilities have formed their own organizations and have been pressing for economic integration into mainstream society, particularly in employment. The gay/lesbian movement has also taken action to define the changes that need to take place within the workplace if they are to be treated equally and with dignity.

Increasingly the question has been asked as to "which women" are moving ahead in the union movement. If it is only white, straight and non-disabled women that are making advances and having their needs met, then the improvements will largely affect those women already relatively well off compared to others. The union movement has begun to respond to some of these more diverse needs. Before examining what unions have done on these subjects, there follows a brief examination of the issues involved.

Racism

Canada has a long history of racism to its discredit, practised against many different groups.[1] The native Beothuk people of Newfoundland were exterminated in the 18th century, while other native peoples were deprived of their land and confined to designated reservations. Native children were forcibly removed from their families to residential schools and religious practices were banned by law. Despite the underground railway that helped American slaves flee north, slavery was not a particularly American institution. From the arrival of the first slave in New France in 1628, slavery flourished for two hundred years until prohibited by British legislation in 1833. Six of the sixteen legislators in the first Parliament of Upper Canada owned slaves.

In the west, Chinese men were initially admitted to work on the railways, but were later subject to a head tax. Chinese women were not allowed entry and Chinese men were prohibited by law from marriage to white women. In 1907 anti-Asian riots in British Columbia damaged the homes and businesses of many Chinese and Japanese people. Native and Asian peoples were denied the right to vote, legislation that remained unchanged until the late 1940s for Asians and until 1960 for aboriginal people. During World War II Japanese Canadians were stripped of their possessions with no compensation and interned in camps. At the same time the government steadfastly refused to allow Jews from Europe to enter the country to escape the Nazi holocaust, and only 5,000 were permitted entry during the whole period from 1933 to 1945.

In recent decades Canadians have tended to ignore this history and have thought of themselves as a tolerant, multicultural society. The current practice of racism in Canada has been called "gentle" discrimination, in which the dominant white majority subtly and quietly excludes minority group members in order not to disturb the status quo.[2] Different ethnic groups have had to insist that racism be recognized. Attitudinal research has shown that fifteen percent of Canadians exhibit blatantly racist attitudes, while another 20 to 25 percent are not free of some racist tendencies.[3] As one writer has concluded:

> Racism in Canada ... has been practised systematically by the Canadian government and people in general from the very beginning of Canadian history. It is not an aberration from our way of life, thinking and behaviour. It is a normal, expected and entrenched part of people's behaviour and their attitudes.[4]

Despite variations in background, education and class among visible minorities, numerous studies have produced similar and depressing conclusions. While some visible minority workers certainly obtain skilled and well-paid employment, there is no doubt that they are more often excluded from the work force, ghettoized in the lowest level of work, given little chance for training or advancement and paid less than white majority workers. A 1985 study in Toronto sent black and white applicants, matched by sex, education, experience, dress and even personality to apply for the same jobs, and found that whites were offered the possibility of employment three times more often than the blacks. The black applicants were also subject to negative and abusive treatment in almost one-quarter of the situations.[5]

A survey of city employees in 1986 found that only 8.5 percent of the workers were visible minority in Toronto and only 3.9 percent in North York, although the population was 12 to 20 percent non-white. In Saskatoon, although 10 percent of the city's population was native in 1986, less than one percent of city staff were of native origin.[6] Similarly in Winnipeg, where the population is 6 percent visible minority and 10 percent aboriginal people, only 4.5 percent and 1.3 percent respectively of the city staff were from these groups.[7]

As it is more difficult for many visible minority workers to find work, it is not surprising that their rates of unemployment are higher than for the population in general. In 1986 the rate of unemployment was 10.2 percent among visible minority men compared to 9.6 percent for all men, and while it was 11.5 percent for visible minority women, the rate was 11.2 percent among the total population of women. Among the native population unemployment is a much more serious problem, double the general average. In 1986 the unemployment rate among aboriginal men was 24 percent and among aboriginal women the rate was 22 percent.[8]

These unemployment figures are drawn from the Statistics Canada 1986 Census data, where the term "visible minority" includes eleven groups: Blacks, Chinese, Filipinos, Indo-Pakistanis, South East Asians, West Asians and Arabs, Japanese, Koreans, Latin Americans, Other Pacific Islanders, and those of multiple visible minority origin. Together these groups comprise 6.4 percent of the labour force, a total of 831,500 workers. Figure 7-1 shows that Chinese and Black workers together constitute almost half of all

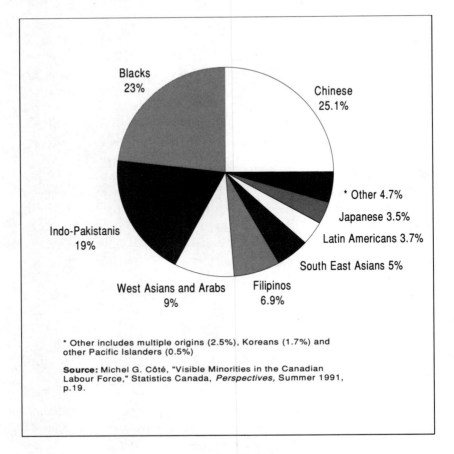

Figure 7-1

Visible Minorities in the Labour Force, 1986
(Total 831,500)

visible minority workers. Aboriginal people form another 2 percent of the labour force.

Both visible minority and native workers earn less than other Canadians. Despite a higher level of education than other Canadians, visible minority workers earned on average 10 percent less than other Canadians in 1985, $24,200 compared to $27,000 (see Table 7-1). There is considerable variation between different visible minority groups. South East Asians, Other Pacific Islanders and Latin Americans earn particularly low incomes, and only two groups, the Japanese and West Asians and Arabs, earn higher

Table 7-1: Average Employment Income for Full-Time and Full-Year Work in 1985

	Total	Women	Men
Visible Minority Workers	24,200	18,900	27,900
Aboriginal Workers	23,200	18,500	26,400
Other Canadian Workers	27,000	20,100	30,700

Source: Statistics Canada, *Profile of Visible Minorities and Aboriginal Peoples,* 1986 Census.

average incomes than other Canadians.[9] Within every group women earn approximately two-thirds of the men's wage and the pay gap by sex is greater than the gap caused by racial background, although both are significant. In many cases women from visible minorities suffer a double jeopardy, appearing at the bottom of the heap, paid less than white men, visible minority men, and white women. Immigration policies and language training programs discriminate against women, reducing their opportunities in the labour market.[10] In her study Boyd concludes "foreign born visible minority women have the lowest average earnings of all."[11]

Aboriginal workers earned even lower wages than visible minority groups in general at an average of $23,200, 14 percent less than other Canadians (see Table 7–1). As with other racial groups, aboriginal women workers are paid two thirds of the wages of aboriginal men. They earn less than other Canadian women, and also less than the average earned by all visible minority women, although in some cases the women of specific minority groups earn less than aboriginal women.

Unions have the capacity to play an important role in obtaining a more equal place for visible minority and aboriginal people within the work force. This involves both lobbying for employment equity legislation and helping to implement it, particularly by educating union members about racism and protecting racial minority workers from harassment. Although only 6 percent of union members are visible minority and native workers, the concentration of racial minorities in urban centres and certain regions of the country is significant. Where visible minority workers are concentrated, as in Toronto and Vancouver, they have a much stronger presence from which to press for recognition and progress within the labour movement. Women constitute 51 percent of visible minority and aboriginal union members, giving them a stronger voice within the racial minority community than women have had in the union movement overall.[12]

Persons with Disabilities

There are a total of 3.3 million people with disabilities in Canada, which includes physical, developmental, mental, visual, hearing, learning and invisible disabilities. This means that 14 percent of the population is identified as having a disability, making it a common experience rather than a rare event.

Considering those living outside of institutions and between the ages of 15 and 64 years, there are 1,767,640 people with disabilities. However, these persons with disabilities, and especially women with disabilities, are much less likely to be in the labour force than other Canadians. In 1985, 51 percent of persons with disabilities were not in the labour force, compared to only 22 percent of people without disabilities. Moreover, over 30 percent of these persons with disabilities were not prevented from working by their disability.[13] As Figure 7-2 shows, 88 percent of non-disabled men were in the labour force, compared to only 58 percent of men with disabilities. Among women, 68 percent of the non-disabled were in the labour force, compared to just 37 percent of women with disabilities.

Among those disabled people who are in the labour force, unemployment is a serious problem. In 1985 15 percent of persons with disabilities in the labour force were unemployed compared to 10 percent of the non-disabled. More than one out of every four unemployed workers with disabilities (27 percent) had found the lack of suitable employment to be the major barrier. Again, disabled women are affected even more negatively than disabled men, their rate of unemployment being 17 percent compared to 14 percent for men with disabilities.

The exclusion of disabled persons from the labour force has a dramatic effect on their incomes. In 1985 63 percent of persons with disabilities had incomes of less than $10,000 a year, compared to only 15 percent of all Canadians. It is especially difficult to escape from the poverty of disability pensions and social assistance when employment income must be sufficient to cover the costs of

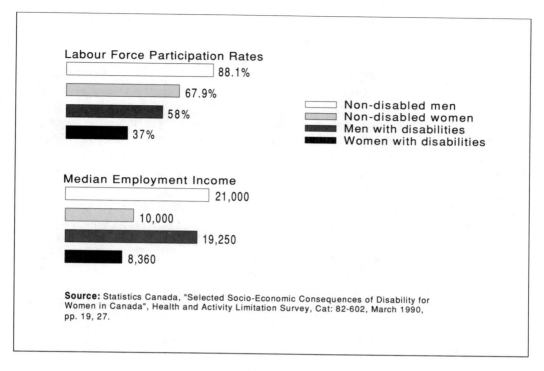

Labour Force Participation Rates

88.1%
67.9%
58%
37%

☐ Non-disabled men
▨ Non-disabled women
■ Men with disabilities
█ Women with disabilities

Median Employment Income

21,000
10,000
19,250
8,360

Source: Statistics Canada, "Selected Socio-Economic Consequences of Disability for Women in Canada", Health and Activity Limitation Survey, Cat: 82-602, March 1990, pp. 19, 27.

Figure 7-2:

Labour Force Participation Rates and Median Employment Income for Disabled and Non-Disabled Men and Women in Households, Aged 15-64, 1985

medicine, technical aids and attendant care, as well as general living expenses.

Women with disabilities are even more likely to be impoverished than men with disabilities. Considering total income from both employment and government sources for all people over 15 years of age, in 1985 non-disabled men had a median income of $20,855, disabled men $12,980, non-disabled women $10,000 and disabled women $8,175. Looking at just income from paid employment for people aged 15 to 64 years of age, the median for non-disabled men was $21,000 and for disabled men $19,250. For women the figures were much lower at $10,000 for non-disabled women and $8,360 for disabled women (see Figure 7-1). It is clear that gender has a greater impact upon income, and particularly upon employment income, than does disability, although both are significant.

For men with disabilities, employment means a substantial improvement in income, but this is not the case for women with disabilities.

Despite the International Decade of Disabled Persons, ending in 1992, there has been little progress for persons with disabilities in recent years. The Canadian Human Rights Act prohibits discrimination against disabled persons, but the legislation is limited not only because it is complaint-based and its procedures very lengthy, but also because employers are not required to make adjustments in order to hire disabled workers. The disabled community has lobbied for years to have the law amended so that employers would be required to accommodate disabled workers, and it is expected to be included in amendments to the Act currently under consideration. The federal Employment Equity Act includes persons with disabilities, but has had no noticeable impact for any of its target groups because it requires only that employers report the situation, not amend it. The proposed Ontario legislation on employment equity is potentially much more significant, because it will be mandatory for employers to develop and implement employment equity plans, although the details of the legislation are still under discussion.

Given that health and safety is a major concern within the union movement, issues affecting the employment of workers with disabilities would seem like an obvious cause for concern. In 1990, 586,800 workers across the country were accepted as injured on the job by Workers' Compensation Boards, and had to take time off work.[14] It is not known how many of these workers were left with a permanent disability, but certainly there are thousands. Every worker is potentially a person with disabilities. However, rights for disabled persons have not been a priority within the union movement. Because so many disabled people are not employed, workers with disabilities constitute only 6 percent of the total number of employed workers. There is no information on the unionization of disabled people, but clearly the voice of disabled persons within the labour movement is not a loud one. Unlike the situation for racial minority groups, there is no regional concentration to give it greater force. As well, union members with disabilities may be severely marginalized in the labour movement no less than in the workplace if they cannot obtain transportation to meetings, if they cannot get into the building or the room where the meetings are held, and if they cannot hear the debates or see the reports.

Gays and Lesbians

It is estimated that one out of every ten people is gay or lesbian. Therefore more than 2 million adults suffer from the negative effects of homophobia, that is the irrational fear of homosexuality, which leads to discrimination against gays and lesbians.

Because it is possible to hide the fact of being gay or lesbian, lesbians may not face the same difficulties as women of colour or women with disabilities in obtaining employment. However, there follows the necessary decision about whether to continue to be silent in order to avoid stigma and discrimination, or to be open and face the risk of no further training or advances at work, if not actual loss of the job.

Maintaining the secret has serious and stressful implications, including never being really honest about oneself with co-workers, being uncomfortable in many discussions of families and friends, and not being able to talk about spare time activities with any freedom. A lesbian has described the situation as "walking a tightrope," explaining "before you come out at work you have to watch every second word that's coming out of your mouth. I used to lie a lot; I'd talk about boy friends I didn't have." Although this woman had told some friends at work and found them accepting, she continued to want a certain degree of anonymity, saying "I may not be in this job forever; it could be a cloud over my head some time in the future."[15] There is no single, courageous "coming out," because new workers and supervisors, transfers, job changes and new contacts all recreate the situation where the decision must be made again.

If gays and lesbians are open about their sexual orientation at work they may face harassment and discrimination. They are passed over for training and promotions and remain in entry level positions, facing a "glass ceiling" of invisible but effective discrimination just like women in general. During the 1950s and 1960s national security services tried to identify gays and lesbians employed by the federal government, because they were viewed as a security risk and therefore either fired or denied access to high level positions. More recently cases of denied promotion, demotion and verbal abuse have been documented.[16] Many gay men work

Lesbian Teachers

On being open about their sexual orientation:

If they only knew that I'm a lesbian and that their child — a six year-old little thing — is with me. They would just be shocked. They would be pulling their kids out.

I remember when Billie Jean King — as someone put it recently — "was yanked out of her bisexual closet," one of the girls in my home class came to me the next day and said, "Did you read the news about Billie Jean King?" I said "Yes." And she said, "She used to be my favourite tennis player but not any more!" I thought, well, that would be the reaction of a lot of people: I really liked her before but now she's gross.

On the security offered by a sexual-orientation protection clause:

I think I could survive my job (with a protection clause), because I think it would be very difficult to prove that anything that I had ever done was in any way harmful to students that I have taught. On the other hand, I think the feeling of distrust or feeling someone was always there waiting for me to make some kind of move which would validate their concerns might be a little bit too much for me.

I would be protected from firing. I would not be protected from ostracism, or harassment, or from students or from colleagues.

Source: Didi Khayatt, "Lesbian Teachers: Coping at School," Sharon Dale Stone, *Lesbians in Canada*, Toronto: Between the Lines, 1990, pp.82-84.

as hairdressers and waiters, and this ghettoization into low level service jobs reflects the cumulative effects of discrimination.

> If statistics were to be gathered, we are confident they would likely show that we tend to be found in disproportionate numbers in almost all of the low-paying service sector jobs: retail sales, clerical work, food services, personal services and the like.[17]

While sex, race and disability are prohibited grounds for discrimination under human rights legislation, gays and lesbians are still struggling to be included in some jurisdictions. Despite years of discussion and lobbying, at the time of writing in mid–1992, it is still not against the law to discriminate against gays and lesbians in the federal jurisdiction. Only Ontario, Quebec, Manitoba, the Yukon and Nova Scotia have included sexual orientation as a prohibited ground for discrimination under human rights legislation, although other provinces are considering this addition.

Women, visible minorities, native people and persons with disabilities were identified by the Abella Commission as the four target groups for employment equity, and have therefore benefited from research, education and public awareness campaigns on these issues. Gays and lesbians thus far been excluded from consideration for employment equity purposes. It has been suggested that gays and lesbians would not wish to self-identify for the purposes of research and the setting of numerical goals and targets. However, research is most often carried on with a guarantee of anonymity and efforts to rectify discrimination in the workplace are not only based upon numerical assessments. General education to create increased awareness and sensitivity, specific training for managers and workers to reduce discriminatory attitudes, reviewing procedures to eliminate any biases, and protection from harassment are not numerical issues. These types of programs are needed as much by lesbians and gay men as by the identified target groups.

There has been serious lobbying from the gay and lesbian community, with support from other target group organizations and some unions, to be included in both the new Ontario legislation on employment equity, and also in the federal employment equity legislation currently under review.

As discussed in Chapter 3, a serious inequality faced by gay and lesbian workers is the exclusion of their partners and families from a wide range of benefits. Because a spouse is commonly defined as a member of the opposite sex, many employers and insurance carriers have refused to recognize that same-sex spouses should receive coverage under benefit plans. Gay and lesbian workers have been challenging their exclusion in the courts. At the federal level a critical case is now being appealed to the Supreme Court of Canada. Brian Mossop, a federal civil servant, was denied bereavement leave upon the death of his partner's father. With the support of the Canadian Union of Professional and Technical Employees, he complained under the Canadian Human Rights Act that he had been discriminated against on the basis of family status. It was not possible to argue the case on sexual orientation since it is not included in the Act.

At the Tribunal the case was won, recognizing for the first time that same-sex partners might constitute a family, but the decision was appealed. Ten organizations intervened in the appeal, including Equality for Gays and Lesbians Everywhere and the National Action Committee on the Status of Women in support of Mossop and the Salvation Army and Realwomen in opposition. The Court overturned the previous decision, rejecting the idea that a family could include same-sex couples. This case will now be appealed to the Supreme Court and other cases at the federal level are being held in abeyance until a final decision on this one. As of October 1991 the Canadian Human Rights Commission had received thirty-three complaints from sixteen complainants claiming discrimination in employment benefits for partners of the same sex, including dental coverage, pension benefits, family related leave, bereavement leave and general employment benefits.

In Ontario and Manitoba sexual orientation is included in human rights legislation and yet cases have still been lost, because spouse and/or family are defined to be or assumed to be exclusive of same-sex partners. For example, Karen Andrews, with the support of the Canadian Union of Public Employees, took a case against the Ontario Health Insurance Plan for refusing to cover her partner and her partner's children. Although the Health Insurance Act had no definition of spouse, the Court reviewed other legislation and found 79 Ontario statutes where the word "spouse" referred to a member of the opposite sex, and the case was lost. However, more recently, in September 1992, Michael Leshner won a precedent setting case, when the Ontario Human Rights Tribunal ordered that his same-sex partner should be eligible for survivor benefits from his provincial government pension plan, just as would a heterosexual partner. Moreover, the Tribunal ordered that the reference to persons "of the opposite sex" be deleted from Ontario's definition of marital status, which may affect the many other laws that exclude gays and lesbians.

A similar case was successful in British Columbia. Timothy Knodel, a member of the Hospital Employees Union, complained that the provincial Medical Services Commission denied coverage to his same-sex partner. The court found that there was discrimination and declared that same sex couples were included in the definition of spouse for the purposes of the Medical Services Act. This decision set an important precedent, because the Court found that the discrimination was an infringement of the right to equality under section 15 of the Charter of Rights, even though sexual orientation is not specifically mentioned there.

Unions are directly involved in this process, since the benefit package is often part of a collective agreement. Gays and lesbians have cause for complaint that they pay the same dues as other union members, but have not been receiving the same benefits from their negotiated contracts. Several unions have supported and financed the grievances and complaints of their members on the issue of same-sex spousal benefits. Unions are also grappling with the results of several recent court decisions, including the Mossop case, that have found the union as well as the employer responsible for infringements of human rights because of being party to a discriminatory collective agreement. Gay and lesbian unionists also want their unions to be active in educating the work force to create a less hostile environment, preventing harassment and discrimination at work, and lobbying for legislation to protect the rights of gays and lesbians.

The Union Movement and Minority Group Rights

Labour Centrals

Committees to deal with human rights issues were less common than women's committees both in the labour centrals and in the thirteen unions interviewed for this study. Three Federations of Labour did not have any human rights committee or its equivalent at the time of the interviews — Alberta, New Brunswick, and Newfoundland and Labrador.

A human rights committee existed at the Nova Scotia Federation of Labour, but it had been inactive until revitalized with new members in 1990, and was in the process of planning a conference on human rights. At the Saskatchewan Federation, the human rights committee had been sporadic in its activities, depending upon the interests of the committee members. In the Manitoba Federation the human rights committee deals with race and disability, while lesbian issues remain within the women's committee, and again the human rights committee had only recently been reactivated. With government funding, course modules on racism had been developed, and a conference primarily on aboriginal issues was planned. The Federation had also sponsored an essay writing competition on racism among school children.

In the British Columbia Federation of Labour, the Community and Social Action Committee was established by Convention in

1986 to work on coalition building, human rights, employment equity and international solidarity. An anti-racism campaign included a co-ordinator to do on-site education and an educational kit. Action has been taken to oppose white supremacist groups organizing in the region, by campaigning for businesses to withdraw advertising from community newspapers printing racist material, and by preventing public authorities from making facilities available for the meetings of such groups. In 1990 the Committee organized an employment equity conference, focused primarily on visible minorities and persons with disabilities. A manual has been produced for community groups and unions that examines how they might work together to develop employment opportunities for disabled workers. The Federation also worked with a local gay and lesbian group to adapt a kit on same-sex spousal benefits, prepared by the Canadian Union of Public Employees, for use specifically in British Columbia. Most recently the Health and Safety Committee of the Federation held a conference and worked with the Community and Social Action Committee to include an additional day to examine the employment of persons with disabilities.

In the Ontario Federation of Labour (OFL), union members from different racial backgrounds have been active and have held caucuses at the Conventions since the late 1970s. The OFL held its first anti-racism campaign in 1981, with a statement called "Racism Hurts Everyone," posters, television commercials and a series of pamphlets in seven languages explaining the nature of racism and how to deal with it. There followed regional conferences, fact sheets and training for union activists on racism. In 1985 a second anti-racism campaign produced a guide for unionists called "Steps to Resolving Racial Conflict in the Workplace" and encouraged the development of local human rights committees. The following year the OFL produced another policy paper, "Racism and Discrimination."

Until 1986 one full-time staff person had handled both women's issues and human rights at the Federation, but a second person was hired full-time so that the work was divided. Since then two conferences on human rights have been held. Another important development occurred in 1987 when two seats were added to the Executive Board and it was established that one of them had to be filled by a visible minority person. The name is put forward by a union and is added to the slate. This was the first affirmative action seat for visible minorities within the labour movement.

Since 1988 the OFL has sponsored the largest union literacy program in North America. It is funded by the provincial government, but developed and administered by the Federation. With two full-time staff at the OFL and eight regional co-ordinators, union members are trained to teach English or French and then offer language training to their co-workers at the workplace. Union members wanting to take language classes contribute an hour of their time immediately before or after their shift, usually matched by an hour paid by the employer.

With the Ontario Women's Directorate, the Federation produced a video on employment equity called "Not Just a Foot in the Door" which included a workshop guide for unionists. The Human Rights Committee obtained funding to produce a guide on disability for shop stewards, which explains the issues, the law, employment equity and what should be negotiated into collective agreements for workers with disabilities. Support and lobbying for mandatory employment equity has also been an important part of the OFL's activities and a conference on employment equity is planned for 1992.

Issues of concern to the gay and lesbian community are only just beginning to emerge in the OFL, and there has not been any direct activity on this issue, nor any caucus at Conventions. However, the Federation is a member of the Coalition for Lesbian and Gay Rights in Ontario and has supported amending legislation to provide same-sex spousal benefits.

The Canadian Labour Congress (CLC) has had a human rights committee for many years, but it has recently been revitalized with new members and has become more active. The first CLC human rights conference was held in 1992, and over 300 unionists from across the country attended the conference, and participated in workshops for racial minorities, native people and persons with disabilities. Following some lobbying, a workshop for gays and lesbians was also included. The conference was regarded as an important opportunity for members of minority groups from across the country to meet and share ideas within the union movement. This conference was preceded in December 1991 by the People's Agenda Conference, where many different community groups were invited to meet with the labour movement to share ideas and strategies, including representatives of minority groups. This was also an important step for the union movement in reaching out to community organizations and their concerns.

Delegates to the
1992 convention of
the Canadian
Labour Congress
at the microphone
during the debate
on affirmative
action positions for
visible minorities.

*Courtesy of Photo
Features Ltd.,
Murray Mosher.*

The CLC has a Social and Community Program that deals with
human rights issues and that obtained a grant to work on anti-racism. There is also an ad hoc group working with the National
Employment Equity Network. With input from both the human
rights committee and the women's committee, employment equity
policies and briefs have been developed. In the CLC's education
program, modules on racism and employment equity have been
initiated.

Most recently, a Task Force reviewed the structure of the CLC
and recommended to the 1992 Convention that one executive
position be made available to represent visible minorities. After
organizing and lobbying on the floor of the Convention this was
changed to two seats. The two representatives, one man and one
woman, were elected by a caucus of visible minority unionists.
This is the second affirmative action plan for elected positions
within the union movement for groups other than women, and

only the OFL and the CLC have made such arrangements thus far.

In Quebec, the Quebec Federation of Labour (QFL) has an Immigration and International Solidarity Committee that was established in 1979 and that year held a conference in Montreal on the situation of immigrant workers and the role of unions. The work of the committee declined in the 1980s, but it was re-established at the 1989 Convention. It now has fifteen members, including one woman, and the majority are members of racial minorities. In May 1992 the committee organized a two day training session on multicultural relationships. It has also produced a "Social Guide," with information on immigration and employment legislation and on social programs such as medical and unemployment insurance and pensions.

At its 1989 Convention, the QFL set up a Committee for the Integration of Disabled Persons, which is composed of half union delegates and half representatives from disabled persons' associations and government agencies. It has twenty members, half women and half persons with disabilities. The committee is developing a training course for union members on disability and employment, and is working on a conference to be held jointly with l'Office des personnes handicapées du Québec.

The Confédération des syndicats nationaux (CSN) established an Immigration Committee in 1986 that also deals with issues of race in general. It had already been established that over one-quarter of CSN members in Montreal were not originally from Quebec,[18] and the Committee decided to examine the problems facing these members. In 1988 interviews were conducted with thirty three members from ten Montreal union locals in different industries.[19] These members were from various racial backgrounds and the interviews were held in French, English, Spanish, Creole, Italian, Greek and Chinese. The workers identified language barriers, racism, discrimination against new immigrants and sexual harassment as problems that they faced from employers, clients and co-workers. Only in a small minority of cases had the union played a role in protecting the rights of these workers and in some situations the union itself was a source of difficulty. In one case union activities were boycotted by the members following the election of a black member to the local executive.[20] The results of this study have directed the work of the committee, including its recommendations to the CSN for action.

Language as a Barrier within Unions

These were the comments of one of the respondents to a survey conducted by the Immigration Committee of the Confédération des syndicats nationaux in Montreal.

"It's impossible for me (to take a position on the union executive). You can see that I speak English poorly and no French at all. To do that work, you have to negotiate, you have to be convincing, you have to be able to understand exactly what everyone says. But if I could speak one of these languages really well, that would be something else. Everyone here, we have a lot of experience working in groups, participating in associations, lots of social activities, organizing. If we knew the language, we could do this work."

Confédération des syndicats nationaux, le Comité d'immigration de la CSN, "Résumé du 'Rapport d'enquête sur la situation des membres de la CSN provenant des communautés culturelles'," Montréal, 1989, p.13. (Translation)

The Committee has prepared materials for general distribution in the affiliate unions on racism and how unions can act against it. In May 1990 a day long educational session was organized on racism and discrimination, and a course has been prepared for union staff and officials who service workers from minority ethnic and cultural groups, so that they are better able to respond to the needs of these workers. With government support, a successful pilot project provided French language training during working hours to thirty hotel workers, and the course is now offered at several other work sites. The Committee has also prepared two briefs to government advising a gradual increase in the rate of immigration, and calling for increased resources to help the integration of new immigrants. In March 1991 the Committee produced a thirty-page document called "Des syndicats de toutes les couleurs," for distribution to all affiliate unions. It examines racism in society, discrimination at work and the role of the union movement. The Committee has also worked to make the 21st March, International Day Against Racism and Discrimination, an important date on the union calender, producing brochures and stickers for the occasion.

The CSN has both a working group on gay and lesbian issues that was set up in 1988 and, since 1991, a central committee on the subject. It is the only labour central that has a formal committee to deal with the concerns of gay and lesbian members. The working group has four members, including one woman, and the committee has eleven members, of which one is a woman. All are gays and lesbians. The working group is most concerned with benefit coverage for same-sex spouses and harassment, while the committee is focused upon the issue of employment equity. The members of both the working group and the committee provide support for gays and lesbians and act as representatives in cases of discrimination. They have also provided training to union members through courses on human rights. The committee is collaborating with Concordia University to organize a conference on issues for gays and lesbians.

Very recently, in the spring of 1992, the CSN Executive established a working group on persons with disabilities, particularly to consider the issue of employment equity. The chair of this committee is also the chair of the women's committee of the CSN. The committee is planning a survey of disabled members to obtain information, and a major conference on disability is being prepared for the spring of 1993.

Unions

Of the thirteen unions, seven had no committee to deal with human rights issues. Although the Communication Workers of Canada had no committee, this union has been active in negotiating employment equity plans and has recently obtained funding to examine how to increase the proportion of workers with disabilities in the workplace (see Chapter 3). The issues of employment equity and harassment have been discussed in Chapters 3 and 5, and here the focus will be more upon activities and changes within the unions.

Of the six unions that had some type of committee, their level and focus of activity varied a great deal. The Hotel Employees and Restaurant Employees International Union had a human rights committee only in its Toronto local. In that local the committee was set up in 1984 and has worked closely with the Ontario Federation of Labour on its anti-racism campaign. The United Food and Commercial Workers Union established a human rights committee relatively recently in 1990. It is comprised of thirteen people from across the country, including visible minority, aboriginal and disabled members. Human rights policies have been developed for the union, including recommendations that human rights committees be established throughout the union. In some provinces and locals, committees are already functioning and it is a high priority to develop them across the country. A brochure on human rights has been produced for distribution throughout the union.

In the United Steelworkers, only District Six, which covers Ontario, has established a human rights committee at the district level, and there are committees in some area councils and locals within the district. These committees have focused primarily on racism. The District has developed two day and five day human rights courses that focus on racism called "Solidarity in Diversity: Building a Multicultural Union." Two conferences have been held, one in 1988 on human rights and another in 1991 called "Taking on Racism." The District Committee has also presented briefs on combating racism to the Ontario government's Race Relations and Policing Task Force and the Metropolitan Toronto Board of Commissioners of Police. With government funding, in 1992 the District developed and piloted a one to three hour flexible anti-racism course for delivery to union members at the workplace and sixteen members have been trained to deliver it.

The Canadian Auto Workers (CAW) has had a human rights committee for two years, structured in the same way as the women's committee, with members who have been elected to the CAW Council, some of whom are from visible minority groups. A human rights conference is now held every year, and the most recent one focused on racism. The conference gives impetus and direction to the human rights committees in the locals, which are mandatory under the constitution. The CAW is the only union that mandates the formation of local women's and human rights committees. The main focus of the human rights committees has been on the issue of racism. The committees established in auto plants under negotiated employment equity agreements (see Chapter 3) have concentrated largely upon non-traditional jobs for women and improving the situation for racial minorities, although information has also been collected on workers with disabilities. The union has developed educational programs on human rights, both for a weekend and a week long course, which have been taken by a large number of activists within the union. Most recently the union has taken over the representation of workers formerly with the Confederation of Canadian Unions, predominantly workers in textile plants. As part of that agreement the CAW agreed to establish a store front in downtown Toronto to serve the needs of immigrant workers.

The Public Service Alliance of Canada (PSAC) has had an Equal Opportunities Committee at the national level since 1976, with 18 members each representing a component of the union. Although responsible for equality issues in general, its focus has been primarily upon women's issues, and it has been primarily white, able-bodied and straight women who have sat on the committee, with sometimes a few white, able-bodied straight men. However, at the 1991 Convention of the union it was decided to add seven more seats to the Committee to represent different minority groups, providing two representatives for visible minorities, two for native people, two for persons with disabilities and one for lesbians and gay men. After meetings with gays and lesbians within the union, and with the full support of the seven other minority group members, the National Executive decided to add an eighth seat, so that there could be a gay man and a lesbian included.

The new committee held its first meeting in the spring of 1992 and established subcommittees for its work over the year. The arrangement is to last only for one year, because the new positions do not formally represent Alliance members, but were solicited from among the membership and self-identified as members of minority groups. However, they are to develop a new mechanism for the committee, which would return to a total of eighteen members but also ensure representation of all the minority groups as well as the union's membership in general.

This change in the national level committee follows several other developments within the union. In 1988 the union hired a Human Rights Officer following a decision by the Convention, in addition to another staff person who deals with women's issues. As well, different committees have developed to represent the interests of minority group members.

The Equal Action Group includes both visible minority and aboriginal members in the National Capital Region who have come together "to focus on racism in the Public Service." To this end the group prepared a presentation on the impact on racial minorities of "Public Service 2000," the proposed reorganization of the federal public service. The group has arranged to meet with the President and the National Executive Board of the union to express their concerns, which include the need for more detailed research on different racial groups and their varying experiences. They are also concerned to foster the development of similar groups in other regions. There is already a group that meets on the issue of race relations in Toronto, the Visible Minority Equity Committee. There is also the beginnings of an aboriginal people's network, although it is not formally organized as yet.

The Lesbian and Gay Support Group is a national network, with members primarily in Ottawa and Vancouver but contacts elsewhere. They have been meeting since 1990 and their goals are to support lesbian and gay members, press for equality and eliminate homophobia. Although the master contract prohibits discrimination because of sexual orientation, it also defines spouse as a member of the opposite sex and the group wants to see this changed. The Support Group has been influential in transforming the politics on this issue within the union, and the leadership is much more supportive now than in the past.

The Members with Disabilities Ad Hoc Committee also first met in 1990 to discuss the needs of workers with disabilities with the Human Rights Officer. They have since met with the National Executive to raise their concerns and also made a presentation on the impact of "Public Service 2000" on people with disabilities. This group has produced a document called "Persons with Disabilities" for distribution in the union, outlining what the union should be doing on the issue. This includes accessible meetings, alternative media to print, access to union education, modules on disability for educational programs, employment equity, and accommodation by the employer. Any buildings controlled from the national office are now accessible for mobility disabilities, but only the Human Rights Officer at the national office has a telecommunications device for the deaf and more are necessary in the regions. This Committee is now applying for government funding to hold a conference on disability issues.

Each of these three groups has produced a brief pamphlet describing their goals and announcing their existence. The orientation of the Alliance is primarily towards supporting the development of such groups, encouraging them to set their own goals and determine what activities need to be undertaken. For the first time at the 1991 Convention there was a Human Rights Forum, with speakers from each of the four groups.

The union has a course called "Fighting Discrimination," but it has not been given very often. A four day course was developed for the union staff and has been offered on several occasions since 1990, in order to increase awareness of these issues among both component and regional staff. There is a joint committee of both the staff and the union as employer to develop an employment equity plan to ensure equality for staff within the union.

In the Canadian Union of Public Employees (CUPE) there is a national level committee called the National Working Committee on Racism, Discrimination and Employment Equity, popularly known as the Rainbow Committee. It was formed in 1988 following a decision of the National Convention and has twice reported back to the Convention with recommendations. As a result the union has adopted an anti-racism policy and a campaign with stickers and information leaflets was undertaken. The committee also recommended that a staff person be hired to deal with racism and a full-time Anti-Racism Officer was hired in 1991. As of 1992 the Rainbow Committee has been reconstituted and its 12 members now represent all regions of the country; it includes black, oriental and native minority group members, and half are women.

One high priority has been to sensitize union staff and leadership to racism and to provide human rights training so that problems experienced by racial minority members can be dealt with appropriately. A one day training program was developed for trainee representatives (union members who then form a pool of candidates for new staff positions) and will be given to each new group of trainees. It is planned that one staff person in each region will be identified to receive special training in human rights and become responsible for those issues. Two courses for union members have been developed and piloted, one on racism and another on cross-cultural training. A joint committee is examining an affirmative action program to ensure representation of minority groups on the CUPE staff and a consultant has been hired to provide a one-day workshop for staff to educate them on the issues.

Apart from the national level of CUPE, the most active region on racism has been Ontario, where visible minority members of the union are concentrated. The Ontario Division has had an active human rights committee for many years composed of members from racial minorities and also holds a human rights conference annually. Ontario has also developed an Employment Equity

The first graduates from an employment equity leadership training program set up by the Canadian Union of Public Employees, 1991.

Courtesy of Photo Features Ltd., Murray Mosher.

Leadership Training Program to develop the union skills of racial minority members. Outside of Ontario activities on racism are just beginning. A committee has been established in Alberta, and a resolution has passed in British Columbia to establish a committee there.

A caucus for gay and lesbian members was held at the 1989 CUPE Women's Conference, which lead to a network of contacts. The members of this network actively lobbied for further action within the union. As a result of this activity and the related increase in requests for information on what to bargain into collective agreements, the CUPE national office produced a kit for members in 1990. This comprehensive package includes some general information on homophobia and the experiences of lesbians and gay men, but also provides a very thorough analysis of the issue of same-sex spousal benefits, with concrete information on what locals should negotiate and how to do it. The information is now being updated for a second version of the kit.

Most recently, a Pink Triangle Committee was established at the last CUPE National Convention and held its first meeting in spring 1992.[21] The Committee has seven members from across the country who will now be able to meet several times a year to work on issues of concern. The priorities are to produce a policy paper on homophobia, to develop strategies for political action and to work with the education department of the union on developing materials on the subject.

At the 1991 CUPE National Convention, a resolution that a disabled person be hired on staff with responsibility for working on the concerns of members with disabilities did not reach the floor, but has been approved by the National Executive. A committee on disability has been recommended and approved, but not yet established.

In some situations it has been useful for union members of minority groups to meet outside of the formal union movement to provide support and press for change. Ronnie Leah has described the development of the Ontario Coalition of Black Trade Unionists (OCBTU).[22] It was formed in 1986 out of a conference organized by the Ontario Federation of Labour called "Building the Participation of Workers of Colour in our Unions." There had been some discussion of a similar organization in the United States and people who were interested signed a list. The OCBTU is open to all non-white workers and its objective is to share resources and co-ordinate struggles against racism in both the workplace and the union movement. It also encourages workers to become more involved in their unions.

In British Columbia the Lesbian and Gay Benefits Committee was formed when two women called a meeting to coordinate information around the different cases going through the courts, and thirty people attended. Although it is not limited to union members, the majority of participants are from several different unions. The goals of the group are to provide support to individuals, to raise awareness through education and to develop political strategies. The Committee has developed a workshop on homophobia available for unions and within the community generally. It has been given several times a year, including at Canadian Labour Congress schools and at the B.C. Federation of Labour's women's conference. At Federation Conventions the Committee provides a hospitality suite for gays and lesbians and has organized and lobbied around resolutions on gay and lesbian issues. Members of the group also worked with the Federation to produce a version of CUPE's kit on same-sex spousal benefits, with information specific to British Columbia. Most recently the Committee has applied for government funding to produce a video on the rights of gays and lesbians in the workplace.

In Ottawa a group called Gay and Lesbian Unionists developed in 1992, and includes members from several different unions. The goals are to share information, consider contract language, and encourage committees inside unions. It is also important as a support group for gays and lesbians who are active inside their unions and do not always receive support for their concerns.

Conclusion

The situation in the union movement with regard to human rights is still very varied. While it is clear that some unions and labour centrals have made considerable efforts, there are others that have not begun to deal with the issues affecting minority groups.

Issues of race or disability or gay/lesbianism were often first raised within women's committees or women's conferences, because these forums were more accepting of the problems and more prepared to deal with them. One exception is the women's committee of the Quebec Federation of Labour, which opposes the introduction or handling of these issues in the women's committee, and does not agree with the position taken by many women's committees in English Canada. For example, in 1989 the women's conference of the Canadian Union of Public Employees consisted of a course called Breaking through the Barriers, which focused on women of colour, native women, women with disabilities and lesbians. In the Public Service Alliance the women's conference has sent resolutions on these issues through to the national convention. In some cases it is still the women's committees that deal with gay and lesbian issues, because the formal human rights committee does not highlight the issue.

However, at the same time it is clear that "women" has usually been construed to mean white, able-bodied straight women, and there remains to be some consideration of "which women" sit on women's committees or get affirmative action seats, and how to ensure that they represent the female membership, in all its variations. The complexity of the issue of representation is only beginning to be dealt with, whether among women unionists or in the union movement generally. The question is how to obtain representation throughout the union movement of all union members, men and women, different racial groups, native people, persons with disabilities and gays and lesbians, integrating this with the need to represent members from different regions of the country and in some cases, different unions.

Some initial efforts in this direction have been undertaken, as outlined above. In the collective agreements it will require negotiated employment equity plans, equal access to benefits and protection from discrimination and harassment. Within the union movement there needs to be supportive policy, education at all levels, access to services for persons with disabilities, and coalitions with community groups. Formal affirmative action for elected and staff positions is likely to be as important for minority groups as it has been for women, and the Ontario Federation of Labour and the Canadian Labour Congress have made a start. Organization of union members within the various minority groups, including special committees, caucuses and conferences, is most likely to ensure progress and results.

Courtesy of the CAW.

8

Conclusion

In the 1970s women union members recognized their secondary
position within the labour movement. Women became increasingly aware that they rarely held executive positions, were less
often delegates to conventions than men, and that issues of
particular concern to women received little attention or action. The
problem was primarily perceived as the existence of barriers to the
entry of women, whether that was the opposition of male union
members, the double workload of women's domestic responsibilities, or training for women who felt lacking in experience for union
positions. Women set about pressing for change, organizing wom-
en's committees to discuss the issues and develop strategies,
finding methods to deal with sexual harassment, providing child
care at union meetings and developing special courses for women
union members. Women struggled for the right and the means to
participate in their unions.

The situation has altered. The efforts of many union women,
and some men, have not been unsuccessful. Most unions and union
organizations have established women's committees and caucuses.
Child care has become more commonly provided at union functions, and complaints about sexual harassment receive a more
appropriate reaction than laughter and jeering. More women attend
conventions and speak at them, and women now serve as elected
officers and occupy staff positions in unions. Issues of particular
concern to women, whether equal pay, employment equity or
specific benefits, are found on the union bargaining agenda.
Women are undoubtedly more organized and more vocal than ten
years earlier. And yet, despite this progress, equality remains
elusive.

In general women continue to be under-represented in the
highest union positions, at conventions, and on local executives.
Women with young children still find it difficult to participate in
union activities. Women without family responsibilities more often

become involved, but many continue to find the union environment a relatively unsympathetic one, where they and their concerns are considered of secondary importance and may be ignored or marginalized. The gruelling pace of work, political infighting and structural immobility affect both men and women, but these factors seem to claim more women victims who drop out from exhaustion or disillusionment.

The problem has been reformulated. First of all, the barriers to women's entry into active union participation are more complex and resilient than initially recognized. For example, child care at union functions helps, but is clearly insufficient to deal with the society-wide imbalance in domestic responsibilities between men and women. Similarly, it has been an important step for unions to pass policies opposing harassment, but effective mechanisms for handling harassment in all its forms have proved perplexing and have yet to be fully developed. It has become necessary to rethink some of the old issues, and attempt to deal with a more complex network of disincentives that affect women's union participation.

Secondly, women who broke through the barriers and obtained positions inside the union structure, quickly discovered that "getting in" was not the only problem. Once "in" other obstacles have been identified. Women find themselves grappling with traditional union structures and processes that are initially intimidating and hard to fathom and then also frustrating in their capacity to prevent innovation. Entrenched union structures, developed in response to external constraints and requirements, now serve to inhibit the kinds of changes necessary to involve women. Issues revolve around a small group of experts and prevent democratic participation. Sometimes these structures are based upon decades of male domination linked to an old boy's network that resists penetration. Collective bargaining committees, for example, often seem to exclude women not only because they have long been dominated by men, but also because of a culture of tough negotiating and the way bargaining is organized. Sexism has proved itself to be a hardy combination of structures, customs and ideas; it is not about to succumb to the first onslaught by women.

Increasingly, women have turned their attention not only to breaking down barriers, so that they have the opportunity to be involved in their unions, but to the fact that the unions themselves do not function in a fashion that facilitates their participation. It is no longer only a demand to "let us in," but a larger desire to transform the way that unions operate, and a growing recognition that if unions do not change their structures and methods, perhaps women never will achieve equality. This new agenda is also beginning to include the need to respond to women from different minority groups. For example, the new kind of union organizing that is taking place among homeworkers in the garment industry is culturally sensitive and reaching out into the community. The leaflets handed out at the plant gate and public meetings no longer answer the cause.

Having some degree of power has also created its own challenges. Women union members do not always share the same opinions as the women who obtain leadership positions, nor appreciate the way that it has been accomplished. Even where it is agreed that the woman will represent women's interests, expectations are often high and the constraints experienced by women in positions of influence are not well understood or appreciated. Like men, women who work in unions may be overburdened by the hours of work, but are without wives to look after the children or pack their bags for negotiating trips. Women in these positions may also find themselves relatively isolated, with little enough time to fulfil all the job requirements, let alone to keep in touch with the grass roots network of women that they have emerged from.

With the development of claims for participation by visible minority and aboriginal people, persons with disabilities and gays and lesbians, the question is also asked as to which women are obtaining the newly available positions of power. If they are all white, able bodied and straight, then many women are still being excluded from participation despite the apparent progress. Like the men who earlier held all the positions of power, majority group women are being questioned about whether they are representative of union membership. This question may seem threatening to the women who have only recently obtained a measure of participation themselves, or it may require another commitment of time and energy that is hard to find. However, it offers the opportunity to understand the variety that the word "woman" encompasses and to work for a union movement that is truly inclusive by being responsive to different needs.

The project for obtaining equality for women within unions has become more far reaching, and therefore more demanding. It is no longer simply the case that change has been stalled by male opposition. It is one thing to say that things must alter; it is another to propose in detail what the changes should look like. For example, it is a relatively straightforward thing to determine that there must be more women delegates at conventions, but it is more complex to establish a mechanism to accomplish that, given existing structures of regional and union representation. Similarly, affirmative action seats may be a useful tool for increasing the number of visible minority, aboriginal and disabled people in positions of power, but there are various ways of implementing such arrangements that must be considered. Meanwhile, institutions tend to be self-perpetuating and not given to change without extreme pressure. Union women are simultaneously working within unions, applying pressure for change and developing the appropriate alternatives. Trial and error occur and different approaches are used. Sometimes the desired change, once implemented, does not produce the expected results and the issue must be reformulated and dealt with again. To the extent that this takes place within an environment hostile to change, the task is made that much more exacting.

As women's committees have become an accepted part of union organization, and women's conferences established as regular events, some have lost their initial drive and determination. Becoming part of the union structure and closer to the union leadership may dampen the capacity to raise questions and demand answers. A further dilemma is posed when the leadership to be pressured now includes women who have been part of the movement for change. Concern that as women's committees become institutionalized they have not always been able to retain their own separate agenda has been expressed. Similarly, women's conferences that provide general education and entertainment sometimes no longer operate as working meetings to consider the next steps necessary to bring change and provide a forum to devise strategies for change.

The pace of change in unions and labour centrals has varied greatly; sometimes with a time lag of several years after the steps for change are initiated and before their full impact is felt. Within the same union the situation may vary between different regions, or between what is policy at the central level and what occurs locally. This uneven rate of change within and between unions makes it hard to assess the progress generally. A new policy that may be a step forward in one union can be in place for years elsewhere and found to be of limited value. For example, not all unions and centrals read out their policies opposing harassment at union events, while in other cases this has been done for years and is recognized as only one part of the necessary mechanisms to prevent harassment. Progress has different meanings for union women in different situations and has not necessarily occurred for all union women.

This unevenness in union development on women's issues also means that women may have quite dissimilar union experiences and concerns. Women also have different individual backgrounds within the union and women's movements. What will seem a major step forward to someone new to union women's struggles, may have a quite different complexion for the woman who has been discussing the issue for fifteen years. Opinions vary from how far unions have come, to how little has been accomplished for the effort invested. Women's conferences or other events that bring together women from many points in this broad spectrum face the challenge of meeting the need for different levels of discussion and analysis if some participants are not to be dissatisfied and frustrated.

External to the organization among women is the problem of backlash — the opposition of men. Such opposition is certainly not new, but sometimes it takes on a new, unanticipated guise. Women have now been demanding change for many years and some men express irritation with the issues, claiming that they have already been dealt with. It may be argued that the union has a women's committee, negotiated parental leave and a policy on harassment, so it is time to move on to other questions. In Ontario this argument is of particular concern among women working for pay equity, who fear that the effort around the legislation will exhaust the patience of the union movement with the issue. As well, women now have or are aiming for more powerful positions and more influence in the union movement. The pressure has not ceased with an annual women's conference and affirmative action seats on executives. Women have a stronger voice and are using it to demand more. In some cases as the challenge grows, so does the resistance.

However, women now speak from relatively stronger positions than they had in the past. More women are involved in all aspects and levels of union activity, including an extensive network of women's committees. It is particularly encouraging that so many women are taking union education courses, an indication that the future looks good for women's continued and increasing participation. As a result of all the activity, and despite evidence of a backlash in some situations, there is undoubtedly a more general acceptance that women's concerns need attention. There is now a strong base from which to move forward, a base that will be stronger still if it becomes possible to formulate unified ideas and action for change with other groups that experience discrimination. Women in the union movement have a wealth of experience and knowledge about organizing that will be brought to bear again in assessing the progress and deciding upon directions for the future, including structural change within the union movement itself.

It is a challenge to retain enthusiasm and persistence over the long haul, when progress seems slow and must sometimes be counted in decades rather than in months. Certainly, we have come a long way since the turn of the century, when women were barely accepted within the union movement, if at all. We have also come a long way in the last fifteen years. My first attempt to assess the situation for women in the labour movement, *Women and Unions*, was published in 1980 and now reads like a historical piece, interesting to know what was occurring then, but of little use to describe the current reality. Now women are grappling with new issues and the need to reformulate the old ones, whether that is being in leadership positions, questioning union structures, pressing more social concerns onto the bargaining table, handling backlash, or working with women who face different types of discrimination. It is important and exciting to realize that in ten or fifteen years another book will be necessary to update the progress and gains made by women within the union movement.

APPENDIX I

The Labour Market Activity Survey

Since 1986 Statistics Canada has carried out the Labour Market Activity Survey (LMAS). A questionnaire is attached to the monthly Labour Force Survey in January of each year, and obtains information on all the jobs held by a respondent in the previous year. It asks whether the job was union or non-union, and this information can be analyzed by detailed industrial and occupational categories, by sex, by size of firm, and by part-time and full-time work, among many others. It provides material for a far more detailed analysis of unionization by sex than information previously available through the Corporations and Labour Unions Returns Act (CALURA).

For the purposes of this paper, the most recent data available was for 1989, and was selected on the basis of the last job held by each worker in the year. For people working in December that job would be included, for people who had stopped working before December, but had worked during the year, the most recent previous job would be included. Thus, only one job for each worker is included, and yet the scope of the data is broader than the snapshot of one month provided by the Monthly Labour Force Survey, which includes only workers employed in that month.

Part-time workers are defined in the standard way for Statistics Canada as workers employed for less than 30 hours per week. Included here are workers employed part-time on both a full-year or part-year basis.

Part-year workers refers to workers who were employed full-time but whose jobs lasted for less than 12 months, either because the job both started and ended in 1989, or because the job ended in 1989 but had not lasted a full twelve months. This is not necessarily a sample of only casual or temporary work, because it includes workers who may have quit or been fired from jobs that were ostensibly permanent positions. However, it is a much closer approximation to looking at temporary employment than any other data available.

Industry Codes

Agriculture

01   Agriculture

Non-Agricultural Primary

02   Forestry
03   Fishing and Trapping
04   Metal Mines
05   Mineral Fuels
06   Non-metal Mines
07   Quarries and Sand Pits
08   Services Incidental to Mining

Manufacturing

09   Food and Beverage Industries
10   Tobacco Products
11   Rubber and Plastics Products
12   Leather Industries
13   Textile Industries
14   Knitting Mills
15   Clothing Industries
16   Wood Industries
17   Furniture and Fixture Industries
18   Paper and Allied Industries
19   Printing-Publishing and Allied Industries
20   Primary Metal Industries
21   Metal Fabricating Industries
22   Machinery Industries
23   Transportation Equipment Industries
24   Electrical Products Industries
25   Non-metallic Mineral Products Industries
26   Petroleum and Coal Products Industries
27   Chemical and Chemical Products Industries
28   Miscellaneous Manufacturing Industries

Construction

29   General Contractors
30   Special-Trades Contractors
52   Services Incidental to Construction

Transportation/Communication/Utilities

31   Transportation
32   Storage
33   Communication
34   Electrical Power, Gas and Water Utilities

Trade

35   Wholesale Trade
36   Retail Trade

Finance

37 Finance Industries
38 Insurance Carriers
39 Insurance Agencies and Real Estate Industries

Education/Health Services

40 Education and Related Services
41 Health and Welfare Services

Personal/Business Services

42 Religious Organizations
43 Amusement and Recreation Services
44 Services to Business Management
45 Personal Services
46 Accommodation and Food Services
47 Miscellaneous Services

Public Administration

48 Federal Administration
49 Provincial Administration
50 Local Administration
51 Other Government Offices

Clerical Occupations

411 Stenographic and Typing Occupations
413 Bookkeeping, Account-recording and Related Occupations
414 Office Machine and Electronic Data-processing Equipment Operators
415 Material Recording, Scheduling and Distributing Occupations
416 Library, File and Correspondence Clerks
417 Reception, Information, Mail and Message Distribution Occupations
419 Other Clerical and Related Occupations

Footnotes

Chapter 1
Women and the Early Development of Unions 1881-1921

[1] John Warkentin, *Canada: A Geographic Interpretation,* (Agincourt: Methuen Publications, 1967) p.152, Table 6–2.

[2] Harold A. Logan, *Trade Unions In Canada,* (Toronto: MacMillan, 1948) Calculated from p.19, Table 3, and p.78, Table 4.

[3] Ibid., calculated from p.18, Table 2.

[4] Ibid., p.78, Table 5.

[5] W.A. Mackintosh, *The Economic Background of Dominion-Provincial Relations,* (Toronto: McClelland & Stewart, 1964) p.55.

[6] Mona-Josée Gagnon, "Les femmes dans le mouvement syndical québécois: aspects historiques," in Marie Lavigne and Yolande Pinard, *Les femmes dans la société québécoise,* (Montréal: Boréal Express, 1978) p.147. (Translation).

[7] Alice Klein and Wayne Roberts, "Besieged Innocence: The 'Problem' and Problems of Working Women: Toronto 1896–1914," in Janice Acton et al., *Women at Work, Ontario 1850–1930,* (Toronto: Women's Educational Press, 1974).

[8] Terry Copp, *The Anatomy of Poverty: The Condition of the Working Class in Montreal 1897–1929,* (Toronto: McClelland & Stewart, 1974) p.68.

[9] Sylvia Ostry, "The Female Worker in Canada," 1961 Census Monograph, Ottawa, Dominion Bureau of Statistics, 1968, p.3, Table 1.

[10] Copp, p.49.

[11] Terry Morrison, "Their Proper Sphere," *Ontario History,* 68, March 1976, p.47.

[12] Ibid.; Deborah Gorham, "The Canadian Suffragists," in Gwen Matheson, *Women in the Canadian Mosaic,* (Toronto: Peter Martin Associates, 1976).

[13] Nellie McClung, *In Times Like These,* (Toronto: McLeod & Allen, 1973, first published 1915) p.51.

[14] Genevieve Leslie, "Domestic Service in Canada, 1880–1920," Acton et al., p.71.

[15] Ibid., p.110.

[16] The Corrective Collective, *Never Done: Three Centuries of Women's Work in Canada,* (Toronto: Canadian Women's Educational Press, 1974) p.134; Wayne Roberts, *Honest Womanhood: Feminism, Femininity and Class Consciousness Among Toronto Working Women, 1893 to 1914,* (Toronto: New Hogtown Press, 1976) pp.31–32; Varpu Lindström-Best, "I Won't Be a Slave! Finnish Domestics in Canada, 1911–1930," in Jean Burnet, *Looking Into My Sister's Eyes: An Exploration in Women's History,* (Toronto: The Multicultural History Society of Ontario, 1986) pp.48–49.

[17] Lindström-Best.

[18] Leslie, p.90.

[19] Gregory Kealey, *Working Class Toronto at the Turn of the Century,* (Toronto: New Hogtown Press, 1973) p.10.

[20] Roberts, p.9.

[21] Ibid., p.48.

[22] Ibid., p.17.

[23] Copp, p.129.

[24] Roberts, p.48.

[25] The Corrective Collective, p.99.

[26] Graham S. Lowe, *Women in the Administrative Revolution: The Feminization of Clerical Work,* (Cambridge: Polity Press, 1987) p.145, Table 7.1.

[27] Ibid., p.170.

[28] Judi Coburn, "I See and am Silent:" A Short History of Nursing in Ontario," Acton et al.

[29] Alison Prentice, "Themes in the Early History of the Women Teachers' Association of Toronto," Paula Bourne, *Women's Paid and Unpaid Work: Historical and Contemporary Perspectives,* (Toronto: New Hogtown Press, 1985) p.102.

[30] Elizabeth Graham, "Schoolmarms and Early Teaching in Ontario," Acton et al., p.190.

[31] Jacques Rouillard, *Histoire du syndicalisme québécois,* (Montréal: Boréal, 1989) p.227.

[32] Ostry, p.3, Table 1.

[33] Morley Gunderson, "Work Patterns," Gail Cook, *Opportunity for Choice: A Goal for Women in Canada,* Ottawa, Statistics Canada and C.D.Howe Institute, 1976, p.117, Table 4.8.

[34] Statistics Canada, *Labour Force Annual Averages, 1991,* Cat.71–002, p.B-8, Table 3.

[35] Bettina Bradbury, "Pigs, Cows and Boarders: Non-Wage Forms of Survival Among Montreal Families, 1861–91," *Labour/Le Travail,* 14, Fall 1984.

[36] Ceta Ramkhalawansingh, "Women During the Great War," Acton et al., p.294, Table 1.

[37] See Chapter 2, Table 2-1.

[38] Copp, p.49.

[39] Roberts, p.31.

[40] The Corrective Collective; Margaret Llewelyn Davies, *Maternity Letters from Working Women,* (London: Virago, 1978, first published 1915); Maud Pember Reeves, *Round About A Pound A Week,* (London: Virago, 1979, first published 1913).

[41] Gail Cuthbert Brandt, "Weaving It Together: Lifecycle and the Industrial Experience of Female Cotton Workers in Quebec, 1910–1950," *Labour/Le Travail,* 7, Spring 1981; Joan Sangster, "The 1907 Bell Telephone Strike: Organizing Women Workers," *Journal of Canadian Labour Studies,* 3, 1978.

[42] Joan Sangster, "Canadian Working Women in the Twentieth Century," W.J.C. Cherwinsky and Gregory S. Kealey, *Lectures in Canadian Labour and Working Class History*, (St. John's: Committee on Canadian Labour History and New Hogtown Press, 1985) p.66.

[43] Marie Gérin-Lajoie, "Le syndicalisme féminin," Michèle Jean, Québécoises du 20e siécle, (Montréal: Les Editions Quinze, 1977).

[44] Roberts, pp.10–11.

[45] Leslie, p.96, Table C.

[46] Lori Rotenberg, "The Wayward Worker: Toronto's Prostitute at the Turn of the Century," Acton et al., p.68, Table A.

[47] Roberts, p.17.

[48] Ruth Frager, "Sewing Solidarity: The Eaton's Strike of 1912," *Canadian Woman Studies*, 7: 3, Fall 1986.

[49] Roberts, p.40.

[50] Charles Lipton, *The Trade Union Movement of Canada 1827–1959*, (Montreal: Canadian Social Publications, 1967) p.81.

[51] Michael Piva, *The Conditions of the Working Class in Toronto, 1900–1921*, (Ottawa: University of Ottawa Press, 1979) p.143.

[52] Ibid., p.148.

[53] Roberts, p.49.

[54] Ibid., p.40.

[55] Pat Staton and Beth Light, *Speak With Their Own Voices: A Documentary History of the Federation of Women's Teachers' Associations of Ontario and the Women Elementary Public School Teachers of Ontario*, (Toronto: Federation of Women Teachers' Associations of Ontario, 1987) p.23.

[56] The Corrective Collective, p.90.

[57] Roberts, p.32.

[58] Gregory Kealey, *Canada Investigates Industrialism: The Royal Commission on the Relations of Labor and Capital, 1889 (Abridged)*, (Toronto: University of Toronto Press, 1973) p.42.

[59] Ibid., p.47.

[60] Coburn; Jean Thomson Scott, *The Conditions of Female Labour in Ontario*, Toronto, University Studies in Political Science, 1892, p.16.

[61] Alison Prentice, "The Feminization of Teaching," in Susan Mann Trofimenkoff and Alison Prentice, *The Neglected Majority*, (Toronto: McClelland & Stewart, 1977).

[62] Scott, p.24.

[63] Roberts, p.27.

[64] Lowe, pp.4–5.

[65] Ibid., p.145, Table 7.1.

[66] Ibid., p.48.

[67] Susan Mann Trofimenkoff, "One Hundred and Two Muffled Voices: Canada's Industrial Women in the 1880s," in Veronica Strong-Boag and

Anita Clair Fellman, *Rethinking Canada: The Promise of Women's History*, (Toronto: Copp Clark Pitman, 1986) p.85.

[68] Sangster.

[69] Ibid., p.126.

[70] Copp, p.129.

[71] Ibid., p.130.

[72] Sangster, p.126.

[73] Harold A. Logan, *The History of Trade Union Organization in Canada*, (Chicago: University of Chicago Press, 1928) p.130, Table 7, p.131.

[74] Alice Kessler-Harris, "Where Are the Organized Women Workers?" *Feminist Studies*, 3: 1/2, Fall 1975.

[75] Klein and Roberts, p.220.

[76] Roberts.

[77] Trades and Labor Congress of Canada, Proceedings of the Fourteenth Annual Session, Winnipeg, Manitoba, September 1898, pp.2, 31.

[78] Alice Kessler-Harris, p.97.

[79] Elaine Bernard, *The Long Distance Feeling: A History of the Telecommunications Workers Union*, (Vancouver: New Star Books, 1982) p.18.

[80] Marie Lavigne and Jennifer Stoddart, "Ouvrières et travailleuses," Lavigne and Pinard, p.140.

[81] Veronica Strong-Boag, "The Girl of the New Day: Canadian Working Women in the 1920s," *Labour/Le Travailleur*, 4, 1979, p.153.

[82] Linda Kealey, "Canadian Socialism and the Woman Question, 1900–1914," *Labour/Le Travail*, 13, Spring 1984, p.97.

[83] Klein and Roberts, p.221.

[84] Ibid., p.96.

[85] Nancy Schrom Dye, "Feminism or Unionism? The New York Women's Trade Union League and the Labour Movement," *Feminist Studies*, 3: 1/2, Fall 1975, p.113.

[86] Ramkhalawansingh, p.277, Table E, and p.279.

[87] Marie Campbell, "Sexism in British Columbia Trade Unions, 1900–1920," Barbara Latham and Cathy Kess, *In Her Own Right: Selected Essays on Women's History in British Columbia*, (Victoria: Camosun College, 1980) p.181.

[88] Robin W. Winks, *The Blacks in Canada*, (McGill-Queen's University Press, Montreal) 1971, p.144.

[89] Alicja Muszynski, "The Creation and Organization of Cheap Wage Labour in the B.C. Fishing Industry," Ph D. Thesis, University of British Columbia, 1988, p.135.

[90] Ibid, p.132.

[91] Paul Phillips, *No Power Greater: A Century of Labour in B.C.*, (Vancouver, B.C. Federation of Labour Boag Foundation, 1967) p.9.

[92] Ibid, p.21.

[93] Ibid, p.8, 32.

[94] Ibid, pp.25–35.

[95] Muszynski, p.184.

[96] Gillian Creese, "Organizing Against Racism in the Workplace: Chinese Workers in Vancouver Before the Second World War," *Canadian Ethnic Studies*, XIX: 3, 1987.

[97] Phillips, p.48.

[98] Ibid, p.98.

[99] Creese, p.38.

[100] Agnes Calliste, "Sleeping Car Porters in Canada: An Ethnically Submerged Split Labour Market," *Canadian Ethnic Studies*, XIX: 1, 1987.

[101] Winks, p.372.

[102] Ibid, p.378.

[103] Daniel G. Hill and Marvin Schiff, "Human Rights In Canada: A Focus on Racism," 3rd Edition, Ottawa, Canadian Labour Congress and Human Rights Research and Education Centre University of Ottawa, February 1988, p.26–28.

[104] Klein and Roberts, p.220.

[105] Campbell, p.174–175.

[106] Michelle Lapointe, "Le syndicat catholique des allumettières de Hull, 1919–1924," *Revue d'histoire de l'amérique française*, 32: 4, mars 1979.

[107] Between 1901 and 1915 61 percent of strikes in Canada involved wage disputes, while another 15 percent involved recognition of the union, the hiring of non-union workers or discharge of workers. See Canada, Department of Labour, Report of the Department of Labour, For the Fiscal Year Ending March 31 1916, Sessional Paper No.36, Vol.LII, No.20, Ottawa, 1917, p.91.

[108] Ibid., from 1901 to 1915 workers won just under 35 percent of the strikes over the period.

[109] Ibid.

[110] Ibid.

[111] Linda S. Bohnen, "Women Workers in Ontario: A Socio-Legal History," *University of Toronto Faculty of Law Review*, 31, August 1973.

[112] Johanna Brenner and Maria Ramas, "Rethinking Women's Oppression," *New Left Review*, 144, March-April 1984.

[113] Jacques Rouillard, *Les travailleurs du coton au Québec, 1900–1915,* (Montréal: Les presses de l'université du Québec, 1974) pp.96–97.

[114] Ramkhalawansingh, p.301.

[115] Gregory S. Kealey and Bryan D. Palmer, *Dreaming of What Might Be: The Knights of Labour in Ontario, 1880–1900,* (Cambridge: Cambridge University Press, 1982) pp.57, 379.

[116] Ibid, p.185.

[117] Phillips, p.14

[118] Kealey and Palmer, p.323.

[119] Gregory S. Kealey, *Toronto Workers Respond to Industrial Capitalism, 1867–1892,* (Toronto: University of Toronto Press, 1980) pp.187–189.

[120] Kealey, p.50.

[121] Eugene Forsey, *Trade Unions in Canada, 1812–1902,* (Toronto: University of Toronto Press, 1982) p.139.

[122] Kealey and Palmer, p.97.

[123] Trades and Labor Congress, Proceedings 1883, Toronto, 1884, p.38.

[124] Rouillard, p.41.

[125] Logan, p.189.

[126] Marie Campbell, "Women and Trade Unions in B.C., 1900–1920: The Social Organization of Sex Discrimination," prepared for the Women's Research Centre, Vancouver, June 1978, p.13.

[127] Ibid., p.219.

[128] Klein and Roberts, p.221.

[129] Nancy Forestell and Jessie Chisholm, "Working Class Women as Wage Earners in St. John's, Newfoundland, 1890–1921," in Peta Tancred-Sheriff, *Feminist Research: Prospect and Retrospect,* (Montreal: published for the CRIAW by McGill-Queen's University Press, 1988) p.146.

[130] Klein and Roberts, p.246.

[131] Ibid., p.243.

[132] Ruth Frager, "Sewing Solidarity: The Eaton's Strike of 1912," *Canadian Woman Studies,* 7: 3, Fall 1986, p.196.

[133] Roberts, p.39.

[134] Campbell, "Women and Trade Unions," p.13.

[135] Campbell, "Sexism in British Columbia Trade Unions," p.172.

[136] Ruth Frager, "Class and Ethnic Barriers to Feminist Perspectives in Toronto's Jewish Labour Movement, 1919–1939," *Studies in Political Economy,* 30, Autumn 1989.

[137] Trofimenkoff, p.89.

[138] Karen Dubinsky, "The Modern Chivalry: Women and the Knights of Labour in Ontario, 1880–1891," Masters Thesis, Carleton University, 1985.

[139] Heidi Hartmann, "Capitalism, Patriarchy and Job Segregation by Sex," *Signs,* 1: 3, 1976; Michèle Barrett, *Women's Oppression Today,* (London: Verso, 2nd Edition, 1988); Dorothy Smith, "Women and Trade Unions: The US and British Experience," *Resources for Feminist Research,* X: 2, July 1981.

[140] Gillian Creese, "The Politics of Dependence: Women, Work and Unemployment in the Vancouver Labour Movement Before World War II," in Gregory S. Kealey, *Class, Gender and Region: Essays in Canadian Historical Sociology,* (St. John's: Committee on Canadian Labour History, 1988).

[141] Scott, p.23.

[142] Ibid.

[143] Bohnen, pp.52–53.

144 Sonya O. Rose, "Gender Segregation in the Transition to the Factory: The English Hosiery Industry 1850–1910," *Feminist Studies,* 13: 1, Spring 1987, p.172.

145 Ibid.

146 Trofimenkoff, p.89.

147 Ibid.

148 Hilary Land, "The Family Wage," *Feminist Review,* 6, 1980, pp.55–77; Michelle Barrett and Mary McIntosh, "The Family Wage: Some Problems for Socialists and Feminists," *Capital and Class,* 11, Summer 1980, pp.51–72.

149 Gloria Montero, *We Stood Together: First Hand Accounts of Dramatic Events in Canada's Labour Past,* (Toronto: James Lorimer, 1979), see chapter "Asbestos Miners at Baie Verte 1978;" Arja Lane, "Wives Supporting the Strike," in Linda Briskin and Lynda Yanz, *Union Sisters: Women in the Labour Movement,* (Toronto: The Women's Press, 1983); Meg Luxton, "From Ladies' Auxiliaries to Wives' Committees: Housewives and the Unions," in Meg Luxton and Harriet Rosenberg, *Through the Kitchen Window: The Politics of Home and Family,* (Toronto: Garamond Press, 1986).

150 Creese, p.125.

151 Brandt.

152 Scott, p.25.

153 Nancy M. Forestell, "Times Were Hard: The Pattern of Women's Paid Labour in St. John's Between the Two World Wars," *Labour/Le Travail,* 24, Fall 1989, p.153, Table 3.

154 Sangster, p.65.

155 Creese, p.125.

156 Marilyn J. Barber, "Sunny Ontario for British Girls, 1900–1930," Burnet, p.63.

157 Scott, p.26.

158 Elizabeth Graham, "Schoolmarms and Early Teaching in Ontario," Acton et al., p.196.

159 Bernard, p.91.

160 Marie Lavigne et Jennifer Stoddart, "Les travailleuses Montréalaises entre les deux guerres," *Labour/Le Travail,* 2, 1977, p.183. (Translation).

Chapter 2
Women and the Changing Union Movement

[1] Sylvia Ostry, *The Female Worker in Canada*, 1961 Census Monograph, Ottawa, Dominion Bureau of Statistics, 1968, p.10.

[2] Statistics Canada, Labour Force Annual Averages 1991, Cat: 71–002, p.B–18–19, Table 8.

[3] Bryan D. Palmer, *Working Class Experience: The Rise and Reconstitution of Canadian Labour, 1800–1980,* (Toronto: Butterworths, 1983) p.237.

[4] Ibid.

[5] Eileen Sufrin, *The Eaton Drive: The Campaign to Organize Canada's Largest Department Store, 1948–1952,* (Toronto: Fitzhenry and Whiteside, 1983).

[6] Joe Davidson and John Deverell, *Joe Davidson,* (Toronto: James Lorimer, 1978) Chapter 3.

[7] Statistics Canada, *Corporations and Labour Unions Returns Act,* Ottawa, Cat. 71–202, Report for 1967.

[8] Doug Taylor, *For Dignity, Equality and Justice: A History of the Saskatchewan Government Employees' Union,* (Regina: Saskatchewan Government Employees' Union, 1984).

[9] Bruce McLean, *A Union Amongst Government Employees: A History of the B.C. Government Employees' Union 1919–1979,* (Vancouver: B.C. Government Employees' Union, 1979).

[10] Robert Laxer, *Canada's Unions,* (Toronto: James Lorimer, 1976) pp.237–238.

[11] Ibid.; Warren Caragata, *Alberta Labour: A Heritage Untold,* (Toronto: James Lorimer, 1979) p.144.

[12] Grace Hartmann, "Organizing Public Sector Workers in the Sixties," in Gloria Montero, *We Stood Together: First Hand Accounts of Dramatic Events in Canada's Labour Past,* (Toronto: James Lorimer, 1979) p.188.

[13] Canadian Nurses' Association, *The Leaf and the Lamp,* Ottawa, 1968, p.59.

[14] Laxer, Canada's Unions, p.231.

[15] Pat Staton and Beth Light, *Speak with Their Own Voices: A Documentary History of the Federation of Women Teachers' Associations of Ontario and the Elementary Public School Teachers of Ontario,* (Toronto: Federation of Women Teachers' Associations of Ontario, 1987) p.156; Laxer, *Canada's Unions,* Chapter 23.

[16] Gail McConnell, *Arbos 1983: Memories 1933–1983,* (Saskatoon: Saskatchewan Teachers Federation, 1983).

[17] Marlene I. Yri, "The British Columbia Teachers' Federation and its Conversion to Partisanship, 1966–1972," Masters Thesis, University of British Columbia, 1979.

[18] Robert Germain, *Le mouvement infirmier au Québec: Cinquante ans d'histoire,* (Montréal: Bellarmin, 1985).

[19] André Petitat, *Les infirmières: De la vocation à la profession*, (Montréal: Boréal, 1989), p.173.

[20] Jacques Rouillard, *Histoire du syndicalisme au Québec*, (Montréal: Boréal, 1989), pp.226–300.

[21] Craig Heron, *The Canadian Labour Movement: A Short History*, (Toronto: James Lorimer, 1989) p.118.

[22] Statistics Canada, *Corporations and Labour Unions Returns Act, Part II*, Cat: 71–202, Ottawa, Report for 1989, p.23.

[23] Ibid.

Chapter 3
Bread and Roses — The Advantages of Unionization

[1] Joan McFarland, "Women and Unions: Help or Hindrance," *Atlantis, 4*: 2, Spring 1979; Maureen Baker and Mary-Anne Robeson, "Trade Union Reactions to Women Workers and their Concerns," in Katharine Lundy and Barbara Warme, *Work in the Canadian Context: Continuity Despite Change,* (Toronto: Butterworths, 1981) p.388.

[2] For a summary of the results of nine Canadian studies between 1972 and 1985 see Morley Gunderson and W. Craig Riddell, *Labour Market Economics: Theory, Evidence and Policy in Canada,* (Toronto: McGraw-Hill Ryerson, 1988) p.314, Table 16.1; R. Swidinsky and M. Kupferschmidt, "Longitudinal Estimates of the Union Effects on Wages, Wage Dispersion and Pension Fringe Benefits," *Relations Industrielles/Industrial Relations,* 46: 4, 1991.

[3] Morley Gunderson, "Male-Female Wage Differentials and the Impact of Equal Pay Legislation," *Review of Economics and Statistics,* 57, 1975, pp.467-468.

[4] Julie White, *Women and Unions,* (Ottawa: The Canadian Advisory Council on the Status of Women, 1980) p.58.

[5] Unpublished data from the Labour Force Activity Survey, Statistics Canada; also see Labour Canada, Women's Bureau, Women in the Labour Force, 1990-91 Edition, Ottawa, p.116, which uses the same data base for 1987.

[6] H. Jain and P. Sloane, *Equal Employment Issues,* (New York: Praegar, 1981).

[7] Gunderson and Riddell, p.320; Swidinsky and Kupferschmidt, p.827.

[8] Morley Gunderson, "Labour Market Aspects of Inequality in Employment and their Application to Crown Corporations," *Equality in Employment, A Royal Commission Report, Research Studies,* Commissioner: Judge Rosalie Abella, Ministry of Supply and Services, 1985, p.21.

[9] Debra J. Lewis, *Just Give Us the Money: A Discussion of Wage Discrimination and Pay Equity,* (Vancouver: Women's Research Centre, 1988); Judy Fudge and Patricia McDermott, *Just Wages: A Feminist Assessment of Pay Equity,* (Toronto: University of Toronto Press, 1991).

[10] Rosemary Warskett, "Political Power, Technical Disputes and Unequal Pay: A Federal Case," Fudge and McDermott.

[11] Ibid.

[12] Carl Cuneo, *Pay Equity: The Labour-Feminist Challenge,* (Toronto: Oxford University Press, 1990).

[13] Lewis; Fudge and McDermott; Pat Armstrong and Hugh Armstrong, "Lessons from Pay Equity," *Studies in Political Economy,* 32, Summer 1990.

[14] Roberta Ellis-Grunfeld, unpublished presentation to the conference on Pay Equity: Theory and Practice, York University, Toronto, 14-15 May 1990.

[15] Canadian Union of Public Employees, *Equal Times: CUPE Pay Equity Newsletter*, March 1989 - March 1990.

[16] Labour Canada, Bureau of Labour Information, Collective Agreement Data Base, unpublished data for January 1992. This data includes all contracts covering 200 or more workers in the federal jurisdiction and 500 or more workers elsewhere, a total of 1,235 agreements and 2,434,055 workers.

[17] Jennifer Keck and Daina Green, "Pay Equity for Non-Unionized Women: A Case Study," unpublished paper presented at the Canadian Association of Schools of Social Work Conference, Kingston, June 1991, p.16.

[18] Ontario Pay Equity Commission, "Report to the Minister by the Ontario Pay Equity Commission on Sectors of the Economy that are Predominantly Female, as required under the Pay Equity Act, section 33(2)(e)," Toronto, January 1989.

[19] Canadian Union of Public Employees, *Equal Times: CUPE Pay Equity Newsletter*, March 1989 - March 1990.

[20] Rosemary Warskett, "Wage Solidarity and Equal Value: Or Gender and Class in the Structuring of Workplace Hierarchies," *Studies in Political Economy*, 32, Summer 1990.

[21] Julie White, *Mail and Female: Women and the Canadian Union of Postal Workers*, (Toronto: Thompson Educational Publishing, 1990) p.97.

[22] Hana Aach, "Unions and Affirmative Action," Women's Bureau, Canadian Labour Congress, Ottawa, 1984, pp.53-60.

[23] Lewis, p.50.

[24] Most of the information in this and the following two paragraphs is drawn from Canadian Auto Workers, "Affirmative Action at Work: The Case of the Canadian Auto Workers and General Motors of Canada," A Change Agent Project by the Ontario Women's Directorate and the Canadian Auto Workers, November 1987.

[25] Canadian Auto Workers, "A Commitment to Equality: CAW Brief for the Ontario Employment Equity Consultation," February 1992, pp.5,17.

[26] Canadian Auto Workers, "Bargaining Affirmative Action: The CAW Experience," Presentation by Peggy Nash, Assistant to the CAW President, to the Canadian Labour Congress Women's Conference, November 1990, p.7.

[27] Ibid, p.7.

[28] Communication Workers of Canada, "Qualification Development Program 1991," leaflet.

[29] Communication and Electrical Workers of Canada, "Submission to the Special Committee on the Review of the Employment Equity Act," 17 January 1992, p.4.

[30] Aach, pp.69-101.

[31] Carol Robertson, "The Quebec Scene: An Energetic Women's Committee Pushes Affirmative Action," Canadian Union of Public Employees, *The Facts*, 9: 5, September/October 1987.

[32] Meg Luxton and June Corman, "Getting to Work: The Challenge of the Women Back Into Stelco Campaign," *Labour/Le Travail*, 28, Fall 1991, p.182.

[33] Aach, p.98.

[34] Labour Canada, Bureau of Labour Information, Collective Agreement Data Base, unpublished data for January 1992.

[35] Canadian Labour Congress, "Submission to the Special Committee on the Review of the Employment Equity Act", Ottawa, February 1992, pp.15-16.

[36] Statistics Canada, Employee Compensation in Canada, Cat: 72-169, Ottawa, 1978, p.46, Table 1. This survey was discontinued after 1978.

[37] Pierre L. Siklos, "The Effect of Unionism on Wages, Total Compensation and the Degree of Unionization in Canada," Research Paper Series #8155, School of Business and Economics, Wilfrid Laurier University, December 1981.

[38] Swidinsky and Kupferschmidt, p.832.

[39] Margie Mayfield, "Work-Related Child Care in Canada," Women's Bureau, Labour Canada, Ottawa, 1990, p.113.

[40] The Ombudsman of Ontario, *Annual Report, 1986–87*, Volume II, p.89.

[41] Julie White, *Women and Part-Time Work, (Ottawa: Canadian Advisory Council on the Status of Women,* 1983) p.63.

[42] Ontario Federation of Labour, "Taking Stock and Moving Forward: Union Women in the 1990s," Toronto, 1990, p.28.

Chapter 4
Moving Up: Women into Union Leadership

[1] Statistics Canada, Corporations and Labour Unions Returns Act, unpublished data for 1989.

[2] Statistics Canada, *Corporations and Labour Unions Returns Act, Part II - Labour Unions, Report for 1989*, Cat: 71-202, p.23.

[3] Marg Bail, "Getting 'The Girls' to the Top," *Canadian Dimension*, October 1988, p.9.

[4] Ibid.

[5] Taking into account whether the affirmative action seats were added or designated, removing them leaves women with 56 executive positions out of 314 in total.

[6] National Union of Provincial Government Employees, "National Union Affirmative Action Survey," Ottawa, July 1989, calculated from pp.6–9.

[7] Interview with the Fédération des affaires sociales, Montreal, 22 March 1991, information for June 1989.

[8] Interview with the Canadian Union of Public Employees, Ottawa, 3 October 1990, unpublished information compiled by the union.

[9] Fédération des travailleurs et travailleuses du Québec, "Un syndicalisme en changement," Rapport du comité sur l'acces à l'égalité, XXIe Congrès, Québec, 27 novembre - 1 décembre 1989, pp.4–5.

[10] National Union of Provincial Government Employees, p.4.

[11] Fédération des travailleurs et travailleuses du Québec, p.4, Table 1.

[12] Interview with the Canadian Auto Workers, Toronto, 22 November 1990.

[13] National Union of Provincial Government Employees, p.13.

[14] Interview with the United Nurses of Alberta, Edmonton, 6 December 1990.

[15] Interview with the Ontario Secondary School Teachers Federation, Ottawa, 16 November 1990.

[16] Statistics Canada, *Corporations & Labour Unions Returns Act, Part II - Labour Unions, Report for 1989*, Cat: 71-202, p.23.

[17] Interview with the Canadian Auto Workers, Toronto, 22 November 1990.

[18] Ontario Secondary Schools Teachers Federation, "Handbook, 1990–91," p.77.

Chapter 5
Women's Activities and Issues Inside Unions

[1] Interview with the British Columbia Government Employees Union, Vancouver, 4 December 1990.

[2] National Union of Provincial Government Employees, "National Union Affirmative Action Survey," July 1989, p.5.

[3] Quebec Federation of Labour, "Un syndicalisme en changement," Rapport du comité sur l'acces à l'égalité, XXIe Congrès, Québec, 27 novembre - 1 décembre 1989, p.4.

[4] Julie White, *Mail and Female: Women and the Canadian Union of Postal Workers*, (Toronto: Thompson Educational Publishing, 1990) pp.174–175.

[5] Nancy Guberman, "Working, Mothering and Militancy: Women in the CNTU," Linda Briskin and Lynda Yanz, *Union Sisters: Women in the Labour Movement*, (Toronto: Women's Press, 1983) pp.278–279.

[6] Gary Chaison and P. Andiappan, "An Analysis of the Barriers to Women Becoming Local Union Officers," Working Paper No.W86–09, Faculty of Business Administration, University of Windsor, October 1986.

[7] Mona-Josée Gagnon, "Les femmes dans le mouvement syndical québécois," Marie Lavigne et Yolande Pinard, *Les femmes dans la société québécoise,* (Montréal: Boréal Express, 1977).

[8] Guberman, p.277.

[9] Confédération des syndicats nationaux, "Rapport-étape," Comité de la place des femmes, 3 décembre 1989, pp.10–11.

[10] Guberman, p.281.

[11] Confédération des syndicats nationaux, p.11.

[12] White, p.198.

[13] Graham S. Lowe, "CUPE Staff Workload Study: Report," Population Research Laboratory, University of Alberta, September 1990.

[14] Interview with the United Nurses of Alberta, Edmonton, 6 December 1990.

[15] Interview with the British Columbia Government Employees Union, Vancouver, 4 December 1990.

[16] Canadian Union of Public Employees, System for the Analysis of Labour Agreement Data (SALAD), CUPE Research, 19 November 1990.

[17] Interview with the Manitoba Federation of Labour, Ottawa, 14 November 1990.

[18] Ontario Federation of Labour, "Challenging Harassment," Document 2, 1st Biennial Convention, 25–29 November 1991, p.5.

[19] Ibid, p.1.

[20] United Steelworkers of America, "Sexual Harassment: A Policy to Prohibit and Prevent Sexual Harassment in the Workplace," p.5, and "Preventing Racial Harassment in the Workplace," p.5.

[21] Statistics Canada, *Corporations and Labour Unions Returns Act, Part II - Labour Unions*, Report for 1989, Cat: 71-202, p.23.

[22] Interview with the United Steelworkers of America, Toronto, 23 November 1990.

Chapter 6
Unorganized Women

[1] Statistics Canada, *Corporations and Labour Unions Returns Act, Part II - Labour Unions,* Cat: 71–202, Reports for 1962 to 1989.

[2] The Bank Book Collective, *An Account to Settle: The Story of the United Bank Workers (SORWUC),* (Vancouver: Press Gang Publishers, 1979); Carol Currie and Geri Sheedy, "Organizing Eaton's," Robert Argue, Charlene Gannagé and D.W. Livingstone, *Working People and Hard Times,* (Toronto: Garamond Press, 1987).

[3] Pradeep Kumar and Megan Slobodin, "Changing Unionism in Canada," Queen's Papers in Industrial Relations, Industrial Relations Centre, Queen's University, Kingston, 1987, p.5.

[4] J. Myles, G. Picot and T. Wannell, "Wages and Jobs in the 1980s: Changing Youth Wages and the Declining Middle," Statistics Canada, Labour Market Activity Survey Analytical Studies, July 1988, p.35.

[5] Ibid, p.2.

[6] Economic Council of Canada, "Good Jobs, Bad Jobs: Employment in the Service Economy," Ottawa, 1990.

[7] Ibid, p.12.

[8] Leo Troy, "Is the U.S. Unique in the Decline of Private Sector Unionism?" *Journal of Labour Research,* XI: 2, Spring 1990, p.127, Table 4.

[9] John O'Grady, "Downhill All the Way: The Labour Movement, Wage Polarization, and the Wagner Act Model of Collective Bargaining," presented to the conference on Broadening the Bargaining Structures in the New Social Order, Toronto, 7–8 May 1992, p.3.

[10] Statistics Canada, *Corporations and Labour Unions Returns Act,* Reports for 1986 to 1989.

[11] According to CALURA women comprised 39 percent of all union members in 1989, while the LMAS provides the figure of 42 percent.

[12] John O'Grady, "Beyond the Wagner Act?" unpublished paper, Toronto, February 1991, p.14.

[13] Ibid, p.10.

[14] Rosemary Warskett, "Bank Worker Unionization and the Law," *Studies in Political Economy,* 25, Spring 1988; Elizabeth J. Shilton Lennon, "Organizing the Unorganized: Unionization in the Chartered Banks of Canada," *Osgoode Hall Law Journal,* 18: 2, August 1980.

[15] Nine percent of women are employed part-year, compared to 12 percent of men. There is a concentration of part-year work in the seasonal work of agriculture, other primary industries and construction — all male dominated industries.

[16] See Appendix I for the occupations included under the category "clerical."

[17] The Bank Book Collective; Warskett; Lennon; Currie and Sheedy; Anne Forrest, "Organizing Eaton's: Do the Old Laws Still Work?" *Windsor Yearbook of Access to Justice*, 8, 1988.

[18] Troy, p.127, Table 4.

[19] Carl Cuneo, *Pay Equity: The Labour-Feminist Challenge*, (Toronto: Oxford University Press, 1990).

[20] Geoffrey England, "Part-time, Casual and other Atypical Workers: A Legal View," *Research and Current Issues Series* No.48, Industrial Relations Centre, Queen's University, Kingston, 1987; Norene Pupo and Ann Duffy, "The Ontario Labour Relations Board and the Part-Time Workers," *Industrial Relations/Relations Industrielles*, 43: 3, 1988.

[21] Currie and Sheedy.

[22] Lennon, p.214.

[23] Warskett, p.57–58.

[24] Peter G. Bruce, "The Processing of Unfair Labour Practise Cases in the United States and Ontario," *Industrial Relations/Relations Industrielles*, 45: 3, Summer 1990, p.497.

[25] Confédération des syndicats nationaux, "L'accés à la syndicalisation au Québec," 1984, pp.56–65.

[26] The Bank Book Collective, pp.105–106.

[27] Ibid, pp.74–77.

[28] Bradley J. Pragnell, "Organizing Department Store Workers," *Research Essay Series* No.22, Industrial Relations Centre, Queen's University: Kingston, 1989.

[29] Ibid.

[30] Jeffrey Sack and Tanya Lee, "The Role of the State in Canadian Labour Relations," *Industrial Relations/Relations Industrielles*, 44: 1, 1989.

[31] Norman A. Solomon, "The Negotiation of First Agreements Under the Canada Labour Code: An Empirical Study," *Industrial Relations/Relations Industrielles*, 40: 3, 1985; J.M.P. Korpesho and Mark Thompson, "First Contract Experience in Manitoba," *Is There a New Canadian Industrial Relations?* Proceedings of the 23rd Annual Meeting of the Canadian Industrial Relations Association, University of Manitoba, May 1986; "L'Arbitrage de première convention collective au Québec: 1978–1984," *Industrial Relations/Relations Industrielles*, 42: 2, 1987.

[32] Beatrice J. Miller, "Unmasking the Labour Board: Big Sticks and Bare Bones, First Contract Arbitration," *Our Times*, 6: 8, 1988.

[33] Beatrice J. Miller, "The Problem of Anti-union Petitions," *Our Times*, 6: 7, 1987.

[34] O'Grady, "Beyond the Wagner Act?" p.7.

[35] Ibid, p.9.

[36] Judy Fudge, "The Gender Dimension of Labour Relations Law: Why Women Need Inclusive Unionism and Broader-Based Bargaining," presented to the conference on Broadening the Bargaining Structures in the New Social Order, Toronto, 7–8 May 1992.

[37] Jean Bernier, "Modernizing Juridical Extension," presentation to the Conference, Broadening the Bargaining Structures in the New Social Order, Toronto, 7–8 May 1992; Statistics Canada, *Annual Averages for Canada and the Provinces for 1990 and 1991,* Cat.71–001, 1991.

[38] Confédération des syndicats nationaux, p.32; Jean Boivin, Claude Rondeau, and Jean Sexton, *La syndicalisation dans le secteur privé au Québec,* Les Presses du l'Université Laval, Quebec, 1983; Claire Bonenfant, Présidente du conseil du statut de la femme, "Un Réforme du code du travail doit tenir compte des femmes," presenté lors du Congrès des relations industrielles, Québec, 12 April 1983.

[39] Fudge, pp.21–24.

[40] Warskett, p.42; Lennon, p.202.

[41] Troy; Seymour Martin Lipset, "Comparing Canadian and American Unions," *Society,* 24: 2, January/February 1987; Noah Meltz, "Interstate vs Interprovincial Differences in Union Density," *Industrial Relations/Relations Industrielles,* 28: 2, Spring 1989.

[42] Kumar and Slobodin, p.4.

[43] Pradeep Kumar and Dennis Ryan, "Canadian Union Movement in the 1980s: Perspectives from Union Leaders," Research and Current Issues Series No.53, Industrial Relations Centre, Queen's University, Kingston, 1988, p.7.

[44] Alain Piche, "Organizing for the Future," *Alliance,* 4, March-April 1991, pp.20–21.

[45] Heather A. Clemenson, "Unionization and Women in the Service Sector," Statistics Canada, *Perspectives,* Autumn 1989, p.35; Barry Weisleder "Organizing Substitute Teachers," Argue, Gannagé and Livingstone.

[46] Linda Briskin and Lynda Yanz, *Union Sisters,* (Toronto: The Women's Press, 1983), see section on The Power of Alliances; Dierdre Gallagher, "Affirmative Action," Argue, Gannagé and Livingstone.

[47] Most of the information for this section was obtained from an interview with Alex Dagg, Director for the Ontario Region, International Ladies Garment Workers Union, Toronto, 8 May 1992.

[48] Laura C. Johnson, *The Seam Allowance: Industrial Home Sewing in Canada,* (Toronto: The Women's Press, 1982).

[49] Interview with Alex Dagg, Ontario Director, International Ladies Garment Workers Union, Toronto, 8 May 1992.

[50] Treasury Board Secretariat, Policies and Procedures Group, Personnel Policy Branch, "Working at Home: A Guide to Implementation," 13 March 1992, p.3.

[51] Bert Hill, "Home Work: Productivity is up 95 per cent for 11 Employees Working from Home," *The Ottawa Citizen,* 3 December 1991, p.F1.

[52] Much of the information in this section was obtained from Theresa Johnson, Researcher, Technology Adjustment Research Project, Public Service Alliance of Canada, Ottawa, 14 May 1992.

[53] Hill, p.F1.

[54] Margaret A. Oldfield, "The Electronic Cottage — Boon or Bane for Mothers?" Anna-Maija Lehto and Inger Eriksson, "Proceedings of the

Conference Women, Work and Computerization," Helsinki, Finland, 30 June - 2 July 1991.

[55] Treasury Board, pp.4,42.

[56] Ibid, p.42.

[57] David Pugliese, "Is your home the workplace of the future?" *The Ottawa Citizen,* 9 May 1992, p.J1.

[58] Rusty Linda Neal, "Cleaning Up In Public: Women's Experiences as Subcontracted Cleaners," Masters Thesis, University of Toronto, 1987, p.43.

[59] Julie White, *Mail & Female: Women and the Candian Union of Postal Workers,* (Toronto: Thompson Educational Publishing, 1990).

[60] Information for this section was obtained in part through an interview with Wendy Iler, Canadian Union of Postal Workers, Ottawa, 13 May 1992.

[61] "Union Trying to Work Out Deal for Cleaners," *The Ottawa Citizen,* 20 March 1986, p.A10.

[62] Committee for Cleaners' Rights, "Notes for a Meeting with the Hon. William Wrye, Minister of Labour for Ontario," Toronto, 27 April 1987.

[63] The Canadian Union of Postal Workers, "CUPW Submission to the Consultation Hearings on Proposed Reform of the Ontario Labour Relations Act," Ottawa, 31 January 1992, p.6.

[64] Ontario Federation of Labour, *Focus,* The Ontario Federation of Labour's Bi-Weekly Newsletter, 17 March 1992.

[65] Ibid. 21 January 1992.

[66] Ontario Federation of Labour, "Submission to the Ministry of Labour Regarding Proposed Reform of the Ontario Labour Relations Act," 6 February 1992, p.51.

[67] Ibid. pp.51,53.

[68] Julie Davis, Ontario Federation of Labour, "Exploring Broader Based Bargaining," presentation to the conference on Broadening Structures in the New Social Order, Toronto, 7– 8 May 1992.

[69] Women for Labour Law Reform, "Press Release," Toronto, 4 June 1992 and "An Open Letter to the Minister of Labour on the Approach of the Current Government to Labour Law Reform," undated.

Chapter 7
Racial Minorities, Persons with Disabilities, and Gays and Lesbians

[1] The following historical information was drawn primarily from Daniel G. Hill and Marvin Schiff, "Human Rights in Canada: A Focus on Racism," Third Edition, Ottawa, Canadian Labour Congress and the Human Rights Research and Education Centre University of Ottawa, 1988, pp.11–14.

[2] Canadian Union of Public Employees, National Working Committee on Racism, Discrimination and Employment Equity (Rainbow Committee), "First Report," 1989, p.4.

[3] Hill and Schiff, p.10.

[4] Gurcharn S. Basran, "Canadian Immigration Policy and Theories of Racism," Peter S. Li and B. Singh Bolaria, *Racial Minorities*, (Toronto, Garamond Press, 1983) p.3.

[5] Frances Henry and Effie Ginzberg, "Who Gets the Work?" Toronto, Urban Alliance on Race Relations and the Social Planning Council of Metropolitan Toronto, 1985.

[6] Canadian Union of Public Employees, 1989, p.4.

[7] Debra Pilon, "Double Discrimination: Sexism isn't the only kind of discrimination against women," *CUPE Facts*, 9: 5, September\October 1987, p.45.

[8] Statistics Canada, *Profile of Visible Minorities and Aboriginal Peoples*, 1986 Census, Ottawa, January 1990.

[9] Michel G. Côté, "Visible Minorities in the Canadian Labour Force," Statistics Canada, *Perspectives*, Summer 1991, p.21, Table 3.

[10] Alma Estable, "Immigrant Women in Canada: Current Issues," Ottawa, Canadian Advisory Council on the Status of Women, March 1986.

[11] Monica Boyd, "Gender, Visible Minority and Immigrant Earnings Inequality: Reassessing an Employment Equity Premise," Working Paper 91–6, Carleton University, Ottawa, June 1991, p.19.

[12] See Chapter Six, Unionization of Racial Minorities.

[13] Statistical information on disability from Statistics Canada, The Health and Activity Limitation Survey, "Highlights: Disabled Persons in Canada" and "Selected Socio-Economic Consequences of Disability for Women in Canada," Cat:82-602, March 1990.

[14] Statistics Canada, National Work Injuries Statistics Program, "Work Injuries," Cat:72-208, December 1991, p.11.

[15] Debra Pilon, "Double Discrimination: Sexism isn't the only kind of discrimination against women," *CUPE Facts*, 9:5, September\October 1987, p.45.

[16] Interview with a member of the Public Service Alliance Lesbian and Gay Support Group, Ottawa, 30 June 1992.

[17] NDP Lesbian, Gay and Bisexual Caucus, "Employment Equity Legislation: Why Sexual Orientation Minorities Should be Included," Position Statement to the Employment Equity Commissioner, February 1992, p.6.

[18] Confédération des syndicats nationaux, "Qui sommes nous? Étude de la composition ethnique des syndicats du Conseil central de Montréal," Montréal, June 1985.

[19] Confédération des syndicats nationaux, "Résumé du 'Rapport d'enquête sur la situation des membres de la CSN provenant des communautés culturelles,'" Montréal, 1989.

[20] Ibid, p.16.

[21] The name Pink Triangle comes from the requirement in Nazi Germany that gays and lesbians wear pink triangles for identification.

[22] Ronnie Leah, "Linking the Struggles: Racism, Feminism and the Union Movement," Reprint Series No.93, Industrial Relations Centre, Queen's University, Kingston, 1990, p.12.

Bibliography

- Aach, Hana (1984). *Unions and Affirmative Action*. Women's Bureau, Canadian Labour Congress, Ottawa.

- Acton, Janice et al. (1974). *Women at Work: Ontario 1850–1930* (Toronto: Canadian Women's Educational Press).

- Aggarwal, Pramila (1987). Business as Usual in the Factory. *Resources for Feminist Research* 16 (1) March.

- Ahmad, Zubeida M. (1984). Women's Work and their Struggle to Organize. *Development: Seeds of Change* 4.

- Ainsworth, Jackie et al. (1982). Getting Organized … in the Feminist Unions. In Maureen Fitzgerald, Connie Guberman and Margie Wolfe, *Still Ain't Satisfied: Canadian Feminism Today* (Toronto: Women's Press).

- Akyeampong, Ernest B. (1989). The Changing Face of Temporary Help. *Perspectives on Labour and Income*, Statistics Canada, Cat: 75–001E, Summer.

- Amsterdam, Susan (1982). The National Women's Trade Union League. *Social Service Review* 56 (2) June.

- Andiappan, P., R. Julian Cattaneo, and Daiva Stasiulis (1984). *Attitudes of Female Union Members Toward Their Union: Results of a Survey of Nurses and Clerks in a Canadian City*. Working Paper No.84–00, Faculty of Business Administration, University of Waterloo, April.

- Antos, Joseph R., Mark Chandler, and Wesley Mellow (1980). Sex Differences in Union Membership. *Industrial and Labor Relations Review* 33 (2) January.

- Argue, Robert, Charlene Gannagé, and D.W. Livingston (1987). *Working People and Hard Times* (Toronto: Garamond Press).

- Armstrong, Pat, and Hugh Armstrong (1990). Lessons from Pay Equity. *Studies in Political Economy* 32 Summer.

- Armstrong, Pat, and Hugh Armstrong (1983). Beyond Sexless Class and Classless Sex: Towards Feminist Marxism. *Studies in Political Economy* 12 Fall.

- Backhouse, Constance (1980). The Fleck Strike: A Case Study in the Need for First Contract Arbitration. *Osgoode Hall Law Journal* 18 (4) December.

- Baden, Naomi (1986). Developing an Agenda: Expanding the Role of Women in Unions. *Labor Studies Journal* 10 (3) Winter.

- Badets, Jane (1990). Canada's Immigrant Population. In Craig McKie and Keith Thompson, *Canadian Social Trends* (Toronto: Thompson Educational Publishing).

- Bail, Marg (1988). Getting 'The Girls' to the Top. *Canadian Dimension* October.

- Bailey, Christopher C. (1979). *White Collar Unionization: The Case of the Nova Scotia Government Employees' Association, 1956–1978.* Masters Thesis, Dalhousie University.

- Bailey, John (1989). On Our Own Terms: Same Sex Spousal Benefits. *Our Times* December.

- Baker, Maureen, and Mary-Anne Robeson (1981). Trade Union Reactions to Women Workers and their Concerns. In Katharine Lundy and Barbara Warme, *Work in the Canadian Context: Continuity Despite Change* (Toronto: Butterworths).

- Balkan, Donna (1985). Practising what we preach ... Women, Unions and Affirmative Action. *Canadian Woman Studies* 6 (4) Winter.

- Ball, Ann (1988). Organizing Working Women: The Women's Labor Leagues. *Canadian Dimension* 21 (8) January.

- Bank Book Collective (1979). *An Account to Settle: The Story of the United Bank Workers (SORWUC)* (Vancouver: Press Gang Publishers).

- Barber, Marilyn J. (1986). Sunny Ontario for British Girls, 1900–1930. In Jean Burnet, *Looking Into My Sister's Eyes: An Exploration in Women's History* (Toronto: The Multicultural History Society of Ontario).

- Barber, Marilyn J. (1984). Below Stairs: The Domestic Servant. *Material History Bulletin* 19 Ottawa.

- Barber, Marilyn J. (1980). The Women Ontario Welcomes: Immigrant Domestics for Ontario Homes, 1870–1930. *Ontario History* LXXII (3) September.

- Barker, Jane, and Hazel Downing (1980). Word Processing and the Transformation of the Patriarchal Relations of Control in the Office. *Capital and Class* 10 Spring.

- Barrett, Michèle (1988). *Women's Oppression Today: The Marxist/Feminist Encounter*, Second Edition (London: Verso).

- Barrett, Michèle, and Mary McIntosh (1980). The Family Wage: Some Problems for Socialists and Feminists. *Capital and Class* 11.

- Baxandall, Rosalyn, Elizabeth Ewen, and Linda Gordon (1976). The Working Class has Two Sexes. *Monthly Review* July/August.

- Beattie, Margaret (1986). The Representation of Women in Unions. *Signs* 12 (1) Autumn.

- Beattie, Margaret (1983). Women, Unions, and Social Policy. *Journal of Business Ethics* 2.

- Beckett, Elizabeth (1984). *Unions and Bank Workers: Will the Twain Ever Meet?* (Ottawa: Women's Bureau, Labour Canada).

- Beechey, Veronica (1982). The Sexual Division of Labour and the Labour Process: A Critical Assessment of Braverman. In Stephen Wood, *The Degradation of Labour* (London: Hutchinson).

- Beechey, Veronica (1979). On Patriarchy. *Feminist Review* 3.

- Bélanger, Jacques et Jacques Mercier (1986). Le plafonnement de la densité syndicale au Québec et au Canada. *Relations Industrielles/ Industrial Relations* 41 (1).

- Bergquist, Virginia A. (1974). Women's Participation in Labor Organizations. *Monthly Labor Review* 97 (10) October.

- Bernard, Elaine (1984). Last Back: Folklore and the Telephone Operators in the 1919 Vancouver General Strike. In Barbara K. Latham and Roberta J. Pazdro, *Not Just Pin Money* (Victoria: Camosun College).

- Bernard, Elaine (1982). *The Long Distance Feeling: A History of the Telecommunications Workers Union* (Vancouver: New Star Books).

- Bernier, Jean (1992). Modernizing Juridical Extension. Presentation to the Conference, Broadening the Bargaining Structures in the New Social Order, Toronto, 7–8 May.

- Black, Errol (1988). The State of Canada's Unions. *Canadian Dimension* 21 (8) January.

- Blumfield, Hanita F. (1982). Jewish Women Sew the Union Label: A Study of Sexism and Feminism in the Emerging Unionization of the Garment Industry, New York City. *Humanity and Society* 6 February.

- Boehm, Marina C. (1991). Who Makes the Decisions? Women's Participation in Canadian Unions. School of Industrial Relations Essay Series N.35 (Kingston: Queen's University).

- Bohnen, Linda S. (1973). Women Workers in Ontario: A Socio-Legal History. *University of Toronto Faculty of Law Review* 31 August.

- Boivin, Jean, Claude Rondeau et Jean Sexton (1983). *La syndicalisation dans le secteur privé au Québec* (Québec: Les Presses du l'Université Laval).

- Bonenfant, Claire (1983). Une reforme du code du travail doit tenir compte des femmes. Présenté lors du Congrès des relations industrielles, Conseil du statut de la femme, Gouvernement du Québec, Québec, April.

- Boston, Sarah (1980). *Women Workers and the Trade Unions* (London: Davis-Poynter).

- Boyd, Monica (1991). Gender, Visible Minority and Immigrant Earnings Inequality: Reassessing an Employment Equity Premise. Carleton University, Department of Sociology and Anthropology, Working Paper 91–6, Ottawa, June.

- Bradbury, Bettina (1987). Women's History and Working Class History. *Labour/Le Travail* 19 Spring.

- Bradbury, Bettina (1984). Pigs, Cows and Boarders: Non-Wage Forms of Survival Among Montreal Families, 1861–91. *Labour/Le Travail* 14 Fall.

- Brandt, Gail Cuthbert (1986). The Transformation of Women's Work in the Quebec Cotton Industry, 1920–1950. In Brian Palmer, *The Character of Class Struggle, Essays in Canadian Working Class History, 1850–1950* (Toronto: McClelland and Stewart).

- Brandt, Gail Cuthbert (1981). Weaving It Together: Lifecycle and the Industrial Experience of Female Cotton Workers in Quebec, 1910–1950. *Labour/Le Travail* 7 Spring.

- Breitenbach, Esther (1981). A Comparative Study of the Women's Trade Union Conference and the Scottish Women's Trade Union Conference. *Feminist Review* 7.

- Brenner, Johanna, and Maria Ramas (1984). Rethinking Women's Oppression. *New Left Review* 144 March-April.

- Briskin, Linda, and Lynda Yanz (1983). *Union Sisters: Women in the Labour Movement* (Toronto: Women's Press).

- Bruce, Peter G. (1990). The Processing of Unfair Labour Practise Cases in the United States and Ontario. *Relations Industrielles/Industrial Relations* 45 (3) Summer.

- Burnet, Jean (1986). *Looking into My Sister's Eyes: An Exploration in Women's History* (Toronto: The Multicultural History Society of Ontario).

- Burnham, Fordon (1976). *Civil Servants By The Sea* (Halifax: Nova Scotia Government Employees Association).

- Calliste, Agnes (1988). Blacks on Canadian Railways. *Canadian Ethnic Studies* 20 (2).

- Calliste, Agnes (1987). Sleeping Car Porters in Canada: An Ethnically Submerged Split Labour Market. *Canadian Ethnic Studies* 19 (1).

- Campbell, Marie (1980). Sexism in British Columbia Trade Unions, 1900–1920. In Barbara Latham and Cathy Kess, *In Her Own Right: Selected Essays on Women's History in British Columbia* (Victoria: Camosun College).

- Campling, Robert F. (1987). Employee Benefits and the Part-time Workers. School of Industrial Relations Research Essay Series No.13 (Kingston: Queen's University).

- Canada (1990). A Consensus for Action: The Economic Integration of Disabled Persons. Report of the Standing Committee on the Human Rights and the Status of Disabled Persons. House of Commons, Ottawa, June.

- Canadian Nurses' Association (1968). The Leaf and the Lamp: The Canadian Nurses' Association and the Influences Which Shaped its Origins and Outlook During its First Sixty Years, Ottawa.

- Caragata, Warren. *Alberta Labour: A Heritage Untold* (Toronto: James Lorimer, 1979).

- Carr, Shirley (1975). Women's Year Union Role. *Canadian Labour* 20 (2) June.

- Carroll, William K., and Rennie Warbarton (1989). Feminism, Class Consciousness and Household-Work Linkages Among Registered Nurses in Victoria. *Labour/Le Travail* 24 Fall.

- Cashman, Tony (1966). *Heritage of Service: The History of Nursing in Alberta* (Edmonton: The Alberta Association of Registered Nurses).

- Chaison, Gary N., and P. Andiappan (1986). The Characteristics of Female and Male Local Union Officers. Working Paper No.W86–10, Faculty of Business Administration, University of Windsor, October.

- Chaison, Gary N., and P. Andiappan (1986). An Analysis of the Barriers to Women Becoming Local Union Officers. Working Paper No.W86–09, Faculty of Business Administration, University of Windsor, October.

- Chaison, Gary N., and P. Andiappan (1982). Characteristics of Female Union Officers in Canada. *Relations Industrielles/ Industrial Relations* 37 (4).

- Charles, Nicola (1983). Women and Trade Unions in the Workplace. *Feminist Review* 15.

- Charpentier, Yvette (1977). Participation des femmes aux mouvements syndicaux. In Michele Jean, *Québécoises du 20e siècle* (Montreal: Les Editions Quinze).

- Clemenson, Heather A. (1989). Unionization and Women in the Service Sector. *Perspectives on Labour and Income*, Statistics Canada, Cat.75–001E 1 (2) Autumn.

- Clio Collective (1987). *Quebec Women: A History* (Toronto: The Women's Press).

- Coalition for Lesbian and Gay Rights in Ontario (1991). We Count: Lesbians, Gay Men and Employment Equity. Brief written for the Ontario Legislature, October.

- Coates, Mary Lou (1991). *Work and Family Issues: Beyond Swapping the Mopping and Sharing the Caring*. (Kingston: Industrial Relations Centre, Queen's University).

- Coates, Mary Lou (1988). *Part-Time Employment: Labour Market Flexibility and Equity Issues*. (Kingston: Industrial Relations Centre, Queen's University).

- Cockburn, Cynthia (1984). Trade Unions and the Radicalizing of Socialist Feminism. *Feminist Review* 16 Summer.

- Cockburn, Cynthia (1983). *Brothers: Male Dominance and Technological Change* (London: Pluto Press).

- Conde, Carol, and Karl Beveridge (1986). *First Contract: Women and the Fight to Unionize* (Toronto: Between the Lines).

- Connelly, Patricia (1983). On Marxism and Feminism. *Studies in Political Economy* 12 Fall.

- Cook, Alice, Val Lorwin, and Arlene Kaplan Daniels (1984). *Women and Trade Unions in Eleven Industrialized Countries* (Philadelphia: Temple University Press).

- Cook, Alice (1968). Women and American Trade Unions. *The Annals of the American Academy of Political and Social Science* 375 January.

- Coote, Anna, and Peter Kellner (1980). Powerlessness and how to fight it. *New Statesman* 7 November.

- Copp, Terry. *The Anatomy of Poverty: The Condition of the Working Class in Montreal 1897–1929* (Toronto: McClelland and Stewart, 1974).

- Cornish, Mary (1986). *Equal Pay: Collective Bargaining and the Law* (Ottawa:Women's Bureau, Labour Canada).

- Cornish, Mary, and Laurell Ritchie (1980). *Getting Organized: Building a Union* (Toronto: The Women's Press).

- Cornish, Mary (1975). Women in Trade Unions. *This Magazine* 9 (4) September-October.

- Corrective Collective (1974). *Never Done: Three Centuries of Women's Work in Canada* (Toronto: Canadian Women's Educational Press).

- Costello, Pauline (1984–84). Women and Trade Unions: The Working Women's Charter. *Melbourne Journal of Politics* 15.

- Côté, Michel (1991). Visible Minorities in the Canadian Labour Force. *Perspectives on Labour and Income*, Statistics Canada, Cat: 75–001E, Summer.

- Coyle, Angela (1982). Sex and Skill in the Organization of the Clothing Industry. In Jackie West, *Work, Women and the Labour Market* (London: Routledge and Kegan Paul).

- Creese, Gillian (1988–89). Exclusion or Solidarity? Vancouver Workers Confront the 'Oriental Problem'. *B.C. Studies* 80 Winter.

- Creese, Gillian (1988). The Politics of Dependence: Women, Work and Unemployment in the Vancouver Labour Movement Before World War II. In Gregory S. Kealey, *Class, Gender and Region: Essays in Canadian Historical Sociology* (St. John's: Committee on Canadian Labour History).

- Creese, Gillian (1987). Organizing Against Racism in the Workplace: Chinese Workers in Vancouver Before the Second World War. *Canadian Ethnic Studies* XIX: 3.

- Crispo, John H.G. (1967). *The Role of International Unionism in Canada*, Washington, Canadian-American Committee.

- Crompton, Rosemary, and Gareth Jones (1984). *White-Collar Proletariat: Deskilling and Gender in Clerical Work* (London: MacMillan).

- Crothers, Diane (1971). Unionizing Legal Workers. *Women's Rights Law Reporter* 1 (1).

- Cuneo, Carl J. (1990). *Pay Equity: The Labour-Feminist Challenge* (Toronto: Oxford University Press).

- Currie, Carol, and Geri Sheedy (1987). Organizing Eaton's. In R. Argue, C. Gannagé and D.W. Livingston, *Working People and Hard Times* (Toronto: Garamond Press).

- Danson, Wendy (1978). Are Independent Unions a Quick Solution? *Kinesis* 7 (5).

- Danylewycz, M., and Alison Prentice (1986). Teacher's Work: Changing Patterns and Perceptions in the Emerging School Systems of Nineteenth and Early Twentieth Century Central Canada. *Labour/Le Travail* 17.

- Danylewycz, M. et al. (1983). The Evolution of the Sexual Division of Labour in Teaching, A Nineteenth Century Ontario and Quebec Case Study. *Social History* 16.

- Davidson, Joe, and John Deverell, *Joe Davidson* (Toronto: James Lorimer, 1978).

- Davies, Margaret Llewelyn (1978). *Maternity Letters from Working Women* (London: Virago) (first published 1915).

- Davies, M. (1974). Women's Place is at the Typewriter: The Feminization of the Clerical Labour Force. *Radical America* 8 (4).

- Dent, Mel et al. (1963). *The Story of the Women Teachers' Association of Toronto*, Vol.1 (Toronto: Copp Clark).

- Denton, Margaret (1984). Industrial Sectors and the Determinants of Earnings: Male-Female Differences. Ph.D. Thesis, McMaster University.

- Desjardins, Edouard, Eileen C. Flanagan, and Suzanne Giroux (1971). *Heritage: History of the Nursing Profession in the Province of Quebec* (Montreal: The Association of Nurses of the Province of Quebec).

- Deverell, John (1982). The Ontario Hospital Dispute 1980–81. 19th Annual Meeting of the Canadian Industrial Relations Association, Vol.I, Ottawa, June.

- Dewey, Lucretia M. (1971). Women in Labor Unions. *Monthly Labor Review* 94 (2).

- Dickason, Gladys (1947). Women in Labor Unions. *Annals of the American Academy of Political and Social Science* 251 May.

- Doherty, Bill (1991). *Slaves of the Lamp: A History of the Federal Civil Service Organizations, 1865–1924* (Victoria: Orca Book Publishers).

- Drake, Barbara (1920). *Women in Trade Unions* (London: Labour Research Department).

- Dubinsky, Karen (1985). The Modern Chivalry: Women and the Knights of Labour in Ontario, 1880–1891. Masters Thesis, Carleton University.

- Duffy, Ann, and Norene Pupo (1992). *Part-Time Paradox: Connecting Gender, Work and Family* (Toronto: McClelland and Stewart).

- Dumont-Johnson, Micheline (1980). Des garderies au XIXe siècle: Les salles d'asile des Soeurs Grises à Montréal. *Revue d'histoire de l'amérique française* 34 (1) June.

- Dunsmore, R.R. (1986). Unfair Labour Practice Remedies in Canadian Jurisdictions other than Ontario: Imposed First Agreements. In *Recent Developments in Labour Law*, Canadian Bar Association, Continuing Legal Education, February.

- Dye, Nancy Schrom (1975). Feminism or Unionism? The New York Women's Trade Union League and the Labor Movement. *Feminist Studies* 3 (1/2).

- Dye, Nancy Schrom (1974). Creating a Feminist Alliance: Sisterhood and Class Conflict in the New York Women's Trade Union League, 1903–1914. *Feminist Studies* 2 (2/3).

- Eaton, Jonathan B. (1990). *The Fleck Strike: Law on the Line.* (Kingston: Industrial Relations Centre, Queen's University).

- Economic Council of Canada (1990). *Good Jobs, Bad Jobs: Employment in the Service Economy.* Ottawa.

- Edelson, Miriam (1987). Challenging Unions: Feminist Process and Democracy in the Labour Movement. (Ottawa: Canadian Research Institute for the Advancement of Women).

- Edelson, Miriam (1982). Breaking Down the Barriers: Women and the Nature of Union Work. *Our Generation* 15 (3) Fall.

- Ellis-Grunfeld. Manitoba Pay Equity Legislation. In Mark Thompson, *Is There a New Canadian Industrial Relations?* Proceedings of the 23rd Annual Meeting of the Canadian Industrial Relations Association, University of Manitoba, May, 1986.

- England, Geoffrey (1987). Part-Time, Casual and Other Atypical Workers: A Legal View. Research and Current Issues Series No.48 (Kingston: Industrial Relations Centre, Queen's University).

- Estable, Alma (1986). *Immigrant Women in Canada: Current Issues* (Ottawa: Canadian Advisory Council on the Status of Women, March).

- Evans, Martin G., and Ondrack, Daniel A. (1986). The Effect of Unionization on Wages: Some Canadian Evidence. *Relations Industrielles/Industrial Relations* 41 (3).

- Fahmy-Eid, Nadia et Micheline Dumont (1983). *Maitresses de maison et maitresses d'école* (Montréal: Boréal).

- Farber, Henry S., and Daniel H. Saks (1980). Why Workers Want Unions: The Role of Relative Wages and Job Characteristics. *Journal of Political Economy* 88.

- Feldberg, Roslyn L. (1980). Union Fever: Organizing Among Clerical Workers, 1900–1930. *Radical America* 14 (3).

- Ferland, Jacques (1989). In Search of Unbound Prometheia: A Comparative View of Women's Activism in Two Quebec Industries, 1869–1908. *Labour/Le Travail* 24 Spring.

- Fiorito, Jack, and Charles R. Greer (1986). Gender Differences in Union Membership, Preferences and Beliefs. *Journal of Labor Research* VII (2) Spring.

- Foner, Philip S. (1980). *Women and the American Labor Movement: From World War I to the Present* (New York: Free Press).

- Foner, Philip S. (1979). *Women and the American Labor Movement: From Colonial Times to the Eve of World War I* (New York: Free Press).

- Forestell, Nancy M. (1989). Times Were Hard: The Pattern of Women's Paid Labour in St John's Between the Two World Wars. *Labour/Le Travail* 24 Fall.

- Forestell, Nancy, and Jessie Chisholm (1988). Working Class Women as Wage Earners in St. John's, Newfoundland, 1890–1921. In Peta Tancred-Sheriff, *Feminist Research: Prospect and Retrospect* (Kingston: published for the CRIAW by McGill-Queen's University Press).

- Forrest, Anne (1988). Why Workers Join Unions: The Role of Firm-Size Reconsidered. In Jean Boivan, *Some Aspects of International Industrial Relations*, Proceedings of the 25th Meeting of the Canadian Industrial Relations Association, University of Laval, Quebec, August.

- Forrest, Anne (1988). Organizing Eaton's: Do the Old Laws Still Work? *Windsor Yearbook of Access to Justice* 8.

- Forsey, Eugene (1982). *Trade Unions in Canada, 1812–1902* (Toronto: University of Toronto Press).

- Fortier, Johanne (1978–79). Les femmes et leur engagement syndical. *Canadian Woman Studies* 1 (2) Winter.

- Frager, Ruth (1989). Class and Ethnic Barriers to Feminist Perspectives in Toronto's Jewish Labour Movement, 1919–1939. *Studies in Political Economy* 30 Autumn.

- Frager, Ruth (1986). Uncloaking Vested Interests: Class, Ethnicity and Gender in the Jewish Labour Movement of Toronto, 1900–1939. Ph.D. Thesis, York Univeristy.

- Frager, Ruth (1986). Sewing Solidarity: The Eaton's Strike of 1912. *Canadian Woman Studies* 7 (3) Fall.

- Freeman, R.B., and J.L. Medoff (1984). *What Do Unions Do?* (New York: Basic Books).

- French, Doris (1968). *High Button Bootstraps: Federation of Women Teachers' Association, 1918–1968* (Toronto: Ryerson).

- French, Doris (1962). *Faith, Sweat and Politics: The Early Trade Union Years in Canada* (Toronto: McClelland and Stewart).

- Fudge, Judy (1992). The Gendered Dimension of Labour Law: Why Women Need Inclusive Unionism and Broader Based Bargaining. Unpublished paper presented at the Conference on Broadening the Bargaining Structures in the New Social Order, Toronto, 7–8 May.

- Fudge, Judy, and Patricia McDermott (1991). *Just Wages: A Feminist Assessment of Pay Equity* (Toronto: University of Toronto Press).

- Gabin, Nancy (1979–80). Women Workers and the UAW in the Post World War II Period, 1945–54. *Labor History* 21 Winter.

- Gagnon, Mona-Josée (1978). Les femmes dans le mouvement syndical québécois: aspects historiques. In Marie Lavigne and Yolande Pinard, *Les femmes dans la société québécoise* (Montréal: Boréal Express).

- Gagnon, Mona-Josée (1974). Les femmes dans le mouvement syndical québécois. *Sociologie et Société* 6 (1) mai.

- Gagnon, Mona-Josée (1973). La femme dans l'idéologie québécoise et dans la CSN: Etude idéologie et monographie syndicale. Thèse de mâitrise, Université de Montréal.

- Gannagé, Charlene (1986). *Double Day, Double Bind: Women Garment Workers* (Toronto: Women's Press).

- Gelber, Sylvia (1972). Which Side Are You On? *Canadian Labour* 17 (5) May.

- Geoffroy, Renee et Paule Sainte-Marie (1971). Attitudes of Union Workers to Women in Industry. Studies of the Royal Commission on the Status of Women, No.9, Ottawa.

- Gérin-Lajoie, Marie (1977). Le syndicalisme féminin. In Michele Jean, *Québécoises du 20e siècle* (Montréal: Les Editions Quinze).

- Germain, Robert (1985). Le mouvement infirmier au Québec: Cinquante ans d'histoire (Montréal: Bellarmin).

- Giroux, Claudette (1978). The Role of Women in the Canadian Trade Union Movement. Masters Thesis, Carleton University.

- Gorham, Deborah (1976)). The Canadian Suffragists. Gwen Matheson, *Women in the Canadian Mosaic* (Toronto: Peter Martin Associates).

- Gottfried, Heidi, and David Fasenfest (1984). Gender and Class Formation: Female Clerical Workers. *Review of Radical Political Economics* 16 (1) Spring.

- Gower, David (1990). Employment of Disabled Canadians. In Craig McKie and Keith Thompson, *Canadian Social Trends* (Toronto: Thompson Educational Publishing).

- Gunderson, Morley, and Leon Muszynski (1990). *Women and Labour Market Poverty* (Ottawa: Canadian Advisory Council on the Status of Women).

- Gunderson, Morley, and W. Craig Riddell (1988). *Labour Market Economics: Theory, Evidence and Policy in Canada* (Toronto: McGraw-Hill Ryerson).

- Gunderson, Morley (1985). Labour Market Aspects of Inequality in Employment and their Application to Crown Corporations. *Equality in Employment,* A Royal Commission Report, Research Studies (Ottawa: Ministry of Supply and Services).

- Gunderson, Morley (1982). Union Impact on Wages, Fringe Benefits and Productivity. In Morley Gunderson and John Anderson, *Union-Management Relations in Canada* (Don Mills: Addison-Wesley).

- Gunderson, Morley (1976). Work Patterns. In Gail Cook, *Opportunity for Choice: A Goal for Women in Canada* (Ottawa: Statistics Canada and C.D.Howe Institute.

- Gunderson, Morley (1975). Male-Female Wage Differentials and the Impact of Equal Pay Legislation. *Review of Economics and Statistics* 57.

- Hamed, S.M.A., and J. Sen (1986). Perceived Barriers to Unionization of Women: A Survey of Canadian Union Leaders. In Mark Thompson, *Is There a New Canadian Industrial Relations?* Proceedings of the 23rd Annual Meeting of the Canadian Industrial Relations Association, University of Manitoba, May.

- Hams, Marcia (1984). Women Taking Leadership in Male-Dominated Locals. *Women's Rights Law Reporter* 8 (1–2) Winter.

- Hansen, Barbara (1978/79). A Historical Study of Women in Canadian Banking, 1900–1975. *Canadian Women's Studies* 1 (2) Winter.

- Hartman, Grace (1976). Women and the Unions. In Gwen Matheson, *Women in the Canadian Mosaic* (Toronto: Peter Martin).

- Hartmann, Heidi (1976). Capitalism, Patriarchy and Job Segregation by Sex. *Signs: Journal of Women in Culture and Society* 1 (3).

- Hennessy, Peter H. (1975). Teacher Militancy: A Comparative Study of Ontario, Quebec and New York Teachers. (Ottawa: Canadian Teachers' Federation).

- Henry, Frances, and Effie Ginzberg (1985). *Who Gets the Work?* (Toronto: Urban Alliance on Race Relations and the Social Planning Council of Metropolitan Toronto).

- Heron, Craig (1989). *The Canadian Labour Movement, A Short History* (Toronto: James Lorimer).

- Hickling Johnston Limited (1968). The Status of Women in the Field of Collective Bargaining. Studies of the Royal Commission on the Status of Women, Ottawa.

- Hield, Melissa (1979). Union-Minded Women in the Texas ILGWU, 1933–50. *Frontiers* IV (2).

- Hill, Daniel G., and Marvin Schiff (1988). *Human Rights in Canada: A Focus on Racism.* Third Edition (Ottawa: Canadian Labour Congress and the Human Rights Research and Education Centre University of Ottawa).

- Horodyski, Mary (1986). Women and the Winnipeg General Strike of 1919. *Manitoba History* 11 Spring.

- Howes, Bill (1988). Doorknocking and Databases: Organizing in the Eighties. *Our Times* 6 (8) December/January.

- Humphries, Jane (1981). Protective Legislation, the Capitalist State and Working Class Men: The Case of the 1842 Mines Regulation Act. *Feminist Review*, Spring.

- Humphries, Jane (1977). Class Struggle and the Persistence of the Working Class Family. *Cambridge Journal of Economics* 1.

- Humphries, Jane (1977). The Working Class Family, Women's Liberation, and Class Struggle: The Case of Nineteenth Century British History. *The Review of Radical Political Economics* 9 (3).

- Humphries, Jane (1976). Women: Scapegoats and Safety Valves in the Great Depression. *Review of Radical Political Economics* 8 (1) Spring.

- Huxley, Christopher, David Kettler, and James Struthers (1986). Is Canada's Experience 'Especially Instructive'? In Seymour Martin Lipset, *Unions In Transition: Entering the Second Century* (California: ICS Press).

- Izraeli, Dafna N. (1984). The Attitudinal Effects of Gender Mix in Union Committees. *Industrial and Labor Relations Review* 37 (2) January.

- Izraeli, Dafna N. (1982). Avenues into Leadership for Women: The Case of Union Officers in Israel. *Economic and Industrial Democracy* 3.

- Jacoby, Robin Miller (1975). The Woman's Trade Union League and American Feminism. *Feminist Studies* 3 (1/2) Fall.

- Jain, Harish C., and P. Andiappan (1986). Sexual Harassment in Employment in Canada. *Relations Industrielles/ Industrial Relations* 41 (4).

- Jain, H., and P. Sloane (1981)). *Equal Employment Issues* (New York: Praegar).

- Jamieson, Stuart (1973). *Industrial Relations in Canada* (Toronto: MacMillan).

- Jammal, Nadine (1985). Les femmes dans le discours syndical. *Canadian Woman Studies* 6 (3) Summer/Fall.

- Jensen, Jane (1986). Gender and Reproduction: Or Babies and the State. *Studies in Political Economy* 20 Summer.

- Johnson, Laura C. (1982)). *The Seam Allowance: Industrial Home Sewing in Canada* (Toronto: The Women's Press).

- Kealey, Gregory, and Bryan Palmer (1982). *Dreaming of What Might Be: The Knights of Labour in Ontario, 1880–1900* (Cambridge: Cambridge University Press).

- Kealey, Gregory (1980). *Toronto Workers Respond to Industrial Capitalism, 1867–1892* (Toronto: University of Toronto Press).

- Kealey, Gregory (1973). *Working Class Toronto at the Turn of the Century* (Toronto: New Hogtown Press).

- Kealey, Gregory S. (1973). *Canada Investigates Industrialism: The Royal Commission on the Relations of Labor and Capital 1889 (Abridged)* (Toronto: University of Toronto Press).

- Kealey, Linda (1984). Canadian Socialism and the Woman Question, 1900–1914. *Labour/Le Travail* 13 Spring.

- Keck, Jennifer, and Daina Green (1991). Pay Equity for Non-Unionized Women: A Case Study. Unpublished paper presented at the Canadian Association of Schools of Social Work Conference, Kingston, June.

- Kehoe, Mary (1978). CLC Conference on Equal Opportunity. *Canadian Labour* 23 (1) March.

- Keneally, James J. (1978). *Women and American Trade Unions* (Montreal: Eden Press Women's Publications).

- Keon, Dan (1988). Union Organizing Activity in Ontario, 1970–1986. School of Industrial Relations Research Essay Series No.16 (Kingston: Industrial Relations Centre, Queen's University).

- Kessler-Harris, Alice (1982). *Out to Work* (New York: Oxford University Press).

- Kessler-Harris, Alice (1975). Where Are the Organized Women Workers? *Feminist Studies* 3 (1/2) Fall.

- Kojder, Apolonja Maria (1986). In Union There is Strength: The Saskatoon Women Teachers' Association. *Canadian Woman Studies* 7 Fall.

- Korpesho, J.M.P. (1986). First Contract Experience in Manitoba. In Mark Thompson, *Is There a New Canadian Industrial Relations*, Proceedings of the 23rd Annual Meeting of the Canadian Industrial Relations Association, University of Manitoba, May.

- Kozia, Karen S., and Patrice J. Insley (1982). Organizations of Working Women can Pave the Way for Unions. *Monthly Labor Review* 105 (6) June.

- Koziara, Karen, and David Pierson (1981). The Lack of Female Union Leaders: A Look at Some Reasons. *Monthly Labor Review,* May.

- Koziara, Karen S., and David A. Pierson (1980). Barriers to Women Becoming Union Leaders. In Barbara D. Dennis, Proceedings of the Thirty-Third Annual Meeting, Industrial Relations Research Association Series, Denver, September.

- Krahn, Harvey, and Graham S. Lowe (1984). Public Attitudes towards Unions: Some Canadian Evidence. *Journal of Labour Research* 5.

- Krebs, Edith (1975). Women Workers and the Trade Unions in Austria: An Interim Report. *International Labour Review* 112 (4) October.

- Kumar, Pradeep, and Lynn Acri (1991). *Women's Issues and Collective Bargaining* (Kingston, Industrial Relations Centre, Queen's University).

- Kumar, Pradeep, and David Cowan (1989). *Gender Differences in Union Membership Status: The Role of Labour Market Segmentation* (Kingston, Industrial Relations Centre, Queen's University).

- Kumar, Pradeep, Mary Lou Coates, and David Arrowsmith (1988). *The Current Industrial Relations Scene in Canada, 1988* (Kingston: Industrial Relations Centre, Queen's University).

- Kumar, Pradeep, and Dennis Ryan (1988). Canadian Union Movement in the 1980s: Perspectives from Union Leaders. Research and Current Issues Series No.53 (Kingston: Industrial Relations Centre, Queen's University).

- Kumar, Pradeep, and Megan Slobodin (1987). Changing Unionism in Canada. Queen's Papers in Industrial Relations, 1987–12 (Kingston: Industrial Relations Centre, Queen's University).

- Kuyek, Joan et al. (1985). Strong Women, Strong Unions: Speeches by Union Women. Participatory Research Group and Canada Employment and Immigration Union, January.

- Kuyek, Joan Newman (1979). *The Phone Book: Working at the Bell* (Toronto: Between the Lines).

- Lacelle, Claudette (1982). Les domestiques dans les villes canadiennes au XIXe siècle: effectifs et conditions de vie. *Histoire Sociale/Social History* 15 (29).

- Lafleur, Ginette (1988). L'industialisation et le travail rémunéré des femmes, Moncton, 1881–91. In Peta Tancred-Sheriff, *Feminist Research: Prospect and Retrospect* (Kingston: published for the CRIAW by McGill-Queen's University Press).

- Lafortune, Louise (1985). L'égalité des chances dans l'enseignement … mais pourquoi pas? *Canadian Woman Studies* 6 (4) Winter.

- Land, Hillary (1980). The Family Wage. *Feminist Review* 6.

- Langan, Joy (1975). BCFL Women's Rights Committe *Canadian Labour* 20 (2) June.

- Langan, Joy (1976). Trade Union Women's Committees. *Canadian Labour* 21 (3) September.

- Lapointe, Michelle (1979). Le syndicat catholique des allumettières de Hull, 1919–1924. *Revue d'histoire de l'amérique française* 32 (4) mars.

- Lavigne, Marie, and Jennifer Stoddart. Ouvrières et travailleuses. In Marie Lavigne and Yolande Pinard (1978). *Les femmes dans la société québécoise* (Montréal: Boréal Express).

- Lavigne, Marie et Jennifer Stoddart (1977). Les travailleuses Montréalaises entre les deux guerres. *Labour/Le Travail* 2.

- Laxer, Robert (1976). *Canada's Unions* (Toronto: James Lorimer).

- Leah, Ronnie (1989). Linking the Struggles: Racism, Feminism and the Union Movement. *Socialist Studies/Etudes Socialistes: A Canadian Annual* 5.

- Leah, Ronnie (1987). Organizing for Daycare. In Robert Argue, Charlene Gannagé and D.W. Livingstone, *Working People and Hard Times* (Toronto: Garamond Press).

- Legrande, Linda H. (1978). Women in Labor Organizations: Their Ranks Are Increasing. *Monthly Labor Review* 101 (8) August.

- Lepage, Francine et Anne Gauthier (1981). Syndicalisation: Droit à aquérir, outil à conquérir: Etude sur les travailleuses non syndiquées au Québec. Conseil du statut de la femme, Gouvernement du Québec, Québec.

- Lewenhak, Sheila (1977). *Women and Trade Unions. An Outline History of Women in the British Trade Union Movement* (London: Ernest Benn).

- Lewis, Jane (1985). The Debate on Sex and Class. *New Left Review* 149.

- Lewis, Debra J. (1988). *Just Give Us the Money: A Discussion of Wage Discrimination and Pay Equity* (Vancouver: Women's Research Centre).

- Li, Peter S., and B. Singh Bolaria, *Racial Minorities* (Toronto: Garamond Press, 1983).

- Lindstrom-Best, Varpu (1986). I Won't be a Slave! Finnish Domestics in Canada, 1911–1930. In Jean Burnet, *Looking into My Sister's Eyes: An Exploration in Women's History* (Toronto: The Multicultural History Society of Ontario).

- Lipset, Seymour Martin (1987). Comparing Canadian and American Unions. *Society* 24 (2) January/February.

- Lipsig-Mummé, Carla et Rita Roy (1989). La Population Syndiquée au Québec. *Labour/Le Travail* 23 Spring.

- Lipsig-Mummé, Carla (1987). Organizing Women in the Clothing Trades: Homework and the 1983 Garment Strike in Canada. *Studies in Political Economy* 22 Spring.

- Lipsig-Mummé, Carla (1984). La crise du syndicalisme nord-americain, éléments d'interpretation. *Relations Industrielles/ Industrial Relations* 39 (2).

- Lipton, Charles (1967). *The Trade Union Movement of Canada 1827–1959* (Montreal: Canadian Social Publications).

- Logan, Harold A. (1948). *Trade Unions in Canada* (Toronto: MacMillan).

- Logan, Harold A. (1928). *The History of Trade Union Organization in Canada* (Chicago: University of Chicago Press).

- Lowe, Graham S. (1990). CUPE Staff Workload Study: Report. Population Research Laboratory, University of Alberta, September.

- Lowe, Graham (1987). *Women in the Administrative Revolution: The Feminization of Clerical Work* (Cambridge: Polity Press).

- Lowe, Graham S. (1986). Women, Work and the Office: The Feminization of Clerical Occupations in Canada, 1901–1931. In Veronica Strong-Boag and Anita Clair Fellman, *Rethinking Canada: The Promise of Women's History* (Toronto: Copp Clark Pitman).

- Lowe, Graham (1981). Causes of Unionization in Canadian Banks. *Relations Industrielles/Industrial Relations* 36 (4).
- Luxton, Meg, and June Corman (1991). Getting to Work: The Challenge of the Women Back Into Stelco Campaign. *Labour/Le Travail* 28 Fall.
- Luxton, Meg (1986). From Ladies' Auxiliaries to Wives Committees: Housewives and the Unions. In Meg Luxton and Harriet Rosenberg, *Through the Kitchen Window: The Politics of Home and Family* (Toronto: Garamond Press).
- MacDonald, Glenn M., and John C. Evans (1981). The Size and Structure of Union—Non-Union Wage Differentials in Canadian Industry. *Canadian Journal of Economics* 14.
- MacKenzie, Eric Duncan (1971). The Historical Development of the New Brunswick Teachers' Association, 1902–1954. Masters Thesis, University of New Brunswick.
- Mackintosh, W.A. *The Economic Background of Dominion-Provincial Relations* (Toronto: McClelland and Stewart, 1964).
- MacLean, Annie Marion (September 1899). Factory Legislation for Women in Canada. *American Journal of Sociology* V (2).
- Maki, Dennis R. (1983). Unions as Gatekeepers of Occupational Sex Discrimination: Canadian Evidence. *Applied Economics* 15.
- Maki, Dennis R., and Christenson, S. (1980). The union wage effect re-examined. *Relations Industrielles/Industrial Relations* 35 (2).
- Marchak, Patricia (1975–76). Women, Work and Unions in Canada. *International Journal of Sociology* V (4) Winter.
- Marchak, Patricia (1973). Women Workers and White Collar Unions. *Canadian Review of Sociology and Anthropology* 10 (2).
- Maroney, Heather Jon (1986). Feminism at Work. In Bryan Palmer, *The Character of Class Struggle: Essays in Canadian Working Class History* (Toronto: McClelland and Stewart).
- Martin, Michèle (1988). Feminization of the Labour Process in the Communications Industry: The Case of Telephone Operators, 1876–1904. *Labour/Le Travail* 22 Autumn.
- Mayfield, Margie I (1990). Work-Related Child Care in Canada (Ottawa, Women's Bureau, Labour Canada).
- McCallum, Margaret E. (1989). Separate Spheres: The Organization of Work in a Confectionary Factory: Ganong Bros., St. Stephen, New Brunswick. *Labour/Le Travail* 24 Fall.
- McCallum, Margaret (1986). Keeping Women in Their Place: The Minimum Wage in Canada 1910–25. *Labour/Le Travail* 17 Spring.
- McClung, Nellie. *In Times Like These* (Toronto: McLeod and Allen, 1915).
- McConnell, Gail (1983). *Arbos 1983: Memories 1933–1983*. (Saskatoon: Saskatchewan Teachers' Federation).
- McFarland, Joan (1979). Women and Unions: Help or Hindrance. *Atlantis* 4 (2) Spring.
- McLean, Bruce (1979). *A Union Amongst Government Employees A History of the B.C. Government Employees Union 1919–1979* (Vancouver: B.C. Government Employees Union).

- McManus, Patrick (1988). Nurses win a louder voice. *Western Reporter* 3 (31) 24 October.

- McShane, Steven (1984). A Male-Female Comparison of Participation in a Local Labour Union. Ph.D. Thesis, Michigan State University.

- Meltz, Noah (1989). Interstate vs. Interprovincial Differences in Union Density. *Industrial Relations/Relations Industrielles* 28 (2) Spring.

- Meyerowitz, Joanne J. (1988). *Women Adrift: Independent Wage Earners in Chicago, 1880–1930* (Chicago: University of Chicago Press).

- Middleton, Lucy (1977). *Women in the Labour Movement: The British Experience* (London: Croom Helm).

- Milkman, Ruth (1985). *Women, Work and Protest: A Century of Women's Labor History* (London: Routledge and Kegan Paul).

- Miller, Beatrice J. (1987–88). Unmasking the Labour Board. *Our Times* 6 (7) November, 1987; 6 (8); December 1988; and 7 (1) February, 1988.

- Milkman, Ruth (1987). *Gender at Work: The Dynamics of Job Segregation by Sex During World War II* (Chicago: University of Illinois Press).

- Milkman, Ruth (1980). Organising the Sexual Division of Labor: Historical Perspectives on Women's Work and the American Labor Movement. *Socialist Review* 10 Jan-Feb..

- Montero, Gloria (1979). *We Stood Together. First Hand Accounts of Dramatic Events in Canada's Labour Past* (Toronto: James Lorimer).

- Morrison, Terry (1976). Their Proper Sphere. *Ontario History* 68 March.

- Mossuz-Lavau, Janine et Mariette Sineau (1980). L'ouvrière française et la politique. *Sociologie du Travail* 22.

- Muszynski, Alicja (1988). The Creation and Organization of Cheap Wage Labour in the B.C. Fishing Industry. Ph.D. Thesis, University of British Columbia.

- Muszynski, Alicja (1984). The Organization of Women and Ethnic Minorities in a Resource Industry: A Case Study of the Unionization of Shoreworkers in the B.C. Fishing Industry, 1937–1949. *Journal of Canadian Studies* 19 (1).

- Myles, John, G. Picot, and T. Wannell (1988). Wages and Jobs in the 1980s: Changing Youth Wages and the Declining Middle. Statistics Canada, Analytical Studies, No.17, July.

- Naylor, James (1986). Toronto 1919. *Historical Papers/Communications historiques* 44.

- Neal, Rusty Linda (1987). Cleaning Up In Public: Women's Experiences as Subcontracted Cleaners. Masters Thesis, University of Toronto.

- Neis, Barbara (1988). Doin' Time on the Protest Line: Women's Political Culture, Politics and Collective Action in Outport Newfoundland. In Peter R. Sinclair, *A Question of Survival: The Fisheries and Newfoundland Society* (St. John's: Institute for Social and Economic Research, Memorial University).

- Newby, Nancy J. (1986). *The Sky is the Limit: The Story of the Canadian Air Line Flight Attendants' Association* (Vancouver: Mitchell Press).

- Nichols-Heppner, Barbara A. (1984). Women in Public Sector Unions in Quebec: Organizing for Equality. Ph.D. Thesis, McGill University.

- O'Cleireacain, Carol (1986). Women and the Future of the Labor Movement. *Social Policy* 16 Winter.

- O'Grady, John (1992). Downhill All the Way: The Labour Movement, Wage Polarization, and the Wagner Act Model of Collective Bargaining. Presentation to the conference on Broadening the Bargaining Structures in the New Social Order, Toronto, 7–8 May.

- O'Grady, John (1991). Beyond the Wagner Act? unpublished paper, Toronto, February.

- Oddo, Maruja (1985). FTQ: Pour l'égalité au-dela des mots. *Canadian Woman Studies* 6 (4) Winter.

- Oldfield, Margaret A. (1991). The Electronic Cottage — Boon or Bane for Mothers? In Anna-Maija Lehto and Inger Eriksson, *Proceedings of the Conference Women, Work and Computerization.* Helsinki, Finland, June-July.

- Ontario Pay Equity Commission (1989). Report to the Minister by the Ontario Pay Equity Commission on Sectors of the Economy that are Predominantly Female, as required under the Pay Equity Act, section 33(2)(*e*). Toronto, January.

- Ostry, Sylvia (1968). The Female Worker in Canada. 1961 Census Monograph (Ottawa: Dominion Bureau of Statistics).

- Palmer, Bryan D. (1983). *Working Class Experience: The Rise and Reconstitution of Canadian Labour, 1800–1980* (Toronto: Butterworths).

- Panitch, Leo, and Donald Swartz (1988). *The Assault on Trade Union Freedoms* (Toronto: Garamond Press).

- Paquette, Janice (1986–87). Issues of Concern to Women in Current Public Sector Union Negotiations in Quebec. *Resources for Feminist Research* 15 (4) December 1986/January 1987.

- Parr, Joy (1990). *The Gender of Breadwinners: Women, Men and Change in Two Industrial Towns, 1880–1950* (Toronto: University of Toronto Press).

- Parr, Joy (1985). Women Workers in the Twentieth Century. In W.J.C. In Cherwinski and Gregory S. Kealey, *Lectures in Canadian Labour and Working Class History*, Committee on Canadian Labour History and New Hogtown Press.

- Pennell, Joan (1990). Consensual Bargaining: Labor Negotiations in Battered-Women's Programs. *Journal of Progressive Human Services* 1 (1).

- Pentland-Smith, Janice (1978). Provisions for Women in B.C. Union Contracts. Unpublished, available in Julie White, *Women and Work: A Resource Kit.* Women's Programme, Secretary of State, Ottawa.

- Petitat, André (1989). *Les infirmières: De la vocation à la profession* (Montréal: Boréal).

- Phillips, Paul. *No Power Greater: A Century of Labour in B.C.* (Vancouver: B.C. Federation of Labour Boag Foundation, 1967).

- Piva, Michael J. (1979). *The Condition of the Working Class in Toronto, 1900–1921* (Ottawa: University of Ottawa Press).

- Ponak, Alan, and Larry F. Moore (1981). Canadian Bank Unionism: Perspectives and Issues. *Relations Industrielles/Industrial Relations* 36 (1).

- Poole, Michael (1981). *Theories of Trade Unionism* (London: Routledge and Kegan Paul).

- Porter, Marilyn (1978). Consciousness and Secondhand Experience: Wives and Husbands in Industrial Action. *Sociological Review* XVI (1) March.

- Pragnell, Bradley J. (1989). Organizing Department Store Workers. Research Essay Series No.22 (Kingston: Industrial Relations Centre, Queen's University).

- Prentice, Alison et al. (1988). *Canadian Women: A History* (Toronto: Harcourt Brace Janovich).

- Prentice, Alison (1985). Themes in the Early History of the Women Teachers' Association of Toronto. In Paula Bourne, *Women's Paid and Unpaid Work: Historical and Contemporary Perspectives* (Toronto: New Hogtown Press).

- Prentice, Alison (1975). The Feminization of Teaching in British North America and Canada, 1845–1875. *Social History* 3.

- Pupo, Norene, and Ann Doris Duffy (1988). The Ontario Labour Relations Board and the Part-Time Workers. *Relations Industrielles/Industrial Relations* 43 (3).

- Rands, Jean (1972). Toward an Organization of Working Women. In *Women Unite* (Toronto: Canadian Women's Educational Press).

- Raphael, Edna E. (1974). Working Women and their Membership in Labor Unions. *Monthly Labor Review* 97 (5).

- Red Apple Collective (1978). Socialist-Feminist Women's Unions: Past and Present. *Socialist Review* 8 (2) No.38, March-April.

- Reeves, Maud Pember (1979). *Round About A Pound A Week* (London: Virago), (first published 1913).

- Reiter, Ester (1988). The Interchangeable Worker and Fighting Back: Identifying Some Strategic Issues. *Labour/Le Travail* 21 Spring.

- Reiter, Ester (1991). *Making Fast Food: From the Frying Pan into the Fryer* (Montreal: McGill-Queen's University Press).

- Reitz, Jeffrey G. (1981). *Ethnic Inequality and Segregation in Jobs*, Research Paper No.12, Centre for Urban and Community Studies, University of Toronto, May.

- Roberts, Wayne (1976). *Honest Womanhood: Feminism, Femininity and Class Consciousness Among Toronto Working Women, 1893–1914* (Toronto: New Hogtown Press).

- Robinson, Marguerite E. (1967). *The First Fifty Years* (Saskatoon: The Saskatchewan Registered Nurses Association).

- Robinson, C., and N. Tomes (1984). Union Wage Differentials in the Public and Private Sectors: A Simultaneous Equations Specification. *Journal of Labor Economics* 2.

- Rooney, Francis (1978–79). SORWUC. *Canadian Women's Studies* 1 (2).

- Rose, Sonya O. (1987). Segregation in the Transition to the Factory: The English Hosiery Industry 1850–1910. *Feminist Studies* 13 (1) Spring.

- Rose, Sonya O. (1986). Gender at Work: Sex, Class and Industrial Capitalism. *History Workshop* 21 Spring.

- Rosenthal, Star (1979). Union Maids: Organized Women Workers in Vancouver, 1900–1915. *B.C. Studies* 41 Spring.

- Rouillard, Jacques (1989). *Histoire du Syndicalisme au Québec* (Montréal: Boréal).

- Rouillard, Jacques (1974). *Les travailleurs du coton au Québec, 1900–1915* (Montréal: Les Presses de l'Université du Québec).

- Rubery, Jill (1980). Structured Labour Markets, Worker Organisation and Low Pay. In Alice H. Amsden, *The Economics of Women and Work* (Harmondsworth: Penguin).
- Russell, Bob (1991). A Fair or a Minimum Wage? Women Workers, the State, and the Origins of Wage Regulation in Western Canada. *Labour/Le Travail* 28 Fall.
- Sack, Jeffrey, and Tanya Lee (1989). The Role of the State in Canadian Labour Relations. *Relations Industrielles/ Industial Relations* 44 (1).
- Sangster, Joan (1985). Canadian Working Women in the Twentieth Century. In W.J.C. Cherwinski and Gregory S. Kealey, *Lectures in Canadian Labour and Working Class History*, Committee on Canadian Labour History and New Hogtown Press.
- Sangster, Joan (1989). *Dreams of Equality: Women on the Canadian Left, 1920–1950* (Toronto: McClelland and Stewart).
- Sangster, Joan (1985). The Communist Party and the Woman Question, 1922–29. *Labour/Le Travail* 15 Spring.
- Sangster, Joan (1979). The 1907 Bell Telephone Strike: Organizing Women Workers. *Labour/Le Travailleur* 4.
- Scott, Jean Thomson (1892). *The Conditions of Female Labour in Ontario* (Toronto: Toronto University Studies in Political Science).
- Scott, Paul (1984/85). Equality in Employment: A Royal Commission Report. *Currents: Readings in Race Relations* 2 (4) Winter.
- Sen, Joya (1984). Women's Participation in the Canadian Labour Market and Barriers to their Unionization. Ph.D. Thesis, University of Toronto.
- Sexton, Jean (1987). L'Arbitrage de Première Convention Collective au Québec: 1978–1984. *Relations Industrielles/ Industrial Relations* 42 (2).
- Sexton, Patricia Cayo (1982). *The New Nightingales: Hospital Workers, Unions, New Women's Issues* (New York: Enquiry Press).
- Shilton, Elizabeth Lennon (1980). Organizing the Unorganized: Unionization in the Chartered Banks of Canada. *Osgoode Hall Law Journal* 18 (2) August.
- Siklos, Pierre L. (1981). The Effect of Unionism on Wages, Total Compensation and the Degree of Unionization in Canada. Research Paper Series #8155, School of Business and Economics, Wilfrid Laurier University, December.
- Simpson, W (1985). The Impact of Unions on the Structure of Canadian Wages: An Empirical Analysis with Microdata. *Canadian Journal of Economic* 18.
- Smith, Dorothy (1981). Women and Trade Unions: The US and British Experience. *Resources for Feminist Research* X (2) July.
- Solden, Norbert C. (1978). *Women in British Trade Unions 1874–1976* (Dublin: Gill and MacMillan).
- Solomon, Norman, P. Andiappan and Dan Shand (1986). Canadian National Union Presidents: An Empirical Study. *Relations Industrielles/ Industrial Relations* 41 (3).
- Solomon, Norman (1985). The Negotiation of First Agreements Under the Canada Labour Code: An Empirical Study. *Relations Industrielles/ Industrial Relations* 40 (3).
- Solomon, Norman (1984). The Negotiation of First Agreements in Ontario: An Empirical Study. *Relations Industrielles/ Industrial Relations* 39 (1).

- Solomon, Norman, and R. Grant (1983). Canadian Trade Unionism and Wage Parity for Women: Putting the Principle into Practice. *Journal of Business Ethics* 2.

- Spinks, Sarah (1973). Women on Strike: Dare and Wardair. *This Magazine* 7 (1) May-June.

- Stasiulis, Daiva (1987). Rainbow Feminism: Perspectives on Minority Women in Canada. *Resources for Feminist Research* 16 (1) March.

- Staton, Pat, and Beth Light (1987). *Speak with Their Own Voices: A Documentary History of the Federation of Women Teachers' Associations of Ontario and the Elementary Public School Teachers of Ontario* (Toronto: Federation of Women Teachers' Associations of Ontario).

- Steedman, Mercedes (1986). Skill and Gender in the Canadian Clothing Industry, 1890–1940. In Craig Heron and Robert Storey, *On the Job: Confronting the Labour Process in Canada* (Montreal: McGill-Queen's University Press).

- Stone, Sharon Dale (1990) *Lesbians in Canada* (Toronto: Between the Lines).

- Strong-Boag, Veronica (1986). Pulling in Double Harness or Hauling a Double Load: Women, Work and Feminism on the Canadian Prairie. *Journal of Canadian Studies* 21 (3) Fall.

- Strong-Boag, Veronica (1979). The Girl of the New Day: Canadian Working Women in the 1920s. *Labour/Le Travailleur* 4.

- Sufrin, Eileen (1983). *The Eaton Drive: The Campaign to Organize Canada's Largest Department Store, 1948–1952* (Toronto: Fitzhenry and Whiteside).

- Sugiman, Pamela (1982). The Sales Clerks: Worker Discontent and Obstacles to its Collective Expression. *Atlantis* 8 (1).

- Sutton, John R. (1980). Some Determinants of Women's Trade Union Membership. *Pacific Sociological Review* 23 (4) October.

- Swidinsky, R., and M. Kupferschmidt (1991). Longitudinal Estimates of the Union Effects on Wages, Wage Dispersion and Pension Fringe Benefits. *Relations Industrielles/Industrial Relations* 46 (4).

- Taylor, Barbara (1979). The Men Are As Bad As Their Masters. *Feminist Studies* 5 (1).

- Taylor, Don, and Bradley Dow (1988). *The Rise of Industrial Unionism in Canada: A History of the CIO* (Kingston: Industrial Relations Centre, Queen's University).

- Taylor, Doug (1984). *For Dignity, Equality and Justice: A History of the Saskatchewan Government Employees' Union* (Regina: Saskatchewan Government Employees Union).

- Tentler, Leslie Woodcock (1979). *Wage Earning Women: Industry, Work and Family Life in the U.S. 1900–1930* (New York: Oxford University Press).

- Till-Retz, Roberta (1986). Unions in Europe: Increasing Women's Participation. *Labor Studies Journal* 10 (3) Winter.

- Tilley, Louise A., and Joan W. Scott (1978). *Women, Work and Family* (New York: Holt Rinehart and Winston).

- Todres, Elaine M., Barabara J. (1987). Falk and Frances S. Welch. Women's Issues and Industrial Relations: The Challenge of Pay Equity Legislation in Ontario. In Harish Jain, *Emerging Trends in Canadian Industrial Relations,*

Proceedings of the 24th Meeting of the Canadian Industrial Relations Association, Hamilton, June.

- Townson, Monica (1975). Organizing Women Workers. *The Labour Gazette*, June.

- Tremblay, Louise-Marie (1970). *Le syndicalisme québécois: idéologies de la CSN et de la FTQ 1940–1970* (Montréal: Les Presses de l'Université de Montréal).

- Tremblay, Marielle (1985). Un syndicalisme au masculin: la CEQ et la question des femmes. Thèse de doctorat, Université du Québec à Montréal.

- Trofimenkoff, Susan Mann (1986). One Hundred and Two Muffled Voices: Canada's Industrial Women in the 1880s. In Veronica Strong-Boag and Anita Clair Fellman, *Rethinking Canada: The Promise of Women's History* (Toronto: Copp Clark Pitman).

- Troy, Leo (1990). Is the U.S. Unique in the Decline of Private Sector Unionism? *Journal of Labour Research* XI (2) Spring.

- Ursel, Jane (1986). The State and the Maintenance of Patriarchy: A Case Study of Family, Labour and Welfare Legislation in Canada. In J. Dickinson and B. Russell, *Family, Economy and State* (Toronto: Garamond Press).

- Van Raaphorst, Donna L. (1988). *Union Maids Not Wanted: Organizing Domestic Workers 1870–1940* (New York: Praegar).

- Vance, Catherine (1968). *Not by Gods But by People: The Story of Bella Hall Gauld* (Toronto: Progress Books).

- Vohanka, Sue (1982). Getting Organized in the CCU. In Maureen Fitzgerald, Connie Guberman and Margie Wolfe, *Still Ain't Satisfied: Canadian Feminism Today* (Toronto: Women's Press).

- Walker, Eva K. (1963). *The Story of the Women Teachers' Association of Toronto*, Vol.2 (Toronto: Copp Clark).

- Warburton, Rennie (1986). The Class Relations of Public Schoolteachers in British Columbia. *Canadian Review of Sociology and Anthropology* 23 (2) May.

- Ward, Susan (1980). Helena Gutteridge: Votes for Women and Trade Unions. Barabara Latham and Cathy Kess, *In Her Own Right: Selected Essays on Women's History in B.C.* (Victoria: Camosun College).

- Warkentin, John (1967). *Canada: A Geographic Interpretation* (Agincourt: Methuen Publications).

- Warskett, Rosemary (1990). Wage Solidarity and Equal Value: Or Gender and Class in the Structuring of Work Place Hierarchies. *Studies in Political Economy* 32 Summer.

- Warskett, Rosemary (1988). Bank Worker Unionization and the Law. *Studies in Political Economy* 25 Spring.

- Warskett, Rosemary (1987). Legitimate and Illegitimate Unionism: The Case of SORWUC and Bankworkers Unionization. Paper presented to the Political Economy Sessions of the Canadian Political Science Association, Hamilton, Ontario, June.

- Warskett, Rosemary (1981). Trade Unions and the Canadian State: A Case Study of Bank Worker Unionization, 1976–1980. Masters Thesis, Carleton University.

- Watson, Louise (1976). *She Never Was Afraid: The Biography of Annie Buller* (Toronto: Progress Books).

- Watt, Ian (1980). Linkages Between Industrial Radicalism and the Domestic Role Among Working Women. *Sociological Review* 28 (1).

- Weisleder, Barry (1987). Organizing Substitute Teachers. In Robert Argue, Charlene Gannagé and D.W. Livingstone, *Working People and Hard Times* (Toronto: Garamond Press).

- Wertheimer, Barbara (1977). *We Were There* (New York: Pantheon Press).

- Wertheimer, Barbara, and Ann Nelson (1975). *Trade Union Women* (New York: Prager Press).

- Wetzel, Kurt, Donna E. Soloshy, and Daniel G. Gallagher (1988). Factors Shaping Union Commitment Among Women Unionists. Paper presented at the Learned Societies, University of Windsor, June.

- White, Jerry P. (1990). *Hospital Strike: Women, Unions and Public Sector Conflict* (Toronto: Thompson Educational Publishing).

- White, Julie (1990). *Mail and Female: Women and the Canadian Union of Postal Workers* (Toronto: Thompson Educational Publishing).

- White, Julie (1983). United We Stand. In Patti Schom-Moffatt and Cynthia Telfer, *The Women's Workbook* (Toronto: Between the Lines).

- White, Julie (1983). *Women and Part-Time Work* (Ottawa: Canadian Advisory Council on the Status of Women).

- White, Julie (1980). *Women and Unions* (Ottawa: Canadian Advisory Council on the Status of Women).

- White, Pamela M. (1990). Ethnic Origins of the Canadian Population. In Craig McKie and Keith Thompson. *Canadian Social Trends* (Toronto: Thompson Educational Publishing).

- Winks, Robin W (1971). *The Blacks in Canada: A History* (Montreal: McGill-Queen's University Press).

- Women's Bureau, Labour Canada (1987). Equal Pay: Collective Bargaining and the Law. Conference Speeches. Ottawa.

- Wood, W.D. (1959). An Analysis of Office Unionism in Canadian Manufacturing Industries. Ph.D. Thesis, Princetown University.

- Yri, Marlene I. (1979). The British Columbia Teachers' Federation and its Conversion to Partisanship, 1966–1972. Masters Thesis, University of British Columbia.

Index

Date Due
